Elizabeth Packard

ELIZABETH PACKARD

A Noble Fight

Linda V. Carlisle

UNIVERSITY OF ILLINOIS PRESS
URBANA, CHICAGO, AND SPRINGFIELD

Library of Congress Cataloging-in-Publication Data
Carlisle, Linda V., 1947–
Elizabeth Packard : a noble fight / Linda V. Carlisle.
p.   cm.
Includes bibliographical references and index.
ISBN 978-0-252-03572-2 (cloth : alk. paper)
1. Packard, E. P. W. (Elizabeth Parsons Ware), 1816–1897. 2. Psychiatric
hospital patients—Illinois—Biography. 3. Social reformers—Illinois—Biography.
4. Women social reformers—Illinois—Biography. 5. Mentally ill—Commitment
and detention—United States—Case studies. 6. Mentally ill—Civil rights—
United States—Case studies. 7. Husband and wife—United States—Case studies.
8. Married women—Civil rights—United States—Case studies. 9. Women's rights—
United States—Case studies.
I. Title.
RC464.P33C37   2010
362.2'1092—dc22[B]   2010016579

For my husband,
Donald C. Bush,
and
my parents,
V. G. and Bee Carlisle

Contents

LIST OF ILLUSTRATIONS ix

ACKNOWLEDGMENTS xi

Introduction 1

1 "All the Love His Bachelor Heart 16
Could Muster"

2 "New Notions and Wild Vagaries" 24

3 Breaking the Mold 35

4 Free Love and True Womanhood 44

5 "The Forms of Law" 57

6 Andrew McFarland and Mental Medicine 68

7 "A World of Trouble" 78

8 "An Unendurable Annoyance" 91

9 From Courtroom to Activism 104

10 "My Pen Shall Rage" 118

11 Shooting the Rattlesnakes 132

12 Vindication and "Virtuous Action" 145

13 Triumph and Disaster 155

14 Working in Her Calling 165

15 "Great and Noble Work" 177

16 Final Campaigns 190

NOTES 201

BIBLIOGRAPHY 233

INDEX 251

List of Illustrations

1. Elizabeth and Theophilus Packard, Jr. 37
2. Packard resists her removal to the asylum 62
3. Dr. Andrew McFarland, superintendent of the Illinois State Hospital for The Insane, ca. 1860 68
4. Illinois State Hospital for the Insane, Jacksonville, ca. 1860 72
5. Judge Charles R. Starr 104
6. Attorney Stephen R. Moore 106
7. Kankakee County Court House 108
8. Elizabeth Packard 124
9. James B. Bradwell 133
10. Myra Colby Bradwell 134
11. Illinois Senate debating Packard's Personal Liberty Bill, 1867 136
12. Samuel Ware Packard 155

Acknowledgments

I AM DEEPLY INDEBTED to those who read and commented on early drafts of this book, including Professor Kay Carr at Southern Illinois University Carbondale (SIUC) and Professors Ellen Nore, John A. Taylor, James Trent, Mary Ann Boyd, Charlotte Frisbee, and Shirley Portwood at Southern Illinois University Edwardsville (SIUE). The late Dr. John Y. Simon, SIUC, read many drafts and asked the tough questions that led to valuable insights. I will always be grateful for his guidance and the opportunity to work with such an extraordinary scholar and individual.

Special thanks are also due to writer Barbara Sapinsley, who generously shared her research material on Elizabeth Packard. Our conversations were a delight and her suggestions invaluable.

I appreciate the encouragement I received from former Director Gary Denue, former Dean Jay Starratt, Dean Regina McBride, and my colleagues at Lovejoy Library, SIUE. Special thanks to our Interlibrary Loan staff, Deidre Johnson, Hope Myers, and Bessie Richards, who obtained numerous, often obscure, print and microfilm documents for me and also to Tony Leopold and Ginger Strickland for their assistance in digitizing the illustrations.

Financial support for this research came from a King V. Hostick Award provided by the Illinois State Historical Society and the Illinois Historic Preservation Agency. The Graduate School at Southern Illinois University Edwardsville also provided much appreciated support.

At the Illinois State Historical Library in Springfield, Connie Butts, Cheryl Schnirring, and Mary Michals provided assistance during my visits to the library and telephone inquiries. Kim Efird at the Illinois State Archives in Springfield provided assistance in locating and citing nineteenth-century records of the Illinois General Assembly.

Other librarians, archivists, and their staffs in various other states also provided invaluable assistance. Diane Richardson, special collections librarian, went far beyond the call of duty to assist during and following my visit to the Oskar Diethelm Library, New York Hospital–Cornell Medical Center, which was then in temporary quarters at the New York Academy of Medicine. David Farrell, curator, History of Science and Technology Program & associate university archivist at Bancroft Library, University of California at Berkeley provided valuable assistance during my visit there. Jack Eckert, reference librarian, and the staff of the Rare Books and Special Collections unit at Francis A. Countway Library of Medicine, Harvard Medical School, Cambridge, Massachusetts, were also a great help. My thanks also go to Dr. Fred Altaffer and the Central Office Research Review Committee of the Massachusetts Department of Mental Health for granting permission to use records of the Worcester Insane Asylum.

Elizabeth Slomba, university archivist at the University of New Hampshire, located and copied reports of the New Hampshire Insane Asylum for me. Ned Pocengal, library assistant, located and scanned useful manuscript items from the Harvey Cushing and John Hay Whitney Medical Library at Yale University. I also received assistance from Elizabeth Marzuoli, reference archivist at the Massachusetts State Archives, and from Linda Brown, Mary Bennett, and Kevin Knoot at the Iowa State Historical Society–Iowa City. Megan Schulz, reference librarian, Kansas State Library, located valuable information for me in records of the Kansas legislature.

Many others, too numerous to name, provided assistance at the New Hampshire Historical Society; Congregational Church Library and Archives in Boston; Chicago Historical Society; Historical Society of Oak Park and River Forest; Kankakee County Historical Society; Manteno Historical Society; Kankakee Public Library; Manteno Public Library; Jacksonville Public Library; Mt. Pleasant (Iowa) Public Library; St. Louis Public Library; Cook County Recorder of Deeds; Cook County Assessors & Treasurer's Mapping Department; Cook County Probate Court; Office of the Morgan County Clerk in Jacksonville, Illinois; and Illinois Regional Archives Depositories at Northeastern Illinois University, Illinois State University, and the University of Illinois at Springfield. Research is clearly not a solitary process, and this project could not have been completed without the courtesy and expertise of those individuals.

Finally, I gratefully acknowledge the support given by my extraordinary husband, Donald C. Bush, who must feel that he married both me and Elizabeth Packard on that June day in 1997. You have been my best friend, staunchest cheerleader, willing and uncomplaining assistant, and loving companion throughout the research and writing of this book, and no words can express the love and appreciation I feel in return.

Introduction

IN THE SPRING OF 1875, a distraught Mary Todd Lincoln, wife of the slain president, was involuntarily committed to a private mental hospital in Batavia, Illinois, by a court order requested by her son, Robert Lincoln. Fifteen years earlier, an unknown Illinois woman named Elizabeth Packard was also involuntarily committed to a state mental hospital in Jacksonville. There are remarkable connections between the two cases. Both women contested their confinement, both were examined and declared insane by Dr. Andrew McFarland, both had explored Spiritualism, and both were befriended by Chicago attorneys and activists James and Myra Bradwell.

For three decades following her release, Elizabeth Packard traveled the United States lobbying for laws to protect the civil rights of married women and the mentally ill. Historians have noted that the Illinois laws that governed Mary Lincoln's institutionalization in 1875 were among the most stringent in the nation because of Packard's reforms. Among these laws was Packard's law requiring a jury trial at which individuals might defend their sanity prior to commitment. The law was intended to prevent false commitment of individuals by relatives with perfidious motives; however, opponents decried it as a public humiliation of the insane and their families. In practice, Robert Lincoln's lawyers subverted the law by notifying Mrs. Lincoln of her impending trial only a few hours beforehand and by then appointing a lawyer for her who supported her commitment. It was, however, Packard's law protecting the rights of mental patients to send and receive mail that enabled Mrs. Lincoln to correspond with attorneys James and Myra Bradwell, who then pressed successfully for her release.[1]

Elizabeth Packard's resistance of her own commitment and the laws she was later instrumental in passing changed the jurisprudence of insanity in the United States. As one historian has noted, "modern-day civil commitment codes have their genesis" in Packard's campaign.[2] After Packard, involuntary commitment and management of mental institutions in the

United States would be shrouded in legislation protecting the civil liberties of those deemed insane.

Who then was Elizabeth Packard and what propelled her into the role of reformer? Packard was the wife of Reverend Theophilus Packard, Jr. who, alarmed at her heretical religious ideas, exasperated by her assertiveness, and appalled at her suggested affair with another man, declared her insane. Confined for three years in the Illinois Hospital for the Insane under the care of Dr. Andrew McFarland, Packard emerged from the asylum in 1863 determined to campaign for laws to protect the personal liberty of those alleged to be insane. Unable under existing laws to recover her children or personal property from her husband, she also became an advocate for equal rights for married women.

Packard called her story "The Great Drama," and indeed it was. With tales of a heartless husband, a conspiring doctor, a mother torn from her children, and unrequited love, Hollywood could write no better plot. Indeed to some, her story seems like a clichéd romance employing stale themes of a wronged, but strong, woman beset by male tyrants and villains. However, historians of women will recognize themes of oppression and struggle for identity and voice that have been repeated in generation after generation of women from ancient times to the present. Still, to know Elizabeth Packard, the historian must look beyond both the melodrama of her books and her representations of herself as victim and heroine.

Despite the drama in her writing, Packard did not thrive on public attention or spectacle. She did not, for example, join the lyceum circuit or appear in popular public forums, as did other public women of her day. Instead, she approached her public work methodically, one might even say "professionally," following the example of her antithesis, Dorothea Dix. She sought out powerful reformers (Gerrit Smith and Wendell Phillips) and politicians (President Ulysses S. Grant, state governors, and legislators) to advance her cause and worked to influence them personally as well through pen and press. As she worked for asylum reform, she became increasingly knowledgeable about new practices in asylum management and the legalities surrounding commitment laws. In studying the whole of her life, it becomes evident that her appeals for reform were based on much more than the emotion and melodrama of her personal story.

A public figure from the 1860s to the 1890s, Packard gained national notoriety as she lobbied legislatures, literally, from coast to coast. However, unlike Dorothea Dix, Packard won few friends in America's fledgling psychiatric profession. While Dix worked with asylum doctors to build institutions for care of the insane, Packard sought to change the asylum system and limit the authority of the doctors. This earned Packard the disdain and animus of early psychiatrists.

Despite opposition from the Association of Medical Superintendents of Institutions for the Insane (AMSAII), forerunner of the American Psychiatric Association, Packard achieved extraordinary success as states from Maine to Washington Territory passed, with variations, many of her laws. Furthermore, her persistent critique joined a chorus of other voices that, together, compelled America's emerging psychiatric profession to develop more exacting criteria for defining, diagnosing, and treating mental illnesses.

Packard fueled her campaign with sensational books and pamphlets about her personal experience, and supported herself with income from her "publishing business." But, beneath the veil of a female scribbler peddling a combined asylum narrative and Gothic romance, Packard addressed some of the most compelling social questions of nineteenth-century America: What civil rights are due married women? What rights and liberties are due those individuals deemed to be insane? What boundaries may a society reasonably impose on an individual's beliefs and behaviors?

Thus, Elizabeth Packard's life story is important on many levels. It is an intellectual history in which we see the interaction of Revolutionary ideology, Calvinist thought, and popular religion in shaping an individual's worldview. Packard's meld of religious ideas that mixed traditional and novel beliefs along with her insistence on "personal liberty" reflects the tumultuous intellectual environment of her time. It was an era in which traditional religion, based in shared creeds and theology, was yielding under pressure of the Second Great Awakening to a religious expression based on individual experience and private belief systems. This phenomenon, which historian Nathan Hatch called the "democratization of American Christianity," gave birth to self-defined popular religious expression that called into question both past traditions and "expert knowledge."[3]

The shift from the communal, hierarchical society of colonial times to a more democratic and individualistic society created an intellectual conundrum that is reflected in Packard's demands for freedom of conscience and speech: To what extent—at whose expense—should one demand individual rights? What is a reasonable balance between striving for personal liberty and sacrificing for the common good? Which of us, for example, would sacrifice our children's welfare for a perceived greater good? Indeed, Elizabeth Packard would struggle at intervals throughout her life to balance what she viewed as dual, yet conflicting duties to her family, to self, and to the God, who, she believed, called her to reform work.

Packard's story is also social history, demonstrating how changing societal views of mental illness resulted in the development of new institutions. While Enlightenment philosophy inspired new views of mental illness, the cultural shift from communally oriented to individual-oriented society led to changing views of who was responsible for care of the mentally ill. Gradually, over the eighteenth and nineteenth centuries, responsibility for care of the insane moved from the family and immediate community to charitable institutions and the state. Medieval views of the mentally ill as animal-like creatures in need of restraint or exorcism gave way to hopes for treatment and even cure, allowing for the introduction of "moral treatment."

Developed by French physician Philippe Pinel, moral treatment called for humane care that stressed minimal use of physical restraint in favor of a psychologically oriented therapy.[4] Moral treatment prescribed confinement of the individual in a pleasant, orderly environment that fostered a return to sane behavior. York Retreat, built in England in 1792 by Quaker philanthropist William Tuke, was among the earliest institutions established for moral treatment of insanity. In the United States, moral treatment was instituted as early as 1834 at the Vermont Asylum for the Insane in Brattleboro.

Both moral treatment and public acceptance of societal responsibility for care of the insane expanded in the 1840s through the work of Dr. Thomas Kirkbride and Dorothea Dix. Dix lobbied for funding for state-sponsored asylums, while Kirkbride, superintendent of the Pennsylvania Hospital for the Insane, developed national models both for moral treatment and for the design of institutions that would foster that treatment.

Influenced by Tuke's York Retreat, the Kirkbride plan called for a central, multistory building, with a series of symmetrical wings on each side. The wings were arranged so windows on both sides provided both natural light and views of an attractive pastoral landscape. Reformer Dorothea Dix worked with asylum superintendents to persuade state legislatures to establish state-funded institutions for the insane modeled on the Kirkbride plan for both buildings and moral treatment.

Unfortunately, by the time Elizabeth Packard was confined in the Hospital for the Insane in Jacksonville, Illinois, it was apparent that many of these institutions were falling short of the hopes and ideals of their founders. While moral treatment was clearly an enormous advance over earlier treatment, and certainly beneficial for some, it was not useful in all cases. Even when desirable, it was increasingly difficult to practice moral treatment in the large, public asylums of the mid-nineteenth century.

The demographic transformation wrought by urbanization and immigration added further impetus to changing perceptions of proper care and treatment of the insane. Increased immigration and concentration of population in cities both coincided with the growth of mental institutions and created additional stress on those institutions. Overcrowding, false expectations for cure, and the necessity of long-term care for incurables along with the difficulty of managing a large, expensive institution and its staff were but a few of the difficulties confronting asylum superintendents. By the mid-nineteenth century, public faith in these institutions had been shaken by the complex realities involved in institutional care and treatment of the insane.

As early psychiatrists confronted these administrative challenges, they were also grappling with definitions, typology, and treatment modalities. Proceedings of nineteenth-century AMSAII conferences reveal the impassioned debates of a profession still seeking consensus on basic definitions and causes of insanity. What denoted the line between insanity and merely eccentric ideas or odd behavior? Were "minor mental maladies" a form of insanity? The answers often reflected religious ideas and contemporary culture more than scientific theory or proven evidence. The doctor who sought to rely on methodical evidence or theory still had to contend with powerful religious and cultural undercurrents expressed in the beliefs of patients' families and the general public, not to mention the state officials who controlled funding for public mental hospitals.

Surrounding all of these issues was the jurisprudence of insanity, which raised questions not only of individual rights and liberty, but also professional turf. Who had final say in the laws that governed commitment and care of the mentally ill individual: the family, the local doctor, the asylum doctor, the judge, the jury, the attorney? What civil rights did the mentally ill retain? The answer could mean the difference between liberty and involuntary commitment to a mental institution. In the case of the criminally insane, it could be the difference between treatment, prison, or execution.

Thus changing beliefs regarding care and treatment of the mentally ill have, historically, involved broader cultural shifts that affected institutions, organizations, and laws. Elizabeth Packard's challenge to the institutions, organizations, and laws of her time reflected yet another shift in the history of care and treatment of the mentally ill. It marked the end of large public mental hospitals and a trend toward varied treatments for differing types and degrees of mental illness.

Packard's story also reveals how the fact of her sex shaped her beliefs, defined her role in society, and made her vulnerable to commitment to an insane asylum. Packard was a transitional woman who lived in the blurred margin between traditional and progressive views of women's proper place in society.[5] She deeply valued her roles as wife and mother, and accepted the home as woman's natural sphere. However, influenced by the writing of domestic feminists such as Catharine Beecher, she expected to be granted a degree of authority and certain basic rights within that sphere. A daughter of the Early Republic, she held liberty as her highest value. It was unthinkable to her that anyone—male or female, slave or free—could be denied freedom of expression, liberty of conscience in religious matters, or protection of basic human rights. These progressive views would create difficulties for Packard in her marriage and community.

The intellectual, social, and cultural fluidity of nineteenth-century America both expanded societal boundaries and made it more difficult to discern the limits of acceptable beliefs and behaviors. How far beyond the norm an individual could venture depended not only on the nature of one's ideas and actions but also on geography, class, association, and sex. This was particularly true for women. For example, nineteenth-century woman's rights advocates found much support in New England, where, in notable instances, husbands and wives teamed in the dual crusades for abolitionism and woman's rights. Couples like the Theodore Welds, the Gerrit Smiths, and the James Motts found support among likeminded associates.[6] The boundaries for these individuals were expanded by class position, the support of spouses and associates, and their location in a geographical region where reform movements were essentially the norm. But Elizabeth Packard, as the wife of a Calvinist minister in a rural Midwestern community, would not enjoy such advantages.

Nevertheless, buoyed by the optimism of new ideas, Packard confidently expressed her opinions and demanded her rights with apparent disregard for the boundaries the wife of an orthodox minister was expected to respect. Driven by intellectual curiosity and a sense of religious calling, she contested the gender-specific norms that defined her place in law and society. Radically for a woman in her position she demanded the right to think for herself declaring, "I though a woman, have just as good a right to my opinion, as my husband has to his, although he is a professed minister of Christ."[7]

Thus, ultimately Elizabeth Packard's story is about boundaries. In pursuit of personal liberty, Packard pushed the intellectual, cultural, and social limits of her day, naively at first, but later deliberately. In so doing, she breached reinforcing boundaries of gender and religion, and became ensnared in the indeterminate definitions of insanity espoused by the emerging profession of psychiatry.

Packard was controversial in her own time and remains so today. Some question whether her reforms truly benefited the insane. Certainly her laws requiring greater external oversight of asylums and postal rights for patients succeeded in decreasing the likelihood of false commitments and patient abuse. Many, however, believe that her law requiring a jury trial for both women and men prior to involuntary commitment was a too extreme response to what she considered a radical violation of her civil rights.

Packard advocated family and charitable care for the mentally ill in private homes. However, she also recognized the need for institutions to care for those who had no family or friends or who were too deranged to be managed at home. While she indeed called for the "asylum system" of her time to be destroyed, she also called for it to be "raised anew" in a "more righteous" form. Her campaign for formal external oversight of asylums and for patients' right to send and receive mail uncensored assumed the presence of institutions for care of the insane. She truly sought to protect the civil liberties of the insane, not to return them to the almshouses of an earlier day or to the streets where, today, we unfortunately find many who need care. Even with its flaws, hers was a thoughtfully conceived, good faith effort to address what we now know is one of the more complex, persistent, and intractable social problems facing modern society.

Packard's noble crusade was also at times vengeful as she determined to hang her husband and doctor "on the gallows of public opinion" for relegating her to an insane asylum. She considered herself the heroine of her Great Drama and presented herself as such in all her writing. Conversely, she presented her husband and doctor as villains who falsely relegated her to an insane asylum for ulterior motives. All will not agree with her assessment.

Certainly, the pioneers of American psychiatry were not the autocratic villains that Packard portrayed them as. They were, almost to a man, deeply concerned for the welfare of the insane and devoted to the profession they believed offered the most hope for those afflicted with mental illness. Nor was Packard's husband a complete villain. As a minister he was deeply disturbed by his wife's rejection of orthodox religion. A devoted father, he was mortified at the "new notions and wild vagaries" that she was teaching their children. Against his expectations for a loyal and faithful wife, Elizabeth's demands for equal rights and personal liberty did, indeed, seem crazy to him. When all else failed, sending her to a hospital for the insane seemed to him the only way to protect his children and restore peace in his family, church, and, indeed, community.

Packard was clearly "anti-psychiatry." Her personal experience of psychiatry and, to an extent, general medicine was negative. Her Jacksonian trust in the good sense of common folk and suspicion of elitism led her to prefer "natural" homeopathic remedies. This certainly reflects the tenor of the times in which she lived wherein the expert opinions of professionals were held suspect by common opinion. Unfortunately, once Packard and others who shared her concerns squared off with the psychiatric profession, there was little opportunity for unimpassioned dialogue that might have led to compromise and better laws. Fault here can certainly be shared by both sides.

The question of Packard's sanity became a central issue in her life. Her husband and doctor firmly believed her to be insane, while other contemporaries viewed her with respect. While there may appear to be ample evidence on both sides of the question, one must always remember that insanity is a culture-bound concept. What seems perfectly sane in one time or place may seem less so in another time or place. My personal belief is that both Elizabeth and Theophilus Packard would probably have benefited from separation and a "rest cure" at the height of their conflict in 1860. That she required confinement in a mental hospital seems doubtful when even her doctor, Andrew McFarland, conceded that he "searched in vain" for evidence of derangement for the first two years of her incarceration. The persona she presented to legislatures, journalists, and friends apparently convinced them she was quite sane. Even her critics described her as intelligent, articulate, and attractive and the *Chicago Tribune* called her the "wise friend of the insane." Perhaps, in the end, the question of her sanity is indeed, as one historian suggested, a "moot point" that will remain a matter of opinion.[8] Whatever her mental state, it certainly does not diminish her accomplishments nor lessen her value as an actor in history.

While Packard would never be granted the historical acclaim of Dorothea Dix, she was acknowledged in her own time as a force for change in protecting the civil rights of asylum patients and married women. Her influence on psychiatric professionals is evident in their repeated references to her in national meetings and their concerted efforts over three decades to block or amend her legislation. Without ascribing too much credit to the efforts of any single individual, it is safe to say that Packard's case was a tipping point in effecting change in the laws governing civil commitment and protecting the civil rights of those deemed insane.

·American architect R. Buckminster Fuller once said that "Human integrity is the uncompromising courage of self-determining whether or not to take initiatives, support or co-operate with others, in accord with all the truth and nothing but the truth, as conceived by the divine mind, always available in each individual." Certainly, Elizabeth Packard showed uncompromising courage in her resolve to live according to the truth that she believed the "God within" had revealed to her. She was determined to change laws that imperiled her own liberty of conscience and civil rights and she transformed that personal need into courageous action to protect civil rights of other vulnerable groups in her society. Even apart from her historical significance to psychiatry and the movement for woman's rights, hers would be a story worth telling.

A NOTE ON SOURCES

The primary sources consulted for this book include Elizabeth Packard's books and pamphlets, Theophilus Packard's diary and letters, Andrew Mc-Farland's reports and letters, and the proceedings of the AMSAII as published in the *American Journal of Insanity* (*AJI*). Other sources include newspapers, articles, reports, public records, and legal documents. As much as possible I have endeavored to let these sources speak for themselves, with the following caveat.

In her writing, Elizabeth often re-created dialogue with the principals in her story. These recalled conversations, of course, cannot be accepted as accurate and truthful. Packard, her husband, and her doctor each wrote (often long after the event) to persuade others that their ideas and actions were correct. Thus, their writing is the truth only as they constructed it in their own minds and for their own purposes.

Where there is disagreement among my sources—and that is often—I have tried to juxtapose their opinions. I have also qualified their remarks with phrases such as "according to Packard," "he recorded," "she recalled," and the like to clarify whose perspective is being presented. Whenever possible, events they described have been corroborated with other sources. However, for the most part, I found that they spoke accurately about the events they mention, although their interpretations of those events differ.

Nevertheless, the source materials remain problematic. The sheer volume of published work produced by Elizabeth Packard tends to drown out any competing voices. Indeed, her skill in promoting herself and her cause, not to mention her colorful, quotable style, make it difficult to give fair voice to others. While Theophilus Packard's diary reveals his personality and opinions, his voice is restrained in his effort to disclose as little detail as possible while defending himself. This restraint is less evident in his letters of defense published in various newspapers in response to his wife's books and legislative activities. Andrew McFarland's persona and views are quite clear in his various published reports, letters to newspaper editors, and personal correspondence. Still, the voluminous and persistent cries of a "woman wronged" tend to outweigh the words, if not the deeds, of both of these men.

Nevertheless, I do find that Elizabeth Packard, if not the heroine, is the most interesting and historically significant individual in this story. This position is not due to the imbalance of sources, but is based on the breadth of her impact on public opinion, law, and policy surrounding care and treatment of the mentally ill.

There are several secondary sources that deal with Packard and I am indebted to the researchers who produced them, particularly those who specifically discussed Packard's case. For nearly a century, most published discussion of Packard came from Andrew McFarland's colleagues in the psychiatric profession. It was, not surprisingly, mostly negative. For example, Dr. William R. Dunton, in a 1907 article for the *Johns Hopkins Hospital Bulletin,* quickly concurred with McFarland's assessment that Packard was insane. He found the fact that the narrative in her book, *Modern Persecution,* was "not consecutive," was "of itself" an indication of "mental instability." Dunton was also the first to suggest in writing that her condition may have been related to her sex, specifically either to menopause or to a "conjugal psychosis."[9]

Apparently unaware that Packard continued in her opinions and reform activity well into her seventies, he reported that, "after she had accomplished certain reforms she seems to have settled down to a quiet life, possibly at the expiration of her climacteric and the subsidence of the mental symptoms." He speculated that the difference in age between Packard and her husband might have been "an added factor."[10] In a "Further Note on Mrs. Packard" published the following year, Dunton reported that he had read her four-volume *Great Drama* and was convinced that she was not only insane, but also "unchristian" since she apparently "had no hesitation in publishing the same material under different titles." He noted that, nevertheless, she appeared to have supported herself comfortably from sales of the book.[11]

In a 1913 article in the *American Journal of Insanity,* Dr. Richard Dewey, who served as president of the AMSAII in 1895–96, concurred with the profession's stance that Packard's legislation was "retrogressive."[12] Dewey believed the Illinois law by which she was committed was clearly unconstitutional, and opened to Packard "a brilliant career as a martyr to tyrannical legislation . . . in which she manifested a high order of ability to muster and organize her forces."[13] Dewey conceded, "All things considered, the question of her insanity seems to require further elucidation."[14]

By the mid-twentieth century, Packard was receiving routine mention in histories of American psychiatry. Alfred Deutsch, for example, noting that most asylum narratives by former patients had little effect, called Packard's books "a notable exception" that led to changes in lunacy laws. He granted that her behavior after her release from the Jacksonville asylum "was so intelligent, and her ability so striking, as to lend weight to her charge that she had been 'railroaded.'"[15]

Not until the 1960s did the work of revisionist and feminist historians enable new perspectives on Packard's life and work. Although he did not know of Packard, Michel Foucault in *Madness and Civilization* (1961) challenged earlier scholarship and launched a scholarly debate as to whether asylum building was the result of progressive benevolence or, as Foucault suggested, a form of social control. Important contributors to this discussion included historians David Rothman, Andrew Scull, and Gerald Grob.

Meanwhile, psychiatrist Thomas Szasz and feminist writer Phyllis Chesler used the Packard case to support their argument that psychiatry has historically been a biased and oppressive force in society.[16] Chesler also compared Packard to women such as Anne Hutchinson and Mary Dyer, who were punished for exhibiting independent religious ideas. Like Szasz, she argued that "witches and mentally ill patients" were created "through the social interaction of oppressor and oppressed."[17]

As the foregoing suggests, Packard frequently served as a polemical example for either pro- or anti-psychiatry writers. A notable exception was an article on Packard by Myra Himelhoch and Arthur Shaffer, published in the *Journal of American Studies* in 1971. The authors identified her crusade as "anti-institutional and anti-psychiatrist" and concurred that some of the policies she sought may have been shortsighted. However, they believed Packard was correct in demanding better safeguards in the commitment process as well as in her judgment that asylums often failed to be therapeutic. They applauded Packard for seeking justice rather than pity for the mentally ill and for demanding for them the same constitutional rights that other citizens enjoyed.[18]

By the latter decades of the twentieth century, historians began to suggest that the asylum narratives by former patients such as Packard should not be dismissed as flawed visions of reality. Jeffrey Geller, for example, argued that women's asylum narratives "should be seen as neither more nor less valid than contemporaneous accounts by professionals." Geller examined the connection between gender, mental illness, and women's "roles as wife, daughter, victim, and advocate." He cited Packard's case as a notable illustration of a woman's powerlessness in her role as wife.[19]

Geller and Maxine Harris later excerpted portions of Packard's books, *Modern Persecution* and *The Great Drama,* in a collection of asylum narratives entitled *Women of the Asylum: Voices From Behind the Walls, 1840–1945.* They observed that, insane or not, the women writers of asylum narratives were "still keen observers of their environment, meticulous chroniclers of their own experiences, and often poetic and witty recorders of their subjective mental and emotional state."[20]

Similarly, Susan J. Hubert (*Questions of Power: The Politics of Women's Madness Narratives,* 2002) argued that the autobiographical writing of women believed to be mentally ill provided distinctive perspectives for understanding the history of psychiatric treatment in the United States. Hubert suggested that, through their asylum narratives, women such as Packard rejected "both institutional practices and the male prerogative to define and limit the experiences of women." These women used writing as a tool to rebel against the authority of the medical establishment as well as to advocate reform.[21]

Some historians, however, continued to show disdain for Packard well into the twentieth century. In a biographical sketch of Packard in *Notable American Women, 1607–1950* (1971), for example, John C. Burnham defended Andrew McFarland as "a highly respected physician" and condemned Packard's laws for reinforcing "old stereotypes and suspicions" and "undermining public confidence" in physicians and mental hospitals. He suggested that Packard chose to write sensational, asylum exposés rather than books about women's rights knowing the asylum narratives would attract more readers.

When writer Barbara Sapinsley asked Burnham's advice for her book about Packard, he told her he "thoroughly disapprove[d] of any attempt to resurrect Mrs. Packard," adding that "her motivation was personal and vindictive" and that she had ruined the career of one of the ablest psychiatrists of the nineteenth century.[22] Burnham advised Sapinsley that there were "any number of women who worked effectively and constructively for women's rights who might better be popularized."[23]

Sapinsley rejected Burnham's advice and completed her book on Packard, but searched in vain for a publisher for it for nearly two decades. When *The Private War of Mrs. Packard* was finally published in 1991, it became the first book devoted entirely to Packard. Sapinsley's substantial research, conducted primarily during the 1960s, was aided by recollections and documents from Packard's direct descendants, with whom Sapinsley was personally acquainted. This book remains a valuable source of information about Packard not readily available from other resources.

Meanwhile, other scholars were beginning to analyze asylum narratives as a genre, often including Packard as an example. For example, Mary Elene Wood (*The Writing on the Wall: Women's Autobiography and the Asylum*, 1994) included Packard's *The Prisoner's Hidden Life* in her examination of literary symbolism in asylum narratives. Wood's analysis of the strategies Packard used to establish authority with her readers enabled a new understanding of her writing. She described Packard's books as a combination of "spiritual autobiography, slave narrative, political treatise, and domestic fiction." In the context of these genres, Wood believed that the apparent disorder in Packard's writing in fact reflected a purposeful interjection of examples and testimonials aimed at reinforcing her credibility.[24]

In a 2003 article for the *Alabama Law Review,* Jennifer Rebecca Levison called on historians to "transcend ahistorical and somewhat restrictive labels" such as "feminism" and "separate spheres" in order to better understand Packard. She positioned Packard "as a border woman" comparable to nineteenth-century women such as Charlotte Bronte, Margaret Fuller, and Elizabeth Stoddard who struggled to reconcile "conservative and radical tendencies."[25]

Still other historians have studied Packard's interaction with or influence on notable contemporaries. Mark Neely and R. Gerald McMurtry (*The Insanity File: The Case of Mary Todd Lincoln,* 1986) considered the impact of Packard's case on Mary Todd Lincoln's 1875 commitment proceedings.[26] Jane Friedman (*America's First Woman Lawyer: The Biography of Myra Bradwell,* 1992) discussed Bradwell's use of the editorial power of her *Chicago Legal News* to block efforts to repeal Packard's Personal Liberty Law.[27] Meanwhile, David Lightner (*Asylum, Prison, and Poorhouse: The Writings and Reform Work of Dorothea Dix in Illinois,* 1999) briefly compared Packard with celebrated reformer Dorothea Dix.[28]

While several historians have considered Packard's impact on the jurisprudence of psychiatry, few legal scholars have examined her views on marriage and divorce. An exception is Hendrik Hartog who, in a 1988 article entitled "Mrs. Packard on Dependency," analyzed Packard's demand for her right to be a married woman and her understanding of the force of law as well as her definition of manliness and her views on the rights of husbands. In a later book, *Man & Wife in America* (2000), Hartog discussed the impact of coverture on women's lives and the variety of ways in which it could be used both for and against women's interests. In this context, he cited Packard as an example of the nineteenth-century wife's dependency and "need to be 'trusted' by her husband." He recounted an incident in which Packard's husband refused to give her $10 from her patrimony so that she could visit her brother in a distant community. Hartog suggested that Packard related this incident strategically, knowing that other women "would understand this dialogue as an expression of a husband's ordinary rights (and as an expression of a near-abusive—and foolish—insistence on those rights)."[29]

In another legal history, Norma Basch (*Framing American Divorce,* 1999) included Packard as an example of the "deep antipathy" nineteenth-century women held toward "matrimonial boundaries." Basch found irony in the fact that, although Packard contested "every vestige" of her husband's marital authority, she continued "to frame marriage in terms that naturalized coverture" by insisting that man was woman's "natural protector."[30]

In recent decades even official histories of psychiatry began to describe Packard, if not favorably, at least more neutrally. In *The History and Influence of the American Psychiatric Association* (1987), published by the American Psychiatric Press, Walter Barton described Packard as "an effective crusader" and noted that some scholars believed her commitment was the result of collusion between her husband and doctor.[31] In *Out of Bedlam: The Truth about Deinstitutionalization* (1990), Ann Braden Johnson traced the origin of organized advocacy for the mentally ill to Packard's campaign in the 1860s.[32] In a similar vein, Gerald Grob (*The Mad Among Us,* 1994) noted that demands for patients' rights by those such as Packard led to the founding of the National Association for the Protection of the Insane and the Prevention of Insanity in 1880.[33] Likewise, Elizabeth Lunbeck (*Psychiatric Persuasion: Knowledge, Gender, and Power in Modern America,* 1994) mentioned Packard briefly as an example of former patients whose calls for reform brought to an end the "halcyon years" of American psychiatry and asylum building. Judith Lynn Failer (*Who Qualifies for Rights?* 2002) noted Packard's impact on the development of standards for involuntary commitment.

Each of the above scholars has contributed to my understanding of Packard and her place in history. Yet, despite the recurring interest in Packard and attention to elements of her story, historians have yet to provide a comprehensive, scholarly biography that brings together the many dimensions of her life and work. That is the purpose of this biography. In particular, I hope to extend discussion of her religious ideas and political ideals, first by showing the varied influences that led to her personal theology and then by demonstrating how this theology inspired her political stance on personal liberty and women's equal rights. Most important, I hope to demonstrate her influence on the psychiatric profession as revealed in her interaction with

Andrew McFarland and in the reaction of the profession to her proposed reforms. This account goes beyond previous works in documenting the extent and influence of her legislative activities. Finally, I hope to present her story in the context of a historical era in which ideas about gender, religion, and insanity were fluid and often dependent upon one's immediate society.

Elizabeth Packard's life and work invites further research. Her writing certainly is worthy of further analysis by literary scholars. Research in other states might well reveal that her legislative efforts were even more widespread than documented to date. It would also be useful to search for more complete information regarding her interactions with the other reformers she mentions. Finally, new theoretical perspectives could examine her life apart from the concepts of oppression and separate spheres that dominate her presentation of herself. I hope this biography of Packard provides a springboard for those future scholars.

1 "All the Love His Bachelor Heart Could Muster"

ELIZABETH PARSONS WARE WAS BORN in Ware, Massachusetts, on 28 December 1816. She was the fifth child born to Reverend Samuel and Mary Tirrill Ware, but the first to survive infancy. Two sons, Samuel and Austin, were born later and also survived to adulthood. When ill health forced her father to leave the ministry, the family moved to nearby Conway, Massachusetts, where they remained until Elizabeth was about sixteen. As a teenager, she boarded at the Conway, Massachusetts, home of Reverend Daniel Crosby while attending Mr. Bradford's school.[1]

Around 1832, the Ware family moved to Amherst, Massachusetts, where Elizabeth attended Amherst Female Seminary, which had opened for classes that same year. Unrelated to Amherst College, the female seminary was the first institution at Amherst established explicitly for women's higher education. Elizabeth Ware's name appeared among the 191 students listed in the school's 1835 catalogue.[2]

During those years, the Wares took in boarders from Amherst College, and it was under those circumstances that Elizabeth met young Henry Ward Beecher, a classmate of one of their boarders. She recalled that Beecher taught Sabbath school at the Congregational church she attended.[3] Within little more than a decade, Beecher would become one of the most popular preachers in America. As an adult, Elizabeth would follow his teaching and avidly read his columns in *The Independent*, a widely circulated Congregationalist periodical. The personal theology that she later developed drew in part from the combined influences of Beecher's exuberant teaching and her Congregationalist upbringing. However, Beecher's less orthodox ideas and inquisitive spirit matched hers far more than the strict Calvinism of her parents.

After completing her studies at Amherst Female Academy, Elizabeth became the principal at Randolph Academy in West Randolph, Massachusetts. But her brief teaching career was interrupted when, two months after her nineteenth birthday, she became ill with what she described as "a derangement which followed a severe brain fever."[4] Dunglison's *Dictionary of Medi-*

cal Science (1854) cross-listed "fever, brain" with "cerebral, Phrenitis," which was characterized by high fever, headache, "redness of the face and eyes, intolerance of light and sound, watchfulness, and delirium, either furious or muttering." The disease was believed to be caused by sunstroke, inebriation, or "violent mental emotions, etc."[5] The recommended treatment was bleeding, purging, and "application of ice to the shaved head" and "the avoiding of irritation of every kind."[6]

When Elizabeth's symptoms failed to improve with conventional treatment, her father took her to nearby Worcester Hospital for the Insane, which had opened just three years earlier. Under the leadership of Dr. Samuel B. Woodward, the Worcester facility became a national model and Woodward earned international recognition as "the leading American authority of mental diseases."[7] Elizabeth was admitted on 27 January 1836 as a patient of Dr. Woodward.

Woodward's first entry in her patient record, dated 6 February 1836, read: "Came by Judge of Probate—insane for 5 weeks. At times considerably excited, her mood is variable. She is at times calm, at others has a considerable excitement. She is very pleasant at present." Woodward's next note suggests contemporary understanding of the causes of mental illness as he recorded, "Her father supposes that she laced too tight and that as a teacher she has had too much mental effort."[8]

Her patient record did not mention brain fever nor did it describe symptoms consistent with brain fever, such as redness of face, intolerance of light and noise, severe headache, and high fever. Woodward did specify that in addition to "considerable excitement of the nervous system," she also suffered from such physical symptoms as sores and amenorrhea. The medications he prescribed for her included magnesium sulfate (commonly called Epsom Salts and used as an antacid and laxative), tincture of opium (a pain reliever and sleep aid), moderate opiates, morphine, a myrrh amalgamation called "the Griffiths mixture" (for amenorrhea with anemia), and Thebaine (a mild stimulant used to elevate mood).[9]

According to Felter's *Eclectic Materia Medica, Pharmacology and Therapeutics* (1922), myrrh was "an ingredient of the celebrated Griffith's Mixture (Mistura Ferri Composita) for the amenorrhea of chlorosis and other forms of anemia."[10] Dunglison's *Dictionary of Medical Sciences* indicates that mistura ferri composita was a "tonic and emmenagogue (used to induce menstruation) . . . useful wherever iron is indicated."[11]

Woodward apparently believed the derangement was caused by something other than the generalized delirium associated with a high fever. He noted on

16 February, for example, "Her mind is rational on some topics and greatly insane on others." This was an interesting observation that foreshadowed her diagnosis decades later as a monomaniac on the subject of religion. Although Woodward provided no hint about the topics on which he considered her irrational, the implication was established that, by the age of nineteen, Packard was expressing views "on some topics" that some considered irrational.

After three weeks Woodward recorded that Packard's sores were better, she was "calm and rational," and she was "improving in a very favorable manner." Suggesting that the Wares' only daughter was, perhaps, a bit spoiled, Woodward noted that she wanted "indulgences" and had "doubtless had them to a great extent."[12]

Two days before releasing her, Woodward wrote that her health was "greatly improved" and added, "She is industrious . . . and at all times now very pleasant—Thebaine withdrawn." On 18 March 1836, Elizabeth was discharged "in a very favorable state [with] her mind free from insanity, her health restored and all the operations of the system going on favorable." Woodward closed the case with the note that his patient was "an interesting and intelligent girl."[13]

Packard's confinement at Worcester is significant for several reasons. Although she accepted the opinion that her illness was "occasioned by an excess of mental and physical effort combined," she blamed "malign medical treatment" during her initial illness for her derangement. She believed she had been unnecessarily bled and purged "with allopathic drugs when tonics alone were required to sustain the excessive action of the brain." (Allopathic was defined as "relating to the ordinary method of medical practice, in contradistinction to the homeopathic.")[14] She attributed her recovery to time, not medical treatment, and explained that finally "the blood had had time to form again so that I could control my mind."[15]

Whether her record at Worcester provides early evidence of a mental disorder or merely reflects nineteenth-century norms and medical knowledge will likely remain a matter of opinion. It has been well documented that, for women of the Victorian era, the label of insanity was easily acquired and nearly impossible to overcome. It was believed that female organs could produce hysteria and other mental symptoms. Hence, to be female was to live within a body viewed as inherently weak, both physically and mentally. Some historians suggest that, in that era, "Few young women could escape neurasthenia (a blanket term for nervous disorders) even in the best of circumstances."[16]

Certainly, the Worcester hospitalization marked the beginning of Packard's general distrust of formal medicine and doctors as well as her disillusionment with the notion that men could be depended upon as women's "protectors."

She was mortified that her father had taken her to an asylum "needlessly and unkindly" and in so doing exposed her to the stigma of insanity.[17]

Packard wrote little about the next few years, during which she stayed at her parents' home; however, the next significant event she recorded was indeed momentous. Late in 1838 or early 1839, she received a proposal of marriage from Theophilus Packard, Jr., a longtime associate of her father. She had known him since she was ten years old. However, she wrote that he became her "suitor for only a few months" before their marriage.[18] In a later book, she told readers that she chose to marry him ("out of hundreds of other beaux") because she believed he was a good man who could help her become a more "perfect person in Christ Jesus' estimation."[19] What she did not say was that, at age twenty-two, with her education completed and health restored, marriage was the expected next step in her life. Theophilus Packard, Jr. was well respected, financially established, and from a good family. She accepted his proposal, believing that he loved her "with all the love his old bachelor heart could muster."[20]

THEOPHILUS PACKARD, JR.

In 1816—the year his future wife was born—fourteen-year-old Theophilus Packard, Jr. was boarding with the family of Judge Paine in Ashfield, Massachusetts, and attending the academy of Reverend Alvan Sanders. By then he had studied Latin for two years under his father and had learned grammar and arithmetic at the common school near his home in Shelburne.[21]

Born in Shelburne on 1 February 1802, Theophilus was the oldest of eight children (two boys and six girls) of Reverend Theophilus Packard, Sr. and Mary Tirrill Packard. He described his family as close and loving with "kind parents" who nurtured him on the orthodox, evangelical religion of New England's established Congregationalist Church.[22]

The senior Packard was well qualified to tutor his son. The respected pastor of Shelburne's Congregational church held a doctor of divinity degree from Dartmouth College and was a leader in both education and ecclesiastical affairs. A trustee at Williams College from 1810 to 1825, he was instrumental in founding Amherst College in 1821 and was later among those who helped Mary Lyon establish nearby Mt. Holyoke College, the first women's college in the United States.[23]

By 1817, Theophilus, Jr. was sufficiently schooled to accept a teaching position at the common school he had once attended. There he found "scholars both larger and older than myself" and soon discovered that "More patience was requisite than I possessed, to teach and govern little children congregated together in a schoolroom." Despite the "somewhat irksome" nature of the job, he granted that his experience as a teacher "was somewhat profitable."[24]

In 1817, he began an intermittent college career interrupted by frequent illnesses and the necessity of sharing the family's financial resources with his younger brother, Isaac, with whom he was very close. In the summer of 1819 at age seventeen, he attended several revival meetings in Shelburne and decided it was time "to obtain religion." But he admitted that "during all this season of alarm and anxiety," he experienced no "genuine conviction of sin."[25] Even the sudden death of Isaac the next summer did not move him toward conversion despite his brother's deathbed admonition that he should prepare to meet him "at the bar of Christ." Heartbroken, Theophilus returned to Williams College, but soon went back home, unable to study and profoundly "depressed in spirits."[26]

The following year, he joined the first class at Amherst College and began to consider a future profession. He was drawn to the ministry, but considered himself "altogether unfit" since he still lacked the heartfelt conversion experience that he understood was "indispensably necessary to make a good, faithful and useful minister." Finally, during his senior year (1823), the elusive conversion finally occurred.[27] With this prerequisite in place, he could now follow his father into the ministry.

In the fall of 1824 he enrolled at Princeton, then a stronghold of strict Calvinism, to study theology under his father's friend, Reverend Archibald Alexander, and men like Charles Hodge, who once boasted that, during his five-decade tenure at Princeton, "no theological novelty" had been taught.[28] Theophilus enjoyed his studies and made numerous friends at Princeton; however, by the spring of 1825 he was once again ill. He left Princeton before the end of the term, thus marking the end of his formal education.

By summer he was incapacitated by "dyspepsia." When medications failed to help, he decided the "best remedy" was an "abstentious diet," "judicious exercise," regularity in all his habits, and a determined effort to maintain a "cheerful state of mind."[29] This was, in fact, the recommended treatment for dyspepsia, "a state of the stomach, in which its functions are disturbed, without the presence of other disease."[30] Dyspepsia was associated in both medicine and literature with a sour disposition as well as a sour stomach. The *Oxford English Dictionary* defines dyspeptic as "showing depression of spirits like that of a person suffering from dyspepsia; morbidly despondent or gloomy." It is a description that aptly characterized Theophilus Packard's temperament.

In October 1826, Theophilus received a license to preach from the Franklin Association of Ministers.[31] Soon afterward, he embarked on his first missionary assignment, which was a two-month commission from the Massachusetts Domestic Missionary Society to Tisbury Island (part of Martha's Vineyard, off the coast of Massachusetts). He enjoyed life on the island, but found "evangelical religion was at a low ebb" there. He made a list of the families who attended his worship services and forty-five years later wrote that he "still preserve[d] it among my papers."[32] In the winter of 1828, he returned home and accepted an invitation to serve with his father as co-pastor of the Shelburne Congregational Church.

Indeed, Calvinist religion was beginning to ebb throughout New England. By the 1820s several groups had broken with Calvinist orthodoxy, and sectarian bias in the Shelburne community is clear in Theophilus's account of the opposition from local Unitarians to his appointment as co-pastor. His disdain for "that class" is evident as he recalled they had been waiting for the senior Packard "either to die, or to resign on account of ill health" so that they could replace him with a "preacher of Unitarian sentiments." This group was undoubtedly disappointed at the junior Packard's appointment as co-pastor. Theophilus "carefully preserve[d]" the papers documenting the vote, and recorded in his diary the names of the ninety men who voted for him, the twenty-two who voted against him, and the forty-two who abstained.[33]

On 12 March 1828 Theophilus Packard, Jr. was fully ordained as a Congregationalist minister. He recorded that, over the next few years, he "enjoyed the work of the Gospel ministry," but confessed that he "found it laborious work to write out suitable sermons." He added that "the low state of religion in the church and parish" left him anxious and depressed, and he often questioned his fitness for ministry.[34]

In search of self-improvement, he began a regular diary in January 1829. The diary, he said, was written "chiefly for my own gratification and benefit."[35] However, he clearly hoped it would serve as an advice book for his children and later used it to defend his decisions regarding their mother. The diary included instructions to his sister, Sybil Dole, to use it "according to her discretion, allowing my children only to read it when they are at her house—and," he emphasized, "I wish them to read it."[36]

Much of the diary was written in retrospect from the vantage point of old age. The first section, for example, is a narrative autobiography written in 1871. The middle forty or so pages are truly a diary, written between 1829 and 1834. The next section was again written retrospectively and gives brief summaries for each year from 1835 through 1870. This is followed by a few entries written in 1871. The diary ends on Theophilus's seventieth birthday in 1872, thirteen years before his death.

Written in the mode of the Puritan diary in all its breast-beating anguish, Theophilus Packard's diary reveals a well-read and diligent man deeply committed to strict Calvinist principles.[37] It also reflects the interest in education and social reform that was often a byproduct of New England's evangelical Calvinism. Theophilus supported the temperance movement, although he seems to have given up tobacco and "spirituous liquor" as much out of concern for his own health as for principle. He also took a firm antislavery stance in the early 1830s when that position was still suspect as too radical, even in New England.

Even for its genre, Theophilus Packard's diary reveals the depth of his gloom and frustration over the state his of health, soul, and ministry. Depression, ill health, and expectations of impending death are constant themes as he often considered "the flight of time." Even at the age of twenty-two, he was preoccupied by the knowledge that he was "hastily speeding my way out of probation into Eternity."[38] He questioned his fitness for the ministry, writing, "I must quit the ministry, or be a different minister." On his twenty-ninth birthday, 1 February 1831, he wrote that he was "almost startled" that he had survived to that age.[39]

Sectarian strife was a repeated topic of the diary, as conflict continued between Congregationalists and Unitarians in Shelburne. In 1832, the Shelburne school committee, of which Theophilus was a member, refused to rehire a young teacher who "had during the previous year disturbed public religious meetings in town." The teacher's father, who was a Unitarian, sued the school committee for libel. The school committee lost the case and each committee member paid $125 in order to avoid further litigation. In language he would later use to describe denominational conflict in another of his pastorates, Theophilus recorded that "the case was tried amid great sectarian prejudice and passion, and in violation of some of the common usages of Courts . . . The secret of the whole affair of the prosecution," he continued, "was a wish to give a hard stab at Orthodoxy, as appeared most obvious to myself and others."[40]

In 1835 Theophilus toured the trans-Appalachian west, traveling by stagecoach, train, and boat, preaching and visiting ministerial colleagues along the way. By October, he was in Dayton, Ohio, where he attended the Presbyterian Synod's heresy trial of Lyman Beecher, Presbyterian minister and president of Oberlin College.[41] Beecher was part of what historian Nathan Hatch called "the full leadership core" of ministers involved in New England's Second Great Awakening.[42] But by 1835 Beecher had come to believe that human beings possessed the capacity to choose God, which introduced the possibility of human agency in salvation. This, of course, transgressed the strict determinist theology of his predecessors, exposing him to the accusation of Arminianism that led to his trial.

Beecher was acquitted of the charge; however, his trial reflected the splintering of Calvinist theology and also foreshadowed the coming schism in the Presbyterianism into Old School and New School branches. After the schism, the Old School abandoned the 1801 Plan of Union that had permitted Congregationalist ministers to serve in Presbyterian churches.[43] Theophilus did not record his feelings about the Beecher trial or the Old School/New School schism, but this theological conflict presaged coming difficulties in his ministry and personal life.

Theophilus returned home in December 1835, after three months of travel. The next year, at age thirty-four, he invested $850 in a house with six acres near his father's land in Shelburne, but apparently continued to live at his parents' home. Over the next few years, he continued to preach alternate Sundays with his father at the Shelburne church. Recalling the year 1839, he recorded that he "continued on in Shelburne for some time without much to break the monotony of country life." Then, in the next sentence he noted matter-of-factly, "On May 21, 1839, I was married to Miss Elizabeth P. Ware, daughter of Rev. Samuel Ware of South Deerfield, and began to occupy my house June 3, 1839."[44]

The monotony of country life was about to be broken.

2 "New Notions and Wild Vagaries"

IN RECALLING THEIR decision to marry, both Elizabeth and Theophilus Packard intimated that, given the choice again, they would choose differently. His diary entries about their marriage were written many years after the fact and, thus, the immediacy of any happy emotion was surely tempered by subsequent events. Nevertheless, his feelings about marriage appeared to be quite pragmatic. He was settled as a minister and he needed a wife. There seemed almost a touch of regret as he recalled leaving his father's house, which had been his "pleasant and happy home for 37 years," to move into his own home nearby. He lamented retrospectively that he was "not then so fully aware . . . of the sad risk incurred in marrying any person who has once been insane," adding that she appeared to be fully recovered and for years had shown no symptoms of derangement.[1]

Meanwhile Elizabeth, also writing in retrospect, declared that, "next time," she would not marry to suit her father. She observed that the ministers "do club so closely together that they leave the daughter and wife and mother out altogether."[2]

Was it a marriage of convenience? In hindsight, it seems clear that the two were far different not only in age, but also in personality and intellectual bent. Sober and conventional, he was strongly rooted in the Calvinism that his Puritan ancestors brought to seventeenth-century Plymouth Colony, particularly as it had been refined by minister and theologian Jonathan Edwards during the First Great Awakening.[3] High-spirited and inquisitive, she too was marked by a Calvinist upbringing, but her intellectual curiosity led her to question Calvinism's basic tenets and move beyond even the dramatic changes in personal theology that grew out of the Second Great Awakening.

Calvinism was a profound influence on the American psyche, yielding particular attitudes about individual morality, societal goodness, and social relationships that inspired a national ethic of work and industry as well as a yearning to reform both the individual and society. It could also produce a somber and guilt-ridden personality, anxious for personal salvation but fearing damnation. In addition, Calvinism was a religion, indeed a worldview, grounded in hierarchical notions of authority and obedience.

Theophilus Packard exemplified both the positive and negative aspects of Calvinism. An upright, moral, and reform-minded man, he was also anxious, authoritarian, and depressed. Not surprisingly, in marriage he confidently presumed dual authority over his wife and expected from her the respect and deference due him as both her husband and a minister.

Elizabeth Packard was also driven toward improvement of self and society, but she was compelled more by a sense of personal rights and responsibilities than feelings of duty. Although she admitted the need for order in social relations, she valued egalitarianism over authority. In marriage, she expected a democratic, companionate relationship in which her ideas and opinions received equal consideration.

She was influenced by the ideology of the Second Great Awakening, which tended to be Arminian in theology and infused with the Revolutionary values of democracy and individualism. This, however, would prove only the launching point for her religious exploration, which would eventually lead her to Universalism, Swedenborgianism, and Spiritualism. To a striking extent, the conflict between Elizabeth and Theophilus Packard mirrored the theological tension between Calvinism and opposing sects in broader society. Their differing theological perspectives are evident in the personal conversion narrative each recorded.

THEOPHILUS PACKARD'S CONVERSION EXPERIENCE

Saving grace did not come easily to Theophilus Packard, but when it came it conformed to the formulaic pattern recognized by Calvinists as evidence of genuine salvation, and he followed the tradition of Puritan diarists in recording his conversion narrative in detail. "Without any apparent cause," he wrote, "my feelings grew more tender, more intense, more painful." Carefully differentiating his experience from that induced by revivalist enthusiasm, he affirmed, "No extraordinary means were used in my case" to produce an emotional experience. "It was not might or power," he testified, "that caused me to tremble—but a view of my sins and my state and prospects, brought to mind, I can not tell how."[4] He recorded that when the long-sought experience occurred, "a sudden and instantaneous change in my feelings and state of mind took place . . . My despondency, gloom and terror . . . were succeeded by right joy, calm serenity and sweet peace as I never before experienced."[5]

For the remainder of his life, Theophilus venerated New England's Puritan divines and immersed himself in their theology. He recorded with reverence, for example, his visit to the gravesite of Englishman George Whitefield, evangelist of the First Awakening, whose tomb in Newburyport, Massachusetts, was for many years a pilgrimage destination for young ministers.[6] "I visited the Federal St. church," he wrote, "and placed my hand on the skeleton head of George Whitefield . . . that famous preacher whose labors God blessed to the conversion of thousands on both continents."[7]

Reared only twenty miles from Jonathan Edwards's Northampton, Massachusetts, home, Theophilus also visited "the grave of that most godly man, great Theologian, and immortal author" on several occasions.[8] He "read and re-read" the works of Edwards and absorbed "with keen relish" the works of Bellamy, Hopkins, Dwight, Nettleton, and Tyler. These men were associated with the New Divinity movement at Yale and were, like Edwards, strict determinists seeking to revitalize orthodox Calvinism.[9]

But any joy or assurance Theophilus took from religion seemed short-lived as, good Puritan that he was, he engaged in a continuous cycle of spiritual recrimination, fear of damnation, and faint hope of salvation. He struggled to find in his life the blessings that might evidence God's favor on him. But his health was always fragile, the effect of his ministry modest, his financial prosperity temporary, and his family a mixed blessing, at best.

ELIZABETH PACKARD'S CONVERSION EXPERIENCE

An obedient child nurtured on Christian virtues from infancy, Elizabeth apparently lacked the extreme guilt requisite for a Calvinist conversion. She explained that she did not feel like "a great sinner," because she "always had been doing as well as I knew how to do."[10] It was not that she thought her behavior was spotless. She could remember her remorse for speaking impatiently or disrespectfully to her mother and knew "what sorrow for sin was by experience." She viewed this sorrow as evidence of repentance. Thus, she explained, "I didn't put off repentance until the time of revival had come to cry over it then, and go on to the anxious-seat for prayer for pardon."[11]

Nevertheless, she apparently bowed to social and parental expectations for her conversion during a revival meeting in 1831. She described how she and a schoolmate "went out into the broad aisle in the Conway old meeting-house, with about forty others . . . and made public professions of our faith." The only problem was, she recalled, "I didn't know what I was converted from, nor what I was converted unto."[12] Nevertheless, to her surprise, the church determined that her conversion was a "genuine case" and admitted her into membership. Writing decades later she recalled, with tongue in cheek, that she tried to feel that she was a great sinner, but thought she "made a sorry piece of business of it." But when she overheard her pastor assure her father about her conversion, she "concluded to give up my search after conviction, and indulge a hope I had felt it."[13]

Although as an adult she rejected the revivalists' anxious-bench she, like the preachers of the Second Great Awakening, would question clerical and doctrinal authority and claim the right to think for herself in matters of theology. Also like them, she would claim authority from direct revelation as revealed by God through scripture as well as by His presence within each individual and in the natural world. Such notions, simmering in her mind in the first decades of her marriage, would one day lead her into direct conflict with her husband's religion and authority.

Nevertheless, at the time of their marriage in 1839, the two seemed a good match. Both were well educated and from deeply religious families. Both strongly supported the antislavery cause and shared interests in reading, travel, and family life. Their fathers, both Congregational ministers, were longtime friends. She much admired his distinguished father and he respected her father as an elder colleague.

Following a two-week honeymoon traveling in Massachusetts, the Packards set up housekeeping at his house in Shelburne and, for the next dozen years or so, lived apparently unremarkable lives. Theophilus noted that his wife "was very acceptable to the people [of his church], was active and useful among the young people, and did good service in teaching an Infant Class in the Sabbath School for many years." When they entertained visiting ministers, he was pleased that his wife "performed her part most excellently" and "made good impressions."[14]

Likewise she recalled that she was "proud of his popularity as an uncommonly able, talented, and devoted Christian minister." She confessed that her "womanly pride" had often "been flattered at the knowledge of the high esteem in which [her] husband was held, not only by his brother clergymen, but also by all his hearers, almost without exception."[15]

During these years, the Packards expanded their family at the rate of one child every two to three years. Theophilus recorded the birth and baptism of each child with affection and due concern for the child's religious instruction. Recalling the birth of his first son, Theophilus III (nicknamed Theo and Toffy), on 17 March 1842, he wrote that he took "great pleasure" in Theo's growth and development and often took him along on visits to schools and area churches.[16]

He did not mention that his wife had almost died in childbirth. But Elizabeth remembered that "it took three doctors and a great lot of women" to assist in the birth. Despite her preference for homeopathic remedies and suspicion of doctors, she was grateful "for instruments in the hands of a skillful surgeon" at the time of this first child's birth.[17]

On the birth of their second son, Isaac (called Ira), on 24 June 1844, Theophilus again did not mention his wife, but wrote of his "deep and tender interest" in this son, "especially that God would by the Holy Spirit change his heart and convert him into a Christian."[18]

A third son, Samuel Ware, arrived on 2 November 1847. Theophilus recalled Samuel's birth with a cautionary note, writing that he feared "infidel notions and fatal errors will prove the ruin of his soul."[19] Elizabeth recalled that Samuel caused his father "ten times more annoyance than all the other children combined," but added that her husband nevertheless was "partial to him to his injury, and to the expense of the other brothers' feelings."[20]

In 1848, the year after Samuel's birth, Theophilus celebrated his twentieth year as co-pastor of the Congregationalist church in Shelburne. He recorded with satisfaction the demise (apparently temporary) of the Unitarian church in the community, noting its "hostility to evangelical religion." He observed happily that, apart from Shelburne Falls village, nearly all the families in town attended the Congregational church and added, "The Baptists . . . have given up their meetings [and] disbanded their church."[21]

The next year, on 10 May, the Packards welcomed their only daughter, Elizabeth (called Libby by her mother and Lizzie by her father). She was for both parents "an object of most affectionate regard." While Theophilus wrote warmly, "It is exceedingly pleasant to have one daughter in a family of children,"[22] Elizabeth treasured Libby as "another specimen of her mother's womanly organization—kind, loving, gentle, and true."[23]

A fourth son, George Hastings, arrived 18 July 1853. Theophilus wrote that George, like his other children, was from birth "instructed from the Assembly's Catechism, that noble compound of religious truth." He was encouraged that little George showed a desire for conversion, often weeping and asking his father "what he could do to be saved."[24]

Up to the early 1850s, life seemed to go well for the Packards. Their property included a two-story house and six "good acres" worth $100 per acre. Elizabeth described their farmstead in fond detail right down to the picket fence. The sizable house was "painted both outside and in, and nicely papered." It had "a large kitchen, a large pantry and storeroom, a nice arch kettle set in the kitchen, and nine closets." The front and back yards were each "enclosed with a good picket fence." The property included a barn, carriage house, and several outbuildings. An orchard supplied the family with a variety of fruits and berries. Elizabeth noted that "the house was insured for six hundred dollars, at the Mutual Insurance Company's office."[25]

She also noted that the Shelburne congregation paid Theophilus's salary "prompt and well." His salary ranged from $375 to $500, plus gifts from the congregation. It was, she wrote, "money, fully equal to his wants and the wants of his family."[26]

If a healthy family and financial prosperity evidenced God's grace, the Packards were blessed. Religion was, of course, central to their lives. But the interest both gave to finances, property, and childrearing suggests they were also concerned with wealth and social status. They seemed, by all accounts, to be a rising middle-class family, and they subscribed to the mores appropriate for their class. Indeed, as a Congregationalist minister, Theophilus Packard was poised to join New England's elite.

Concurrently, Elizabeth ascribed to the ideals of the true woman and re-publican mother.[27] As the daughter and wife of ministers, she would have heard many sermons admonishing women to model their lives on these ideals and she was deeply influenced by this teaching and its apparent affirmation in scripture.

Clearly, in the early years of their marriage, Packard was proud of her husband's status and relative wealth, and happily supported him in his work. She took pride in her domestic expertise, whether it was in decorating the home or entertaining her husband's associates. She was a dedicated republican mother who reared her children with a mixture of affection, instruction, and discipline aimed at developing godly and faithful citizens.

But, even as Packard embraced domesticity and true womanhood, she absorbed contending interpretations of those ideals as expressed in the novels and advice books of nineteenth-century women writers. Though she mentions none of these by name, their influence on her thoughts and actions is, nevertheless, clear. By the third and fourth decades of the nine-teenth century, women had produced a new genre of literature, the romance novel. The "literary domestics," as one historian called them, were often disregarded by contemporaries (and later some historians) as sentimental "scribblers." Nevertheless, they broke new ground by featuring women as heroines in plots set within woman's private sphere. While they typically espoused normative gender values, their work as writers moved them into the public arena even as their choice of subject matter carried woman's private sphere onto the public stage.[28]

These writers provided a model for Packard who, when propelled into the public sphere, determined to survive by writing and selling books. Like the subjects of the sentimental novelists, she portrayed herself as a true woman and longsuffering heroine. She later compared her life story to the plot of a romance novel: "We have heard of such deep laid plots in romances," she wrote, speaking through the voice of an Illinois legislator, "but we never knew one acted out in real life before."[29]

Perhaps even more influential than the romance writers was the advice of domestic feminists such as educator and writer Catharine Beecher, who exalted domesticity and true womanhood while promoting modest expansion of woman's sphere. As one historian noted, these women helped to redefine the meaning of domesticity.[30] As a schoolteacher in New England in the 1830s, Packard might well have used Beecher's popular textbooks, *Exercises in Grammar* (1829), *Arithmetic Simplified* (1832), and *Primary Geography for Children* (1833). Beecher's most widely read publication, however, was *A Treatise on Domestic Economy,* an advice book published in 1841 that became the Bible of the nineteenth-century cult of domesticity. Aimed at wives (and young women who hoped to become wives) it offered advice on every conceivable aspect of nineteenth-century woman's sphere, from interior design to treatment for a foundered horse.

Packard seems to have patterned her domestic endeavors according to the advice in Beecher's *Treatise.* As Beecher admonished, she maintained an orderly, well-appointed home. Her children were equally well appointed and Packard took pride in designing and tailoring beautiful clothing for them. As Beecher advised, she provided the children with good nutrition and homeopathic healthcare. Rearing six healthy children was a feat in early nineteenth-century America and Packard viewed her children's robust health as evidence of her success as a mother. She also abided by Beecher's advice regarding a woman's personal health, which emphasized the importance of routine, diet, rest, and calisthenics.

Packard's ideas about gender roles also echoed Beecher's views of a well-ordered society in which a system of laws sustained "certain relations and dependencies in social and civil life." Within this structure each individual could "pursue and secure the highest degree of happiness within his reach." In Beecher's philosophy, "a truly democratic state" permitted "each individual . . . to choose for himself, who shall take the position of his superior." Accordingly, no woman was "forced to obey any husband but the one she chooses for herself." Thus, a woman was not "obliged" to take a husband, but once she chose to marry, she was obliged to grant her husband a position of superiority over her. Such relations, Beecher explained, were ordained by God for the good of human society.[31] Packard agreed in principle with these divinely ordained social relations. However, her perspective was tempered by the fact that she, unlike Beecher, was a married woman who understood that reality could sometimes overrun an ideal.

French traveler Alexis de Tocqueville observed that a married woman in America could not "for a moment" escape her restricted sphere "without immediately putting her tranquility, her honor, and even her social existence in peril."[32] Elizabeth Packard would run squarely into this reality. And in a paradox perhaps representative of many women, she would be pushed by necessity into the public sphere by the constrictive nature of the very values she held. In this process, she would ultimately develop a rudimentary "feminist consciousness" as she attempted both to maintain the ideals and status of a true woman and to make her way in the public sphere.[33]

Indeed, as women's historians have demonstrated, domesticity and true womanhood would ultimately prove subversive to patriarchal authority. The same ideals that exalted womanhood also legitimated woman's authority over her domestic sphere and offered the possibility of extending her moral influence over a wider domain. If women were by nature more pious, pure, and domestic than men, should they not exercise authority over affairs beyond the home that affect the home and children? Catharine Beecher thought they should and wrote that, in such matters, a wife's "opinions and feelings have a consideration, equal, or even superior, to that of the other sex."[34]

Elizabeth Packard wholeheartedly agreed and she expected reciprocity with her husband in return for her investment in these values. Thus, she insisted on her right to exercise authority over the practical matters related to the home and children. She also expected her husband to exhibit a measure of respect and consideration for her efforts and opinions. This was fine with Theophilus Packard—so long as her activities and opinions corresponded to his.

Hence, even as the Packards enjoyed what by both their accounts were relatively happy years, fault lines were opening. Not surprisingly, Theophilus Packard's later complaints against his wife would be linked to the notion of "true womanhood," and he would declare that she had failed in each of the four aspects of that ideal. Not only would he despair at her lack of "submissiveness," he would question the correctness of her piety, charge her with neglecting her domestic duties and, ultimately, doubt her purity, that is, her fidelity to him. Indeed, she would find it increasingly difficult to live within the constricting ideals of true womanhood.

By the early 1850s, there was apparently tension between the Packards on both domestic and theological matters. Abruptly, in December 1853, Theophilus resigned as pastor at Shelburne. His leaving would necessitate a complete change in ministerial leadership for the church since his eighty-four-year-old-father was in failing health and would, in fact, die within two years. But, despite the congregation's petition urging him to stay, Theophilus remained adamant about leaving.[35]

For about six months he "supplied destitute churches" in the Shelburne area and rejected offers for church positions at Westhampton, Massachusetts, and Harrington, Connecticut.[36] During this time he worked on family genealogy and also published *A History of the Congregational Churches and Ministers of Franklin County* (1854).

In June 1855, he left the family behind and spent two months traveling in the West. While there, he accepted a one-year position with a church in Lyme, Ohio. He returned to Shelburne mid-August and, that fall, sold his house and adjoining land at auction for $425, half of what he had paid for it fifteen years earlier.[37]

We can only surmise all the factors that went into the Packards' decision to abandon their native New England, extended family, and well-established church for what would essentially be a missionary post in the West. Certainly, Theophilus's earlier interest in missionary work and the West would seem reason enough. He wrote that he was "desirous of residing in the Western country with some hope that my health would be improved in that climate," but then added that his wife was "intensely earnest for the change."[38]

Elizabeth, on the other hand, intimated that the religious climate of New England was becoming uncomfortable for her husband and suggested that even the faithful of his congregation were beginning to resist his strict Calvinism. His sermons, she said, "had one striking peculiarity . . . 'Total depravity.' He would push eastward, westward, northward, and southward, to find some nobleness in human nature to attack—overthrow—and destroy."[39] Suggesting that the move was his choice, she wrote that in those days, "I always let [him] lay his own plans" and then "helped him carry them out—that's all." Still, she "didn't care if he thought it best to break up old associations and start on a new track . . . I was for it," she added. "Anything for peace."[40]

But what old associations did Theophilus hope to break up or to escape? What had disrupted the family's peace and prompted their uprooting? Was his wife among the women who were emboldened by the first murmurings of the woman's rights movement to claim their rights as individuals and citizens? Packard, an avid reader who enjoyed the popular periodicals of the day, undoubtedly knew about the woman's rights convention in Seneca

Falls, New York, in 1848 and the radical "Declaration of Sentiments" signed by many of those present.

Health and hope for domestic peace may indeed have been important factors in the move. But Elizabeth Packard was also correct in her observation that the religious climate in New England had changed dramatically. By the early decades of the nineteenth century, Calvinism had inspired numerous opposition sects. Universalism, Unitarianism, and Transcendentalism, for example, each developed as reactions against the harshness of Calvinist doctrine. As early as 1774, Boston Congregationalist Charles Chauncy had quietly published a defense of universal salvation entitled *The Salvation of All Men, the Grand Thing aimed at in the Scheme of God.* Universalists challenged the doctrines of predestination and election by emphasizing the benevolence of God over His justice. They insisted that all would ultimately be saved through the compassion of a loving God.

Meanwhile, Unitarians disputed the Calvinist understanding of mankind as naturally corrupt. They argued that men and women were not born depraved sinners, but were "God's noblest creation" with a "keen moral sense and reliable powers of reason."[41] They also rejected the Calvinist theology of the Trinity, which they contended suggested three Gods, not a single, unified Being. By 1825, Unitarians, under the leadership of William Ellery Channing in Boston, had formed a separate denomination.

By the early 1830s, Unitarian minister Ralph Waldo Emerson was moving toward even more unorthodox views that came to fruition in the brief but persistently influential Transcendentalist movement. Transcendentalists emphasized individual search for religion over corporate liturgies and doctrines. They considered self-reliance and the responsibility to think for oneself in matters of religion vital and believed the individual must look to his or her own soul, not society, for truth and wisdom.[42]

At the same time, Methodists and Baptists made inroads in New England, due in part to the revivals of the Second Great Awakening.[43] By the late 1840s, heterodox sects such as the Adventists and Campbellites were also multiplying. Adventists, or Millerites, followed the prophetic preaching of former Baptist minister William Miller, who predicted the imminent coming of Christ and "advent" of the millennium, Christ's thousand-year reign of peace on Earth.

Campbellites (later the Disciples of Christ) followed Alexander Campbell, a Scotsman and former Presbyterian preacher who claimed the Bible as sole authority and believed each individual must discover the true meaning of Christianity, free from the opinions of others. All of these threatened the clerical and doctrinal authority of the dominant Calvinist churches, and Congregationalist clergy responded with both preaching and missionary efforts to prevent the erosion of orthodoxy.

From Elizabeth Packard's later writing, it is clear she assimilated concepts from each of these religious groups. Furthermore, she was fascinated by a new phenomenon spreading across the Northeast. In 1848, the spirit world intruded directly on American consciousness as the Fox sisters and their "Rochester rappings" in New York gained national attention. Spirit communication and mesmeric trances became parlor games and lyceum amusement for some, while others saw in them the conjunction of ancient teaching and modern science.[44]

By the early 1850s New England was brimming with new ideas and, as the Packards prepared to leave Massachusetts, Congregationalists were no longer the only, nor even the majority, church in Shelburne. According to Theophilus Packard's history of Franklin County churches, by 1853 Shelburne's 2 Congregational churches together had 202 members, while the Baptists claimed 240 members. Methodists, Unitarians, Universalists, Adventists, Episcopalians, and Shaking Quakers claimed smaller numbers, but were also present within the community.[45] It seemed that the New England way was in decline and orthodoxy was being challenged on many fronts.

Thus, for Theophilus Packard, moving west may well have represented escape from these disconcerting sectarian pressures to an environment where orthodoxy might be reestablished. More specifically, it may have been a way to remove his wife from unorthodox influences.

But to Elizabeth Packard the move west meant freedom—freedom from longstanding social and religious strictures and freedom to explore new experiences and ideas. At each step of the journey she continued to absorb new ideas, sometimes accommodating them to Calvinism, but equally often replacing traditional doctrine with "new notions and wild vagaries" that appalled her husband.

3 Breaking the Mold

"FAREWELL! FATHER, MOTHER, BROTHERS! I leave thee this pleasant September morning, 1854, to seek my Western home in Lyme, Ohio. My little group of loved ones are all in good health and spirits—five in number—the oldest, Theophilus, twelve years of age—the youngest, George Hastings, seventeen months—a nursing babe."[1]

Thus, Elizabeth Packard described the family's departure from their native Massachusetts. A decade later she could still recall in minute detail how she had dressed the children for travel. The older boys (Theo, Isaac, and Samuel) wore overcoats, caps, and gloves and each carried a carpetbag. Daughter Libby wore a "black velvet tunic, lined with dove-colored silke, and trimmed with mazarine blue fringe." Baby George was dressed in a "little blue and white knit wrapper, with long, warm sleeves, and his claret merino cape [was] lined with light silk, and embroidered with scallops and knots, and tied with broad claret-colored ribbon strings." The baby's outfit was completed with a fringed "blue zephyr worsted," mittens, and "black-silk velvet cap, with ear tabs of light-blue satin [and] rosettes, and lace border about the front."[2]

The children were apparently the center of attention as the family left the train at Cleveland and boarded a steamboat bound for Sandusky City. Packard recalled with pleasure the remarks of the "gaily dressed ladies" regarding the children's good conduct and fine clothes. She added proudly that she "had been the sole maker, not only of the clothes, but also of the style, or fashion, in which they were made."[3]

Packard and her husband were striking in appearance as well. He, at age fifty-two, was tall and clean-shaven with wildly curly red hair. She, age thirty-eight, was a petite five-feet-one inch with dark brown hair and eyes. She added, with no trace of false modesty, "Almost any man would jump to help me at any time; for I was neatly and tastefully dressed . . . and I find the men generally like to wait upon good-looking and well-dressed ladies!"[4]

Theophilus Packard's recollections of their journey to Ohio were also detailed. He recalled their date of departure (18 September 1854) and carefully documented the logistics and costs of the trip, which included a stop to visit relatives in Lyons, New York. The cost of train fare for 7 was $57.00 and freight for 6,735 pounds of goods was $83.00. At the time his "whole property" was worth $2,700.[5]

In Lyme, Ohio, the Packards were greeted by members of their new Presbyterian congregation as well as by Theophilus's sister Sybil and her husband, Abijah Dole, who resided there. Theophilus described the parsonage as "convenient" and noted that the people of Lyme were pleasant and, perhaps more important, "generous."[6]

The Packards enrolled their oldest son, Theo, at nearby Oberlin Collegiate Institute for the summer term.[7] By the 1850s Oberlin was a center of revivalist zeal and Arminian "Perfectionism" under the leadership of firebrand preacher Charles Grandison Finney.[8] Finney's "new measures" for gaining converts scandalized orthodox Calvinists; thus, when young Theo apparently "professed to obtain a hope that he had become a Christian," his father was unconvinced. He wrote that while Theo was moral, so far as he knew, he failed to "exhibit the marks and evidences . . . of being a real believer." He then added with emphasis, "God of mercy! Save him from soul destroying Universalism."[9]

It was apparently Elizabeth, however, who wanted to move on from Ohio. Theophilus recorded simply that his "wife was unwilling to stay there any longer."[10] In a later book she wrote that Lyme was too much like Shelburne for her liking.[11]

Thus, although the Lyme congregation offered him a permanent position, on 16 October 1855 the family headed farther west to Iowa, where Theophilus became pastor of a Congregational church. Elizabeth enthused, "The farther I got from the East the better I liked it" and added, "When we got to Mount Pleasant, Iowa, we knew what it was to go West."[12] She was exhilarated by the change, and wrote: "Our New England habits have been broken up. Our mould in which we were cast has been broken up. We have had room for expansive growth. We were too conservative rut thinkers, there."[13]

She quickly settled into her roles as homemaker and minister's wife, and happily shed New England propriety. She thrived on the greater degree of social freedom western society fostered, noting that she liked being able to stay in her working-dress in the afternoon without "fear Cousin Ophelia might call and catch me in it."[14]

She was pleased with their "comfortable house of five rooms" and boasted, "Our twenty large boxes of furniture well furnished our home with a far more

Figure 1. Elizabeth and Theophilus Packard, Jr. Courtesy of The Bancroft Library, University of California at Berkeley.

than the usual share of home comforts than most Westerners can boast of having."[15] She was sure that their freight had made a big impression, and that "the number, magnitude, and weight of his [her husband's] innumerable boxes and barrels," would lead one to "conclude T. Packard, Jr. [was] an important personage, destined to make quite a stir in this Western region."[16]

She recalled that her husband "was a very popular and acceptable pastor." The children also seemed to thrive in Mount Pleasant and their mother believed they enjoyed "the superior advantages of Professor Howe's school," which she "considered as preparatory to a collegiate course."[17]

But leaving Shelburne apparently proved difficult for Theophilus and, Elizabeth noted that "the farther [West] he got the worse it was." She surmised much of the difficulty was that he "couldn't make his Uzzah-power felt so much out here as he could in conservative, old New England."[18]

Indeed, Iowa had proved somewhat resistant to the influence of orthodox clergy. The first significant numbers of Congregationalist ministers had arrived in 1843, in response to Reverend Asa Turner's request to Andover Theological Seminary for an "Iowa Band" similar to the "Yale Band" that had pioneered the denomination in Illinois.[19]

The first Congregationalists in Iowa had "itinerated" (traveled from church to church) in the mode of the Methodists and Baptists. But, according to Iowa historian Leland L. Sage, the Congregationalists soon preferred "to settle into one place, where a well-educated clergyman of fastidious tastes could found and lead a separate and independent church in keeping with Congregational polity." Sage described the settled Congregationalists as "a social and cultural elite" that supported literary societies, lecture courses, and higher education and followed an "inclination to regulate the morals of the whole society" by promoting the temperance movement, anti-gambling laws, and, especially, the antislavery effort.[20]

Theophilus Packard, arriving in Iowa in 1855, was among the "settled" ministers who hoped to plant Calvinist orthodoxy and morality on the western frontier. He was welcomed by the earlier band of ministers, and recorded that he became acquainted with pioneer clergymen that included, in addition to Asa Turner, men such as William Salter, Reuben Gaylord, J. J. Hill, and "many ministers in that part of the country."[21]

Still, although by 1856 Iowa's population exceeded half a million, few were Congregationalists. Indeed, Iowans were predominately southern in heritage and many did not welcome "Yankee" Congregationalists, particularly as tensions over slavery escalated during the 1850s.[22] So, while Elizabeth was enthusiastic about their new home in Iowa, Theophilus was troubled. He wrote that he "found the society different from Eastern society" and noted that Congregationalism in general was "not in very good order" there. Worse yet, his church was "small and [the] society feeble."[23] Furthermore, his hopes for removing his wife from unorthodox religious influences had also been disappointed. She continued to nurture unorthodox ideas and soon surrounded herself with a circle of like-minded friends.

Packard's closest friend in Iowa was Mrs. P. H. J. Fisher, a neighbor from Shelburne who had followed the Packards westward. Fisher was, like Packard, a spiritual seeker and she soon left their Congregationalist society to attend the local Universalist church. Packard recalled Theophilus's displeasure with the whole matter, writing, "Of course, Mr. Packard regarded Mrs. Fisher's influence over me as very detrimental."[24]

Packard kept up with news back East by reading two periodicals, *The New Englander* and *The Independent*. *The Independent* was a religious publication aimed at New Englanders who had emigrated westward and was originally founded to foster Congregationalism in the West. The paper also carried news for several other denominations as well as national news, foreign affairs, and commentary on all aspects of church and society. By the mid-1850s it had become increasingly radical and republican in tone, especially with regard to slavery.

Both Packards would have sympathized with *The Independent*'s antislavery position. But Elizabeth also avidly followed the editorials contributed by her childhood acquaintance, Henry Ward Beecher. Beecher, a past editor of *The Independent,* was by then a nationally recognized religious figure. Although he, like Theophilus Packard, was an ordained Congregationalist minister, Beecher had mastered the art of equivocation when it came to Calvinist doctrine. His romantic analogies drew on the beauty of nature or events of everyday life as much as doctrine or scripture, and his preaching typically emphasized love, mercy, and beauty rather than fire and brimstone. But just as he seemed to abandon orthodox doctrine completely, he would avoid heresy by oratorical circumlocution.

Packard also read *The New Englander,* the periodical her husband had condemned in his college account book as "wretched." Packard noted that it was an article in this magazine that provoked her interest in Spiritualism, which she was determined to investigate despite "a most strenuous opposition" from her husband and his church.[25]

While Packard was happy with her new western surroundings, she was increasingly unhappy with her husband. More and more, she chafed at his authoritarian ways and resisted his domination. For example, when phrenologist O. S. Fowler came to town, she determined to attend his lyceum in defiance of her husband's edict to the contrary. In a successful ploy, she told Theophilus that an influential deacon from his church was going to Fowler's lecture at the Campbellite church. She hinted that this deacon believed the pastor should likewise "keep up with the age" or risk losing his position. A reluctant Theophilus apparently attended the program and was duly mortified when Fowler brought the entire Packard family onstage to "read" their heads.[26]

Theophilus makes no mention of this incident in his diary, but his wife made much of it in a later book. According to Elizabeth, Fowler told her husband that his mind was "working like an old worn out horse in a tread mill."[27] Meanwhile, she reported that Fowler applauded her physical and intellectual virtues, declaring that she "had the best head he had ever seen on a woman."[28] Fowler undoubtedly amused the audience when he told Elizabeth that she was "too benevolent," then opined, "You are like the roast pig of the West, who went round with a butcher knife in his back, crying, to every one he met, 'Help yourself to a slice!'" She was gratified to think that even "if my husband don't understand and appreciate me, the phrenologists do."[29]

Clearly there was by now little harmony in the Packard marriage. Taking heart from the phrenologists' opinions and the sympathy of her friends, Elizabeth increasingly disregarded her husband's wishes in various matters. She apparently discomfited him by inviting two visiting Universalist ministers to stay at their house. She wrote that, although she "knew she would be scolded as soon as the company left," she felt that offering such hospitality was "the Christian thing to do."[30]

She said that "by redoubling [her] diligence at home" she could find time for her own "missionary work" in the community. However, Theophilus was apparently concerned not only about the friends she was attracting but also about her public image and influence. He apparently ordered her to stay home and stop neglecting her family.[31] Elizabeth viewed this as an attempt to "break down [her] popularity and influence over the minds and hearts of the people."[32] It was about this time, she recalled, that he began to suggest openly that she might be insane. She added that this "fancied neglect of my duties, was the food by which he fed this serpent of lies."[33]

Elizabeth countered her husband's accusations with charges of her own, declaring it was he, not she, who neglected his duties. "He hated his ministerial duties," she wrote, "they were his drudgeries, his burdens, which he was always trying to shirk." In an added dig, she wrote that in Mount Pleasant he could not get by with preaching "over his sermons the third and fourth time."[34]

That Elizabeth neglected the family is doubtful, given the great pride she took in her home and children. Indeed, both Packards appeared to be devoted parents who were much concerned about the physical and moral welfare of each of their children. But they often disagreed dramatically as to what the children should be taught and when they should be disciplined. After one such disagreement, she reported that an irate Theophilus dragged her into his study and read to her the scripture passage that began, "Wives obey your husbands . . ." She added, "Recollecting that I had learned the lesson by heart, having heard him repeat it to me so many times, [I] thought it was not necessary to take another that time." So, she told her readers, she left him standing there and went downstairs "to seek in solitude that rest for my spirit which I could not expect to find in the society of my husband's arbitrary will."[35]

In defending her devotion to domesticity, Packard pointed to the family's good health and prosperity, and noted that, since their marriage, her husband had saved $100 to $250 each year. "If this is the result of my 'neglecting' my family duties," she declared, "I say it is very profitable neglect, so far as pecuniary profits are concerned."[36]

But, in fact, the Packards were no longer prospering. Their financial resources had been sorely depleted by two long-distance moves in little more than a year and by the expense of buying and remodeling the house in Mount Pleasant. Theophilus noted that the move from Ohio to Iowa had cost $65 for his initial scouting trip, $48 transportation for the family, and $178 freight on 13,335 pounds of goods. He had also spent $1,200 for the house in Mount Pleasant and another $1,000 for the addition to it. Furthermore, he reported that his new congregation furnished "only a meager support" for their minister.[37]

Other factors may also have contributed to Theophilus's discontent with their situation in Mount Pleasant. As the nation spiraled toward civil war, Iowa became a principal route for abolitionists heading from New England to Kansas. Their intent was to bring that state into the Union as a free state, either by vote or by violence. Senator Charles Sumner's "Crime Against Kansas" speech in May 1856, and the subsequent life-threatening assault on Sumner by a proslavery southerner, had further inflamed the nation. In Kansas, tension mounted between Free Soilers who opposed slavery and southerners who favored popular sovereignty. Sage's *History of Iowa* tells that "Eastern crusaders" on their way to Kansas "came directly across Iowa . . . to avoid contact with proslavery Missourians."[38] Mount Pleasant, centered in Henry County in extreme southeast Iowa, was evidently near one such route. Theophilus recorded that, during 1856, "many passed thro' town for Kansas," and some from his congregation "went to resist the Missouri 'border ruffians.'"[39]

Still, his greatest concern was clearly his wife. He believed she was "unfavorably affected by the tone of society, and zealously espoused almost all new notions and wild vagaries that came along."[40] Encounters with phrenologists and Universalists were bad enough, but by then she was openly exploring Swedenborgianism and Spiritualism.

Emanuel Swedenborg (1688–1772) was a Swedish scientist, philosopher, and mystic whose followers established the Church of New Jerusalem (or New Church) shortly after his death. Among his many books were such titles as *The Delights of Wisdom Pertaining to Conjugial Love* (1768), *Universal Human; and, Soul-Body Interaction* (1769), and *The True Christian Religion Containing the Universal Theology of The New Church* (1771). As these works were translated into English in the mid-nineteenth century, they precipitated a resurgence of interest in Swedenborg. Numerous European and American intellectuals—among them William Blake, Thomas Carlyle, Henry James, Sr., John Greenleaf Whittier, Edward Everett Hale, and Harriet Beecher Stowe— were fascinated by his philosophy, which was frequently discussed in the periodicals of Packard's time.[41]

Swedenborgianism, popular among the literary avant-garde, was beyond the reach of most ordinary people. But, Spiritualism, which utopian socialist John H. Noyes described as "Swedenborgianism Americanized," captivated the popular imagination.[42] Spiritualism was built, in part, on the works of Andrew Jackson Davis, whose book *The Principles of Nature; Her Divine Revelations and Voice to Mankind* was published in 1847, the year before the Fox sisters popularized the notion of spirit communication. Davis claimed his book was based on revelations he had received in a visitation from the spirit of Swedenborg.

Combining elements of mesmerism, clairvoyance, and Swedenborg's mystical teaching, Davis's "harmonial philosophy" proposed that spirit communication could reveal divine truths to guide human lives, advance psychology and philosophy, and promote medical cures. Spiritualism confirmed the existence of an afterlife and offered hope of communicating with deceased loved ones at a time when death was a regular visitor to most families. As much a social phenomenon as a religious expression, Spiritualism also promoted egalitarian views of women, marriage, and divorce that appealed to many in the nineteenth-century woman's rights movement.

However, any deeper theological, philosophical, or social premises of Spiritualism were soon lost in séances and the staged performances of, usually female, mediums. Over time most Americans came to view it, at best, as an entertaining sideshow. Many, especially those who held orthodox religious beliefs, considered Spiritualism fraudulent, dangerous, or just plain crazy.

After little more than a year in Mount Pleasant, Theophilus was convinced that "In view of all the surrounding circumstances . . . it would <u>not</u> be best for us to remain long in this place." The next summer he made two exploratory visits to Manteno in east-central Illinois, where his sister Sybil and her husband, Abijah Dole, had moved. Soon thereafter, he was invited by the Manteno Presbyterian congregation "to supply them by the year." He purchased a house and ten acres of land in Manteno for $2,500 and in October 1857 moved his family out of Iowa.[43]

4 Free Love and True Womanhood

MANTENO WAS A SMALL farming village platted on the rich prairie of Kankakee County in east-central Illinois. The arrival of the railroad in 1853 encouraged growth and, by the time the Packards arrived there in 1857, the thriving community boasted a depot, grain warehouse, feed mill, general store, saloon, boarding house, hotel, post office, two schools, and three religious denominations—Catholic, Methodist, and Presbyterian. By 1860, the U.S. Census recorded Manteno's population as 861.

The Presbyterian church in this frontier community was a humble mission compared with the prestigious church Theophilus and his father had served in Massachusetts. The congregation had formed with eleven members just four years earlier at a meeting of the Chicago Presbytery of the New School Presbyterian Church, and was still meeting in the Methodist church building.[1] Theophilus noted in his diary that, much like at Mount Pleasant, he found in Manteno a "small, feeble" congregation with its "society in a very loose state" and the "Sabbath greatly desecrated."[2] Membership would barely exceed fifty through the end of the century.

Three years after Theophilus's arrival, the congregation withdrew from the New School Presbytery and joined with the Old School. Recording the change, the church history mentioned politely, "The creedal hindrances being slight, the congregation, at the suggestion of the McCormicks, who were substantial friends of the church, changed its adherence from what was then the new, to the old school branch of the church."[3] This almost certainly understated the impact of the doctrinal shift. That the transition from New to Old School was less amicable than the church history implies is evident in the instability in membership during Theophilus's pastorate (1857–62), during which "large numbers" left the church to form other congregations.[4]

The discord in the church was mirrored in the Packard household as the couple moved farther apart, both intellectually and emotionally. As they arrived in Manteno, Elizabeth was still mulling over unorthodox theologies she had picked up from Shelburne's religious mix of Unitarians, Universalists, Baptists, Shakers, and Methodists. Theophilus apparently attempted to mute her influence over their children, recording that the thought she might teach them that "morality is religion and Universalism is true" filled him with "unspeakable grief."[5]

Theophilus was also worried about his declining prosperity. He noted that his $500 salary was "insufficient even to support my family" and that he had been "greatly embarrassed" as to his property. Because of the "great financial crash" of 1857, he had been unable to sell his property in Iowa and had been forced to borrow money at 30 to 40 percent interest. Nearly $3,800 in debt, he could barely pay interest on the debt or keep up the $100 annual payment on his life insurance. "Verily," he wrote, "I have been reduced to sore straits."[6] Still, noting the kindness of his sister Sybil and her husband, Abijah Dole, he concluded that it was still "much more pleasant to live in [this] place."[7]

By now, Elizabeth's enthusiasm for western life had been replaced by anxiety. She was distressed by her husband's allegations that she neglected her family and alarmed by his insinuation that she was insane. Her "heaviest burden," she said, was her husband's "incessant . . . trespass" on her "inalienable rights." Especially troublesome was his interference with her "maternal rights" to train her children "in the paths of virtue." All this occurred, she said, at a time when she had "no energies to expend in their defense."[8]

"All these aggravated trials," she conceded, had pushed her beyond "all possible limits of human forbearance." She felt that temporary respite was "an absolute necessity, to prevent the bow thus bent to its utmost tension, from breaking."[9] Against her husband's wishes, she began planning a trip to visit friends and family in New York.

Anxious to avoid any appearance that she had deserted the family, Packard described herself to her readers as a "most faithfully devoted" wife dedicated "entirely to the promotion of [her husband's] interests." She explained that she had never before left the family for an extended trip, while her husband had left "repeatedly and often" to visit his friends and attend meetings.[10] She assured readers that only life-threatening physical and emotional duress could force her to leave, and that she did so only after putting the new Manteno residence in order and making the family's winter clothing.[11] She knew female readers would sympathize with the fact she had performed all this work by herself "with only two day's work of hired help." They would recognize, too, her husband's unfairness in denying her the opportunity to "take a rest" following these labors.[12]

Theophilus apparently opposed her suggestion that they hire a woman to help in her absence, so she assigned various household chores to their older sons. Thus prepared, six weeks after the family's arrival in Manteno, Elizabeth left for New York, taking with her Libby and George, ages seven and four.[13] She later referred to this trip as her "recruiting tour" on which she was "seeking what my soul needed, but could not find at home,—the love and sympathy of friends."[14]

Packard wrote that she arrived at the Lyons, New York, home of her cousins, Angeline and David Field, in December 1857, only to learn that her husband had written in advance to advise them she was insane.[15] She fumed, "Foiled as he now was in his attempts to crush my body beneath the sod, he next began the plot of murdering my spirit, by writing . . . that I was an insane person" who could not be trusted. To her relief, they accepted her side of the story.[16]

Elizabeth's parents had raised Angeline Field from infancy, thus the two women considered themselves more sisters than cousins. Safely ensconced at the Fields' home, Packard could finally relax and rest. She apparently enrolled Libby in school and, over the winter, enjoyed visiting other family members and friends, including another cousin, Dr. Fordice Rice, and his wife Laura in nearby Cazenovia.

In those communities, Packard had arrived not only in the bosom of friends, but also in the heart of the nineteenth-century Spiritualist and woman's rights movements. Lyons and Cazenovia were near New York's burned-over district, so called because of the successive revivals and religious movements that had occurred there during the early decades of the century. Cazenovia was not far from Rochester, the birthplace of modern Spiritualism. Even closer was Seneca Falls, where Elizabeth Cady Stanton and Lucretia Mott had launched the national woman's rights movement in 1848. Thus, Packard's choice of New York as a temporary refuge was significant—it was a place where her increasingly radical ideas could indeed find acceptance and nurture.

SPIRITUALISM AND WOMAN'S RIGHTS

Spiritualism and woman's rights were intertwined in many ways. While each reflected a continuum of ideas, both essentially rejected hierarchical relationships and favored more egalitarian relations between the sexes. To that end, both proposed radical changes in the social and political order. Historian Ann Braude has suggested that Spiritualism represented "an extreme case of the rejection of Calvinism" that especially appealed to a generation of New England women who rejected the harshness and authoritarianism of their fathers' Puritan faith. These women, Braude observed, "explicitly associated their rejection of Calvinism with their gender."[17] Thus, it was not coincidental that women were sometimes drawn to both movements.

Packard's simultaneous exploration of Spiritualism and woman's rights supports Braude's observations. While Packard accepted social and political hierarchies as necessary for an orderly society, she agreed with Spiritualists' refusal to accept any authority over individual conscience. She was also in full agreement with their denunciation of the Calvinist doctrines of original sin and divine election. Like many women, she was repelled by the thought that innocent infants were born sinful and damned.

While Packard never fully embraced the woman's rights movement and was not a feminist in the modern sense of the word, her association with Spiritualism and woman's rights advocates introduced elements of feminist consciousness to her personal theology. That she sought, for example, to bring feminine values to her religious beliefs is evident in her views of the Trinity and also in her defense of Eve. She faulted "Calvinistic theology" for limiting the Deity to the male sex. In that theology, God was simply a "lord and tyrant." She believed a truer Christianity would validate woman's equal place in God's creation by acknowledging a female aspect of God. Thus, a true Christian theology should combine both male and female natures "in one perfect whole." "Thus," she reasoned, "the Holy Ghost must be the wife of God," while Christ, the Son, was "the offspring of this holy union."[18]

She also applied this numinous theology to her understanding of true womanhood. Just as God and Christ were "perfectly manly," the Holy Ghost was "perfectly womanly." Thus, the truer a woman was to her natural feelings and impulses, the more closely she could reflect the Holy Ghost within.[19]

Packard extended her concept of an androgynous God to the Incarnation, suggesting that there must logically be a female incarnation of God in correspondence with Christ, the male incarnation of God. She believed God would send a "model woman" to aid women in "becoming like their God-mother—the Holy Ghost."[20] This belief was in keeping with the mystical theology of Spiritualism, which posited a direct correspondence between the Trinity—Father, Son, Holy Spirit—and the earthly family—father, child, and mother. Borrowing from ancient Kabbalah, Spiritualists identified the Holy Spirit with the Shekinah, the female spirit of the universe.[21]

Packard did not believe a female incarnation had yet occurred, but she envisioned a millennialist future in which "the elect lady" would appear and become the bride of Christ, forming a model "for the inhabitants of the new earth."[22]

This concept may well have been borrowed from contemporary Shakers, who believed their founder, Mother Ann Lee, was an incarnation of Christ.[23]

Despite the mystical elements in Packard's thought, she was not a mystic and did not seek or claim mystical union with God. Pure mystical experience required passive receptivity and suspension of reason and intellect.[24] Her Quaker-like "God within" enlightened her conscience and sharpened her reason, but never overwhelmed or submerged her mind or soul.[25] She was unwilling—likely unable—to suspend her reason in favor of nonintellectual revelation and she was suspicious of any religion that required her to do so. She rationalized that, underlying these spiritual mysteries, were undiscovered scientific truths that reason and progress would someday reveal.

Like feminists, Packard struggled with Eve's culpability in the biblical Fall.[26] She decided that Eve was an anomaly and not representative of a true woman since a true woman would better control her appetite and reason. Eve, she said, "acted like a child rather than like a woman" in eating "the forbidden apple." Nevertheless, she felt sympathy for Eve, believing that she been "blamed too much." A sense of sisterhood is suggested as Packard declared, "I shall go in for defending her,—for she is a woman like me."[27]

Packard was also captivated by Spiritualism's romantic conception of marriage as a union of soul mates. According to the doctrine of "spiritual affinities," the natural order contained one true, spiritual mate for each individual.[28] True marriage, they believed, required a spiritual, not legal, bond between two souls. Some completely shunned traditional marriage, arguing that the state had no right to intrude in social relations and that marriage should not be contracted or bound by law. Unfortunately, the ease with which some prominent Spiritualists abandoned one supposed soul mate for another exposed Spiritualists as a group to accusations of sexual promiscuity, or "free love."[29]

Packard would not reject marriage or condone divorce. But her longing for a companionate relationship led her to embrace the notion of spiritual soul mates. Regrettably, her professed "spiritual affinity" for a man to whom she was not married would soon expose her to accusations of both infidelity and insanity.

Although Packard accepted many Spiritualist beliefs, she was at first uncertain about the matter of communication between living and dead spirits. However, her skepticism on this matter vanished when she encountered her first direct "manifestation of modern Spiritualism" in a visit with relatives in Cazenovia.[30]

It happened, she reported, not in a public program or séance but in the quiet of the Rice family's parlor as the family sat talking around a table. Packard recorded that she was astonished when one of the women suddenly announced that a spirit was present and had a message for her. "My fears so triumphed," Packard confessed, "I burst into tears." She described how the woman acting as medium wrote the spirit's message: "My child, prepare for Persecution! Persecution! Persecution!! . . . But, fear not! . . . You will be sustained by these unseen powers, who are using you as their chosen instrument for great good to humanity." The message, Packard reported, was signed by her deceased mother, Lucy Strong Parsons Ware.[31] She recounted this episode noting, "Not a person in the room knew my mother's name, except myself."[32]

This spirit, she continued, also approved her plans to seek the "council of Hon. Gerrit Smith, as is your intention to do next Saturday." Smith, who lived in nearby Petersboro, was a wealthy abolitionist who in a matter of months would help finance John Brown's raid on the federal arsenal at Harpers Ferry, Virginia. He was also a cousin of Elizabeth Cady Stanton and, like her, a leader in the woman's rights movement. Stanton considered him part of her "magnetic circle" of reformers in central New York. Thus, when Packard sought out Smith "to get light on this subject of woman's rights," she was close to the heart of the movement.[33]

The Smiths' Petersboro home had often served as an informal retreat for harried activists. In the 1830s, abolitionists Sarah and Angelina Grimke had prayed with Smith about plans for their first speaking tour. Fearful they would be condemned as "Fanny Wrights," Smith advised them not to speak publicly except in parlors.[34] The Grimkes wintered over with the Smiths, and Angelina Grimke later wrote that Gerrit Smith, whom she thought of as her brother, was "one of the noblest, loveliest men I ever met."[35] Stanton had also enjoyed Smith's hospitality and told the Grimke sisters in an 1840 letter, "The two green spots to me in America are the peaceful abodes of cousin Gerrit & Theodore Weld."[36]

Apparently, Elizabeth Packard was similarly welcomed into Gerrit Smith's home and quickly received his support. She reported that he counseled her to assert her rights to her husband, telling her there was "no other way for you to live a Christian life with such a man."[37] Smith, she said, advised: "When you have done all that forbearance, kindness and intelligence can do to right your wrongs, all that is left for you to do is, to assert your rights, kindly, but firmly, and then leave the issue to God."[38]

Packard recorded that, as she conversed with the Smiths in their parlor, another spirit visitation took place. Again, the spirit's message was for her, this time from her husband's deceased sister, Jane Hastings. Hastings had been one of her "choicest friends—one of the few who seemed to understand and appreciate me while others would misapprehend and therefore misrepresent me."

This spirit told Packard to prepare for "Opposition! Opposition!! Opposition!!!" and encouraged her to "Persevere! Persevere!! Persevere!!!" Packard recalled that the spirit "laughed outright" when she referred to herself as "the weaker vessel" and questioned why "the light of new truths should dawn" in her mind before that of her husband.[39]

Packard's reporting of these incidents served two purposes. First, they suggested supernatural support for her radical ideas. Furthermore, they demonstrated that a woman, although the "weaker vessel," could possess spiritual insight superior to that of her husband. She was careful to remind her readers that Smith did not find her views "in conflict either with reason or common sense." Indeed, she declared, he fully endorsed "each, and all" of her positions.[40] Thus, Packard believed she had received the blessing not only of the spirits but also of one of the more notable reformers of her time.

ABNER BAKER

Although the sequence of events is unclear, it was around this time that Packard found further consolation in a warm friendship with a man named Abner Baker. A native of Cortland County, New York, Baker had moved to Michigan in 1834 and set up business as a boot maker and merchant. A respected citizen of Marshall, Michigan, Baker served on the local school board and the city council and as supervisor of Calhoun County.[41] It is not clear how they met initially, but the Packards' oldest son, Theo, apparently worked in Baker's store.

Baker and Packard had much in common. Both were born in 1816, married in 1839, and had five children. In addition, Baker was described as "a full believer in the writings of Emanuel Swedenborg," a fact that would have immediately attracted Packard's attention.[42]

By then Packard was, by her own admission, "famishing for a man's love."[43] No baby had arrived on schedule two to three years after young George, and discord in the Packards' marriage was nearing open warfare. Packard fell in love with Baker and believed he returned her affection. Their brief liaison seems to have been conducted mostly through an ill-fated exchange of letters. Although the letters were, by her definition "love-letters," Packard would swear to the end that her relationship with her "beloved Abner" was innocent, declaring "there is such a thing as a pure, spiritual love for I know there is—by my own blissful experience."[44]

How could Packard openly profess love for a man who was not her husband and maintain her perception of herself as a true woman? She resolved this quandary by juxtaposing concepts from Swedenborgianism and Spiritualism with the notion of true womanhood. She considered her relationship with Baker as "harmonial marriage"—a spiritual union of like affinities that existed on a completely different plane from legal marriage or sexual intercourse.

Invoking the cult of true womanhood, she explained that Baker filled her natural, womanly desire for a "protector." How could she not love him, she explained. "Can the thirsty, famishing soul help loving the pure, cold water? Neither can I help loving a pure man!"[45] Indeed, she reasoned, it was her God-given right and privilege "to love a true man,—God's representative on earth." Ironically, she then applied the determinist logic of Calvinism to absolve herself of any responsibility or guilt, saying, "God has made it as morally impossible for a true woman to withhold her love from such a man, as it is for the sun to withhold its light and heat."[46]

By employing this logic, Packard could acknowledge that marriage vows were binding while insisting that, so long as she was faithful in all her duties to her husband, it was not immoral to share a "spiritual" love with another man. To many outside her circle of New York friends Packard's explanation would sound like an excuse for "free love."

Packard now fully identified herself with the progressive reformers she met in New York and was certain that "whole band of 'come-outers' . . . with Gerrit Smith at their head" loved and accepted her.[47] Armed with affirmation she now prepared to return home, determined to follow Smith's advice.

Packard arrived back in Manteno, with Libby and George, in early March 1858. She recalled that, to her complete amazement, Theophilus met her with "as loving a welcome as any wife could desire." He suddenly seemed to respect her "rights and privileges as a junior partner in the marriage firm," showering her with "a liberal portion of manly expressed love and sympathy" that made her "heart [leap] for joy."[48]

But Theophilus recalled no such happy reunion. Instead, he recorded that, to his "great grief and annoyance," his wife returned from New York "a zealous Spiritualist" and tried "to teach it to our children as being taught by the Bible."[49] From that time on, he added, his "domestic peace and enjoyment were greatly interrupted."[50]

Nevertheless, within weeks of her return, Elizabeth Packard was pregnant.

For the moment, there was little else her husband could properly do but try to give her his support.

Apparently over the next several months, Packard maintained a clandestine correspondence with Abner Baker, hiding his letters with copies of her own in a linen chest. At some point, Theophilus discovered the letters and confronted his wife with them as proof of what he considered, at the very least, immodest behavior. Not surprisingly, her protests to the contrary were futile.[51]

Describing a lamentable mess, Packard explained how Theophilus threatened to sue Abner Baker, in her words, "for the privilege of writing to his wife—and instructing her in the Swedenborgian views of truth and duty." In later books, she accused Theophilus of attempting to extort $3,000 from Baker for the letters while keeping copies "for the devilish purpose of defaming" her virtue and sending her to an insane asylum.[52] Apparently, Theophilus was dissuaded from suing Baker by "that Christian lawyer, Mr. Kitchel of Detroit, Mich." Elizabeth wrote melodramatically that Kitchel's "timely warning to [her] misguided husband" spared Baker from "the criminal's doom."[53]

Attempting to shine a positive light on a sordid incident, Packard suggested that the Baker episode for a time actually rekindled her marriage. She was touched by her husband's apparent jealousy over Baker. It seemed that Theophilus saw in her letters to Baker that her "heart was yearning for love" and recognized his neglect of her. For a while, she believed Theophilus had forgiven her, and confided that after her return from New York she "experienced more conjugal love and enjoyment of married life" than in all their previous years of marriage.[54]

Once again, however, her husband's recollections differed from hers substantially. He described 1858 as the "most eventful and distressing year" of his life, during which many "sad scenes" occurred concerning his wife. "I draw a veil over some of the scenes of those days," he wrote, "in the belief that less injury will result . . . by this course than by a full record of events." There were, he continued, "such scenes of trial, anguish and agony, that I was unfitted to a great degree for service."[55]

On 18 December 1858, approximately nine months after her return from New York, Packard delivered her last child. While the child's paternity might well have been questioned, it was not. Theophilus recorded, "My son Arthur Dwight was born in Manteno this year . . . I baptized him in public and took a deep interest in his spiritual welfare." He added, "My heart goes out towards him in strong parental love, and I long to have him give evidence of piety."[56]

In January 1859, only a few weeks after Arthur's birth, Theophilus under-took his own recruiting tour back East, taking five-year-old George with him. He visited briefly in New York, but spent most of the trip in Massachusetts, where he convinced Packard's brothers and elderly father, who had not seen her in more than a decade, that she was once again insane. He returned to Manteno in February 1859 after nearly a month's absence.

Evidently it was around that time that Abner Baker appeared unexpect-edly at the Packards' Manteno home. The full purpose of his visit can only be surmised, but ostensibly it involved Theo's employment at Baker's store. A flustered Elizabeth served supper to their guest and Sybil and Abijah Dole were called in to mediate what was undoubtedly a distressing encounter.[57]

After this incident, Abner Baker seems to have disappeared from the Pack-ards' lives. By 1869 he had moved with his family to Nebraska, where he worked first as a merchant, then a farmer, and eventually served as sheriff of Jefferson County. Over time he helped establish the town of Steele City and built a reputation sufficient to merit a paragraph in Andreas's *History of the State of Nebraska.*[58]

Theophilus never mentioned the Baker affair in his diary. He recorded instead that it was his wife's neglect of the family, strange religious ideas, and disruption of his church that convinced him she was insane and required confinement to an asylum. Packard would protest that she was incarcerated for asserting her rights and resisting her husband's domination. But in a sentence buried in the more than 1,600 pages of her last book, she departed from that stance momentarily to confide that it was "Mr. Baker's letters" that brought "a long string of disasters" on her and her children.[59]

For the record, both would point to a dispute involving a Bible class at her husband's church as the crisis that led to her commitment. It was then, in the spring of 1860, that their private discord erupted into painfully public community scandal.

THE BIBLE CLASS

Packard recorded that the Bible class episode began benignly when Abijah Dole, with her husband's blessing, invited her to share her views which, he observed, were "a little different from our own."[60] Packard said that the class, which had six members (all male) when she joined, "soon increased to forty-six, including the most influential members of the community." And, she added, "The effect of these [Bible class] debates was felt throughout the whole community."[61] Her readers probably suspected (as Packard undoubtedly intended) that the invitation to present her views in the class was a ploy to expose her religious ideas as insane.

Indeed, the "honest views" Packard expressed publicly in this class placed her significantly outside Old School Presbyterianism and well beyond even the milder Calvinism of the New School. Packard's views reflected a democratic theology that valued the individual's personal experience of God over theological knowledge. Packard believed that religious truth was revealed directly to the human conscience—"God's vice-regent" in the soul.[62] Ordinary individuals, she proclaimed, were "God's mirrors, untarnished by human dogmas and creeds." Thus, she preferred the opinions of her peers to the opinions of orthodox theologians and ministers, saying, "I don't want my Bible-class to give me Scott's, or Henry's, or Clark's . . . or any other human being's opinions on the point under discussion . . . I want a new and better source of truth—the opinion of the common minds of the common people."[63]

Packard's religious notions also reflected Enlightenment ideals such as reason, liberty, and the belief in nature as the purveyor of God's natural laws. "Reason," Packard declared, "is, and always has been, my polar-star."[64] She understood reason to be that which was not contrary to observed truth and that which could be apprehended by common sense. Thus, she declared, "Whatever opinions and practice conflict with the plain dictates of my own reason and common-sense are of no account with me whatever. I just lay them all by in a heap for the credulous to glut upon to their hearts' content. I seek . . . a reasonable Bible—a reasonable God—a reasonable practice—for this reasonable religion is the only religion I have any reverence or respect for."[65]

Thus, Packard's arguments in the Bible class relied mostly on reason and common sense, occasionally reinforced by scripture. She recounted one notable debate that exemplified this. The topic under consideration by the class was "How Godliness is Profitable" and the question was: "Have we any reason to expect that a Christian farmer, *as a Christian,* will be any more successful in his farming operations, than an impenitent sinner?"[66] The correct answer from a Calvinist perspective was "Yes"—a man's "true moral character" might be judged by his success because success was evidence of God's favor and, thus, a demonstration of divine election.

Packard, of course, disagreed, and gave her "common sense" reasons. They were based on a tripartite view of human nature that probably eluded the understanding of most in the class and offended the Calvinist sensibilities of those who grasped her application of natural law philosophy. Individuals, she explained, existed in "three distinct departments of being"—physical, intellectual, and spiritual. "Each of these three distinct departments [are] under the control of *laws,* peculiar to itself; and these different laws do not interchange with, or affect each other's department."[67] Thus, Packard reasoned, success in business depended upon physical or mental ability, and had nothing to do with morality or spirituality.[68] The class rejected Packard's argument as "irrelevant to the subject, since she had not confined herself to the Bible alone for proof of her position."[69]

Packard insisted that her ideas should be tested against reason, common sense, and her own conscience as well as scripture. Indeed, her personal credo became: "The only infallible rule or guide for us is God's word, as it is interpreted to us through our individual reason and conscience." Packard believed that individuals were personally accountable to God for their actions. Thus, they must be granted the right to choose and live by what they personally understood to be God's truth. This concept of "free moral agency" was essential to her understanding of salvation. Thus, for Packard liberty— free will—was the essential gift of God.[70] Accordingly, she declared, "Any spirit in the body or out of the body, who attempts to *dictate* to the conscience of another, except through the reason of the one they wish to guide, ought to be looked upon as an enemy to their soul's highest interests."[71]

In its self-confidence and obliviousness to personal limitations, Packard's religious exploration reflected the "religious populism" of her time.[72] At that point, it was not evident which of the popular beliefs then swirling in American culture would become mainstream and which would fall by the way. Contemporary periodicals suggested, for example, that spirit communication might have a basis in science.[73] Thus, Packard was not alone in believing that new ideas about "Magnetism, Electricity, Psychology, and Spiritualism" were reasonable. Indeed, she imagined that they would ultimately be "developed into a spiritual science, the laws of which, future generations may be able to apply with as much certainty . . . as the present age depends upon steam as a locomotive power."[74]

In time, Packard would conclude that messages from spirit intermediaries could not be relied upon for truth, since the spirit world, like Earth, contained both good and evil beings. Ultimately she would reject Spiritualism as an "undeveloped state," and decide that it would not be "safe or proper to depend upon it as a guide for human conduct."[75] But, at this point in her life, the new ideas she was exploring seemed viable and, certainly, more reasonable than Calvinism. Thus, she confidently rejected the "musty old" ideas of her husband in favor of what she considered a more "modern" understanding of religion.

Within a few months, church stalwarts of Theophilus's church decided that the growing Bible class, stirred by his wife to freely debate doctrine and scripture, posed "a dangerous influence" that exposed church creed "to the charge of fallibility." Packard recorded that leadership of the class was transferred from the "softhearted" Abijah Dole to the "intolerant" Deacon Josephus Smith. According to Packard, Deacon Smith soon visited Theophilus with a request from the church that his wife cease her discussions in the Bible class.[76]

Elizabeth described a tearful scene in which Theophilus implored her to leave the class while she, sitting on his lap with her arms around his neck, entreated him tearfully, to "be a man" and tell them, "My wife has just as good a right to her opinions as you have to yours, and I shall protect her in that right." Unfortunately, she said, Theophilus mistook her "earnestness for anger" and pushed her away.[77]

Now in open rebellion against her husband and his congregation, Packard publicly requested a letter of dismissal from the Presbyterian Church so that she could join—not with a Spiritualist, Swedenborgian, or Universalist group—but with the local Methodist church. The Manteno Presbyterians not only denied her request but also viewed it as further evidence of insanity. With the support of his congregation, Theophilus now initiated plans to commit his recalcitrant wife to the Illinois Hospital for the Insane in Jacksonville.

5 "The Forms of Law"

BY JUNE 1860, the conflict between the Packards had, quite literally, reached a maddening degree for both husband and wife. Indeed, the entire family was in significant distress and there can be little doubt that Theophilus was truthful in his statement that it was impossible for him to "live with her comfortably in the family." Unable to either cajole or coerce his wife into submission, he had reached an intolerable place in his marriage.

He tried to send her away, at least temporarily, to stay with relatives. On 1 May 1860, her elderly father, Samuel Ware, wrote Theophilus that he was "willing to do anything consistent with my age and infirmity" to help, but thought it unwise to send Elizabeth on the lengthy trip to his Massachusetts home. "As a last resort," Ware wrote, "she should go to some Hospital near at hand."[1] Theophilus also tried to send her for an extended stay with her brother, Samuel, in Batavia, Illinois, forty miles from Manteno. But this plan evidently collapsed in an argument over whether or not she could have $10 to take on the trip.

Few of the remaining options exercised by other men in unhappy marriages were viable for Theophilus Packard. Desertion was the choice of some, who simply walked away from troubled relationships. But desertion would mean loss of his children, home, and position in his church and community. He rejected divorce on religious grounds, even though divorce was by then relatively easy to obtain in Illinois. Indeed, by 1859 Illinois actually led the nation in granting divorces.[2] Of the options available to him, declaring his wife insane was the most practicable and least socially objectionable. Her past history of treatment at an asylum lent credibility to the suggestion that she was once again insane.

Elizabeth, too, was at an impasse in the marriage. She acknowledged her husband's role as head of the family; but found his requirements for submission overwhelming. She explained that her husband's "education" led him to believe "that his marital authority was the foundation stone [of marriage]."

She added, "He, of course, conscientiously claimed, what I was too willing to grant, viz.: *subjection* to his will and wishes."[3]

She wrote that "the moment a husband begins to subject his wife, that moment the fundamental law of the marriage union is violated . . . the husband has taken the first step towards tyranny, and the injured wife has taken the first step towards losing her natural feeling of reverence towards her husband."[4]

She explained: "My husband claims . . . that my rights of property—my parental rights—my rights of opinion—my rights of conscience are all to be subject to his will." She rejected the notion that she must "subject these inalienable rights of womanhood," declaring that "the claims of a moral, accountable agent under God's government" forbad her from doing so.[5] Although she had long resented her husband's treatment of her, she wrote that only recently had she "reached that stage of womanly development where I had the moral courage to defend myself by asserting my own rights."[6]

She knew from experience that in other circles the ideas her husband so strenuously opposed were considered neither aberrant nor disruptive. She knew, too, of many couples who, like the Henry Stantons and the Gerrit Smiths, embraced the same ideas and acted as partners to promote reform. These provided the models to which she aspired. She believed sincerely that she, like those forward-looking reformers, was simply ahead of her time, writing, "It is my fortune . . . or rather *mis*fortune . . . to be a pioneer, just about twenty-five years in advance of my contemporaries,—therefore, I am called crazy, or insane, by those so far in my rear, that they cannot see the reasonableness of the positions and opinions I assume to advocate and defend."[7]

She, of course, had options for dealing with her troubled marriage other than silent submission or open rebellion. But she would reject long-term separation, desertion, or divorce for many of the same reasons her husband did. The decision to stand her ground appears to have been based, in part, on questionable advice from the friends in New York who encouraged her to assert her rights and those in Manteno who assured her, erroneously, that she could not be committed without a trial, at which they were certain she would be proved sane.

In refusing to submit to the authority of her husband and church (and in her flirtation with Abner Baker) Packard challenged nineteenth-century norms for her gender, which were contracted by the expectation that a woman display, not only domesticity, but also piety, purity, and submission.

Unfortunately, what Packard viewed as resistance to oppression and standing up for her rights her husband viewed as "perversity of behavior" and evidence of insanity. To Theophilus, his wife's behavior violated the standards of conduct appropriate for a wife and Christian in a way that threatened his children, church, and community. He was determined to exercise his authority—indeed, his duty—to control her behavior.[8]

By the spring of 1860, Elizabeth was thoroughly alarmed by her husband's threats to send her to an asylum. She discovered that he had written his brother-in-law, George Hastings, in New York the "most slanderous letter a man could possibly write of a woman." The letter, she said, suggested that she "could not be trusted alone, lest I should be 'seduced' to my ruin! . . . That I was the bane of his life, and the curse of his family, the ruination of his children."[9]

Fearing her husband's intentions, she recorded that she began to plan a defense she could present to the court if he indeed attempted to commit her. She arranged for Isaac to secure her personal papers and obtain help if she were taken away suddenly.[10]

Packard recorded that it was about this time that her husband "left the marriage bed," telling her only that he "thought it best." He also brought in a young woman from his church to watch over her.[11] Packard was certain the woman, Sarah Rumsey, was hired to spy on her. In fact, Rumsey later gave a sworn deposition saying that Packard made "bizarre" comments stating that she was "the medium, by which God is to convey truth to this people" and that her husband was "the serpent."[12]

Meanwhile, her husband began gathering letters and sworn depositions from friends and family supporting his intention to commit his wife. One petition, dated 22 May 1860, contained the signatures of thirty-nine individuals who attested to their "full and sad conviction that [Mrs. Packard] is so far deranged that her own good and the good of her family, not only justify but require her husband to have her placed in an Insane Asylum, as speedily as it can be conveniently done."[13]

On 24 May 1860, fifteen members of her husband's church signed a letter to Elizabeth condemning her conduct and urging her to repent. It seemed an odd missive to send to someone who was believed to be deranged and in need of treatment. The letter read accusatorily: "You have grievously sinned against God in trespassing upon the rights and disregarding the authority of your husband, and of this church, and in unjustly censuring and blaming this church, and in abusing and reproaching without good cause the Bible Class, and in casting your influence against your husband's ministry here, and the sacred cause of Bible religion. We feel . . . solemnly bound to reprove and rebuke you, because you have so entirely disregarded the counsels of your husband, your friends, and members of the church to reclaim you."[14]

The parishioners complained further that she had given money to help build the local Roman Catholic Church "in direct opposition" to her "husband's wishes and preaching, and in opposition to the cause our church is aiming to build up."[15] Interestingly, the letter was given, not to Elizabeth, but to her husband "to be used according to his judgment and discretion."[16]

On inquiry to the Jacksonville asylum, Theophilus would have discovered that his wife could actually be committed with relative ease. The form used to admit a young Elizabeth Ware in Massachusetts twenty-four years earlier had required an individual to be "a lunatic so furiously mad as to render it manifestly dangerous to the peace and safety of the community that the said [person] should continue at large."[17] However, the law then in force in Illinois required only that a person must be "evidently insane or distracted" prior to commitment.

More important, this law had been amended in 1851 to relax the commitment procedure for married women in a manner that, essentially, denied them due process. While the law required that a man must receive a formal hearing or trial and verdict of insanity prior to commitment, a married woman could be institutionalized without a public hearing or opportunity to present evidence in her own defense. The pertinent section of the law read: "Married women and infants, who in the judgment of the medical superintendent are evidently insane or distracted, may be received and detained in the hospital on the request of the husband, or the woman, or parent, or guardian of the infants, without the evidence of insanity or distraction required in other cases."[18]

The law was further amended in 1853 to require certificates from two physicians stating that the woman was insane; however, this provided little protection in Elizabeth's case. Theophilus apparently had little difficulty obtaining statements from two local physicians. Dr. Christopher W. Knott provided a certificate stating that he had "visited Mrs. Elizabeth Packard and consider her laboring with derangement of mind upon some subjects."[19] Dr. A. B. Newkirk declared not only that she was mentally insane, but also that he believed it was "unsafe for her husband and children to be exposed to her as it respects their lives."[20]

Even with these requirements met, however, Theophilus continued to gather support, including sworn statements from Reverend Ansel D. Eddy of Chicago and Dr. P. B. McKay of Wilmington, Illinois, both of whom were leaders in his denomination. Both Eddy and McKay endorsed Theophilus's plan to commit his wife.[21] The fact that he felt compelled to seek evidence and support beyond that required by law suggests there was substantial disagreement in the larger community regarding Packard's mental condition.[22]

Indeed, Elizabeth had supporters in the community. Her husband recorded that she went "out among the French Catholics, Universalists and such like people in the town and made horrible representations of my treatment of her." This, he said, had "aroused a rabid excitement against me, outside of my own church and congregation."[23]

In response to these "false and slanderous rumors in the community" he decided to call "a meeting of various classes of people" to defend his position. On 16 June 1860, his informal "jury" of twenty-one met in the Packards' parlor. Those attending included other ministers, the postmaster, the depot master, doctors, merchants, a justice of the peace, farmers, and both "males and females."[24] Theophilus recorded that of those attending none could show evidence that his wife was not insane or that he had mistreated her. "All but one," he declared, "gave their opinion that she was deranged—and that one was a doctor (or quack, Simington by name) who have as his reason for not voting at all, that he had not been consulted in her case."[25] Reverend Simington was pastor of the Methodist church to which Elizabeth had turned for support after leaving her husband's church.

In the end, he reported that some fifty individuals had "certified in writing" their support for committing his wife to an insane asylum. Now, he continued, he was certain that he had "complied with all the requisitions of the law in her case."[26] Indeed, he had gone far beyond the requirements of the law.

Elizabeth declined her husband's invitation to attend the parlor meeting, refusing to participate in what she considered a kangaroo court. She believed he had "completely psychologized his jury into own sentiments and opinions." She was quick to point out that most of her husband's supporters were members of his congregation who were inclined to acquiesce to their pastor and that some present had, in fact, never met her.[27]

On 18 June 1850, two days after this meeting, Theophilus Packard acted on his threat to take his wife to the asylum. According to Elizabeth's dramatic account, she was preparing to dress for the day when she saw him approaching the house with Drs. Merrick and Newkirk from his church and Sheriff James Burgess. When she, surmising their intent, refused to admit the men, Theophilus used an ax to break through the door. She recorded that each doctor entered the room, felt her pulse, and, "without asking a single question," pronounced her insane. "My husband then informed me that the 'forms of law' were all complied with, and he now wished me to dress for a ride to [the] Jacksonville insane asylum!"[28]

Theophilus later explained that the purpose of the doctors' visit that morning was not to assess his wife's sanity but to determine whether she was physically well enough to travel to the asylum safely. He noted that, by then, the required certificates of insanity had already been filed with the hospital in Jacksonville.[29]

Packard recorded that, after shedding a few tears and praying, she determined that she would not be taken away, crying and struggling in an unladylike fashion. She determined to compose herself, appear neatly dressed, and remain as decorous as possible. But she was equally determined to make it clear that she was being removed from the home against her wishes. So, in a symbolic act of resistance that would become her trademark, she refused to

Figure 2. Packard resists her removal to the asylum.
Source: Packard, *Modern Persecution* (1875), vol. I, 64.

walk from the house or into the train station. Instead, she insisted that the men make a "saddle seat" of their hands and carry her, thus primly seated, to her fate.

Word of the crisis at the Packard home apparently spread through town quickly. Packard wrote that a crowd gathered at the train station, which was near their home. She hoped friends would come to her aid, but recalled that, while there were murmurs of dissent and a few shouts, the men present were reluctant to interfere with another man's authority over his family, especially when assured by the sheriff that the "forms of the law" had been met. Elizabeth wrote that as the train pulled away from Manteno for the two-hundred-mile trip to Jacksonville, she looked out the window to see seven-year-old George running alongside the train, crying.

CHOICES AND CONSEQUENCES

The decision to commit Packard was eased by general public acceptance of hospitalization for insanity, due in part to the efforts of asylum superintendents and the campaigns of asylum proponents such as Dorothea Dix. In fact, by the mid-nineteenth century, some mental ailments had become associated with class in a positive way by those who viewed such disorders as a consequence of "excessively refined sensibilities . . . associated with advanced civilization." As historian Andrew Scull observed, such disorders seemed to some a grand "malady to which ladies and gentlemen of quality (but especially ladies of quality) displayed such striking susceptibility."[30] Indeed, the record of Packard's admission to the Jacksonville asylum would state inoffensively that she was "slightly insane" due to "excessive application of body and mind."[31]

From the beginning, Packard protested vehemently that she was not insane, noting that, in the two decades since her institutionalization at the Worcester asylum, she had been "uniformly healthy, cheerful, well and happy." Indeed, she declared, "I hardly think a more healthy, perfectly sound, robust, elastic constitution that I still have . . . [and] my mind is as comparatively sound as my body is."[32]

It is, of course, impossible to know the true state of her mind or degree of any disorder. Certainly, there is evidence that supports both sides of the case. For example, the two men with authority who declared her insane—her husband and her doctor—were reputable individuals who seemed to have considerable support for their views. Furthermore, Packard was by her own admission near a breaking point just prior to her New York trip, and some of her writing while a patient at Jacksonville certainly raised questions about her mental state.

On the other hand, several factors regarding her commitment support her contention that she was institutionalized unnecessarily under an unjust law by a husband who wanted to suppress her influence on his children and church. Even the psychiatric profession would eventually concede that admitting any individual to an asylum merely on the word of "some respected individual" and the "judgment of the asylum superintendent," as Illinois law allowed, exposed the process to a conflict of interest in the public mind, if not in reality.

While commitment laws such as that in Illinois were intended to shield mentally ill women from public humiliation in a court proceeding, such laws unintentionally provided disaffected husbands with a convenient legal means for dispensing with troublesome wives. Contemporary woman's rights leaders, such as Elizabeth Cady Stanton and Susan B. Anthony, were well aware of instances in which a profligate husband had used similar laws to rid himself of a wife while retaining control of her dowry.

Stanton, for example, reported an incident in 1861 in which Anthony illegally concealed a New York woman from authorities, believing she "was the victim of a conspiracy." Stanton explained: "We had known so many aggravated cases of this kind, that in daily counsel we resolved that this woman should not be recaptured if it was possible to prevent it."[33] Using language Packard would later echo, Stanton wrote: "Could the dark secrets of these insane asylums be brought to light, we should be shocked to know the countless number of rebellious wives, sisters, and daughters that are thus annually sacrificed to false customs and conventionalisms, and barbarous laws made by men for women."[34]

Despite such laws, historians have found that, in general, nineteenth-century asylum reports show that men and women were committed in roughly equal numbers. For example, in her study of the Pennsylvania Hospital for the Insane, Nancy Tomes found little difference in the percentage of male and female asylum residents. During the period 1841–83, Tomes noted a relative increase in the number of single women and married men who were institutionalized. She attributed this to greater social acceptance of the asylum as well as increased confidence in asylum therapy.[35]

Indeed, during his first report as superintendent of the Illinois Hospital for the Insane in Jacksonville (1854), Andrew McFarland reported that of the 347 patients admitted in the previous 2 years "the number of males and females has been nearly the same."[36]

However, the Jacksonville asylum's reports for 1860 through 1864, the years most pertinent to Packard's case, show that married women were admitted in larger numbers than men or single women, despite the fact that men then comprised slightly more (53%) of the general population in Illinois at the time.[37] The report for 1860 shows that 32 percent of those admitted were women, with unmarried men next at 26 percent. The 1862 report shows that 28 percent of admissions were married women. Again, single men were next at 24 percent. In 1864 married women comprised 31 percent of those admitted with single men and single women next at 22 percent each.

This trend changed after 1864 following passage in Illinois of the "personal liberty" law, which required a jury trial for women as well as men prior to commitment. The 1866 report, for example, shows that single men were admitted in slightly greater numbers (26%) than married women (25%). And in 1868, the last report submitted by Andrew McFarland, single men led admissions at 32 percent with married women next at 27 percent.

While the sample is small and cannot be considered definitive, these numbers suggest that at the time of Elizabeth Packard's incarceration, married women in Illinois were more likely to be admitted to the Jacksonville asylum than other individuals. This lends some credence to Packard's later accusation that Andrew McFarland was inclined to accept a husband's statement that his wife was insane.

Had Packard received a trial prior to her commitment would a jury have found her sane? Perhaps not. Even with due process, the fact that she was a woman made her vulnerable. Indeed, both her gender and her social position relative to that of her husband facilitated her commitment. Social scientists have explored the historical tendency toward false diagnoses of mental illness in women. Some attributed this to negative presumptions that women's physical and mental constitutions made them inherently weak and susceptible to both physical and mental illness. Others suggested that women were driven to mental illness by idealized expectations and restrictive norms based on gender.[38]

However, as the letter written by her husband's parishioners demonstrates, Elizabeth Packard was not perceived as a "lady" troubled by the spleen, hypochondria, the vapours, hysteria, or a similar mental ailment. Instead, the implication was not so much that she was weak or ill, but that she was dangerous and a threat to her family and community.

Packard declared from the outset that she was committed primarily for her husband's welfare and not her own. The conflict between them, she said, simply "became a problem too deep for him with all his learning and philosophy to solve." Thus, she said, he determined "to stop all further contention by putting an end to his wife's rational existence."[39]

Theophilus Packard was, of course, not a profligate husband. He was, however, a disaffected husband confounded by his wife's demands for her "rights," appalled by her theology, and deeply offended by her presumed relationship with Abner Baker. Furthermore, her general insubordination threatened his reputation. He could be seen both as a man who could not maintain order in his family and as a minister who could not maintain order in his church or community.

His expectations were, of course, reinforced by the social as well as religious and legal structures of their immediate society. The extent to which social control was a factor in commitment has been discussed by various historians, with some suggesting that institutions such as asylums were built as part of an effort by those in authority to control undesirable elements of the population.[40]

Among those who argue against this hypothesis is historian Constance McGovern. Based on her study of four nineteenth-century Pennsylvania asylums, McGovern believed that neither patients nor their families "were passive victims of state policies and institutional programs." She concluded that the impetus for commitment usually came not from the state or other authorities, but from the family and associates of the person deemed insane. McGovern found that even with laws facilitating involuntary commitment and the relative availability of asylums, families arrived at the decision to commit only after exhausting all other methods of dealing with their troubled family members.[41]

To a degree, McGovern's findings hold true in Packard's case. Theophilus recorded that the decision to institutionalize his wife was reached with anguish, under pressure from his church and only after he had "tried in vain" to have other family members "take her for awhile." He explained that by the spring of 1860 his wife's "diseased state of mind" had "caused great disturbance among our people and in the community."[42] As a result, he wrote, "my people requested me to have her removed to a Hospital for the insane."[43]

Clearly, the push for Packard's commitment was initiated by her family and community, not by physicians or by state policies or programs. Although her case does not provide evidence of social control by the state on a grand scale, it does exemplify social control at a local level as her husband and his supporters attempted to curb what to them was socially unacceptable behavior that they believed threatened the welfare of the family, church, and society.

As a man and a husband Theophilus Packard was in an inherently superior status to that of his wife, both legally and socially. Furthermore, as a minister prominent in the community, he ranked near the top of the social hierarchy. He was, thus, among those responsible for protecting order, not only within his family, but also within the community.

Certainly Packard viewed her commitment as an attempt to control her rights of free speech and liberty of conscience. She considered commitment a form of banishment, suggesting that if she lived in the sixteenth rather than the nineteenth century, her husband "would have used the laws of that day to punish me as a heretic." Instead, she said, "he modernizes his phrase by substituting insanity for heresy."[44]

Nevertheless, she had seriously miscalculated her situation in Manteno, and her decision to follow Gerrit Smith's advice to assert her rights ultimately proved disastrous. Hers was not a companionate marriage—and certainly not a "harmonial" one—and her husband would certainly not act to protect her. Nor would either Illinois law or her community protect her. Too late Packard realized that her immediate society could not support her ideals and spirit of inquiry, and those few who did would not contradict the combined authority of a husband and minister to protect her from commitment.

Indeed, Elizabeth Packard had collided with reinforcing boundaries imposed by gender and religion that could not be surmounted by her idealized rights. Thus, she lamented, "In my first struggle [for] my independence, I lost my personal liberty. Sad beginning!" An indomitable spirit is evident as she then declared: "And this is what they call my insanity, and for which I was sent to the asylum to be cured. I think it will be a long time before this cure will be effected. God grant me the quietude of patient endurance, come what will, in the stand I have taken."[45]

6 Andrew McFarland and Mental Medicine

ELIZABETH WAS AT FIRST impressed by asylum superintendent Dr. Andrew McFarland. She described him as a "fine looking gentleman" and was charmed by his sophistication and attentiveness. McFarland, she said, "very gallantly" permitted her ample time to share her thoughts, while her husband "sat entirely speechless." She believed McFarland, unless her "womanly instincts" deceived her, was equally charmed by her.[1]

McFarland's friends described him as urbane, sophisticated, domineering, and so self-controlled as to appear "impassable and cold." But they also knew him as a man who held "tenderest sympathies" for the "poor, afflicted, and distressed."[2] Like the Packards, Andrew McFarland was a product of New England. Born 14 July 1817 in Concord, New Hampshire, he too grew up in

Figure 3. Andrew McFarland as depicted in *Modern Persecution*. *Source:* Packard, *Modern Persecution* (1875), vol. I, unpaged, after title page.

a devoted family as the son of an "eminent Congregational clergyman" and a mother "noted for her great piety and good works."[3]

He graduated from Dartmouth College in 1840, married Annie H. Peaslee of Gilmantown, New Hampshire, in 1842, and graduated from Jefferson Medical College in Philadelphia the following year. After practicing general medicine for several years, he, reportedly, changed to mental medicine after his mother suffered a case of temporary insanity.[4] He began his career in psychiatry as superintendent of the New Hampshire Asylum for the Insane in Concord.

McFarland was, in many ways, representative of the mixture of altruism and elitism that characterized American psychiatrists during the formative years of the profession. Exceptionally well-educated and with strongly held beliefs he was, nevertheless, practicing an undeveloped profession that was still struggling to establish definitions and diagnoses for various types of insanity.

McFarland's life and decision to focus his career on asylum medicine followed the pattern described by historian Constance McGovern in her study of the founding fathers of psychiatry. McGovern discovered that most early psychiatrists shared a New England reform heritage that inspired both ambition and a desire to work in a calling that would be useful to humanity.[5]

McGovern found that many of these men began working in general medicine and turned to asylum medicine after either unsuccessful or unrewarding experiences in general practice. General practitioners often found themselves competing for patients with self-trained "doctors," proponents of homeopathic medicine, and outright charlatans, all of whom became lumped together with them in the public mind. The men who thus turned to mental medicine determined to maintain higher standards for their new specialty, a decision that would later earn them a reputation for elitism.[6]

In 1842, thirteen asylum superintendents founded the Association of Medical Superintendents of American Institutions for the Insane (AMSAII), forerunner of the American Psychiatric Association. Andrew McFarland was among the ten additional men who joined at the Association's second meeting. The group was selective in its membership, even excluding assistant asylum physicians. AMSAII members were also reluctant to associate with other medical organizations. When the American Medical Association formed in 1846, asylum superintendents hesitated to join both because of the "disrepute associated with general medicine" and because of their desire to establish mental medicine as a distinct specialty.[7]

Asylum building had burgeoned in America during the 1840s and 1850s due in part to the efforts of Dorothea Dix in moving the mentally ill out of prisons and poorhouses into hospitals where they could receive treatment. Asylum doctors would be criticized, perhaps unfairly, for devoting too much time to building and managing asylums and too little effort to advancing their profession scientifically. However, as historians have suggested, this initial emphasis on administration was inevitable as these men essentially helped to create the workplace in which to practice their new profession.[8]

These early psychiatrists had embarked on a daunting task of creating a new profession with little theory or research to guide them. At the time McFarland entered the profession there was no formal education for the specialty. Practitioners of mental medicine learned by studying treatment models practiced in Europe and by observing patients in their work as asylum superintendents. By the 1850s there were efforts within psychiatry to achieve consensus regarding terminology and classifications for insanity as well as to improve patient care. But causes for insanity remained mysterious and, when proposed, were often clothed more in philosophy, religion, and popular wisdom than in science.[9]

Religion, a pervasive feature of nineteenth-century America, was an especially significant influence. Historian Norman Dain observed that, even when psychiatrists tried "to place insanity entirely within the domain of medicine and remove it from the sway of theology and superstition," they had to accomplish this without alienating public support by appearing to reject "the conventional philosophical and religious outlook of the middle class." As a result early psychiatrists often tried "to make their scientific theories conform to established religious beliefs."[10]

Lacking scientific theory or a substantial professional tradition, asylum superintendents tended to locate their authority in personal character and claims of disinterested benevolence. Throughout the nineteenth century, the *American Journal of Insanity* abounded in statements suggesting that general practitioners, lawyers, jurists, journalists, and the public were largely ignorant of mental disease and should, therefore, simply accept the professional judgment of those who had devoted their lives to the care and treatment of the insane.

Andrew McFarland, like many in his profession, was concerned not only with the welfare of mental patients, but also with establishing both the credibility of the profession and a legal framework for its practice. He was, in fact, among the first to call for laws governing commitment of the insane, remarking in an 1850 report in New Hampshire on the "loose condition" of the state's laws relating to the insane. He noted that "hardly a year passes without the occurrence of some gross injustice flowing from those statutory deficiencies." However, McFarland's concern was not that individuals were being committed under false pretenses, but that because of public ignorance regarding mental illness, insane persons were being convicted of crimes and imprisoned, rather than provided with treatment for their disease.[11]

In the spring of 1854 McFarland's growing reputation as an expert in mental medicine caught the attention of trustees at the Illinois State Hospital for the Insane in Jacksonville, who traveled to Concord to interview him. Noting his "superior fitness and qualifications," they hired him as superintendent of the Jacksonville asylum.[12]

Thus, as the Packards were leaving New England and settling in Ohio in 1854, McFarland left New Hampshire for the Illinois community that would be his home for the rest of his life. He settled into the superintendent's residence at the Jacksonville asylum with his wife and four children—George, Harriet, Mary, and T. Fletcher, then ages thirteen, ten, eight, and five years.

By the mid-nineteenth century, Jacksonville had emerged from the central Illinois prairie as an educational and cultural center proudly described by residents as the "Athens of the West." Illinois College, established by Yale Congregationalists, was a thriving institution then under the leadership of the Reverend Dr. Edward Beecher. Across town, the Methodists had established the Illinois Female Academy, which later became the coeducational MacMurray College. The community was also proud of its charitable institutions, which included a school for the deaf and blind as well as the Hospital for the Insane, the first institution of its kind in the state. Overall, it was an attractive location for a professional man such as McFarland who appreciated both culture and benevolence.

The family joined the First Presbyterian Church, presided over by Reverend L. M. Glover, and soon became involved in community life. McFarland was among the sixteen charter members of "The Club," an invitation-only group formed "for the purpose of mutual entertainment and instruction."[13] Membership was limited to twenty men that included such well-placed individuals as the Reverend Dr. Julian M. Sturtevant (future president of Illinois College), Professor Jonathan Baldwin Turner (noted education reformer), and Judge Henry E. Dummer (a longtime acquaintance of Abraham Lincoln).

McFarland faced formidable challenges as he took charge as the Jacksonville asylum's second superintendent. By 1854 it was clear that American asylums, although a vast improvement over earlier ways of caring for the insane, were failing to achieve their hoped-for ideals. Overcrowding and high staff turnover frequently compromised patient care. Early claims for cure had proven inflated, and superintendents now faced wrenching decisions about long-term care of those deemed incurable. Furthermore, the large central buildings typical of early nineteenth-century asylums were difficult (and expensive) to maintain. Thus, even as his profession struggled for recognition of its authority, it was coming under increasing criticism in the press as public disillusionment regarding cures and concern about the cost of maintaining state-supported asylums began to grow.[14]

In addition to these difficulties, McFarland was assuming responsibility for an institution that was embroiled in state and local politics even before the first patients were admitted. Legislation to establish the Jacksonville asylum had passed the Illinois legislature in 1847 encouraged by local physicians and town boosters who invited support from reformer Dorothea Dix.[15]

Appointments to the asylum's board of trustees were often political and politics figured in both local and state attempts to control management of the institution.[16] McFarland would have to balance judiciously the continual need for economic support from the state legislature with his desire to maintain professional rather than political control over the affairs of the institution.

Indeed, the previous superintendent had been fired following an investigation by the state legislature and allegations of mismanagement.[17] Many on the hospital staff remained loyal to the former superintendent and did not welcome the change in administration. Thus, McFarland took charge at Jacksonville amid internal dissent, political subterfuge, and public concern about management of the asylum.

Figure 4. Illinois State Hospital for the Insane, Jacksonville, ca. 1860.
Source: Packard, *Modern Persecution* (1875), vol. I, unpaged, after title page.

Clearly aware of the challenges confronting institutions such as his, McFarland commented on the difficulty in maintaining the public trust in his first report. He urged vigorous oversight of the hospital by its trustees, noting that "If an institution is well conducted, it is worth an effort to keep [the public] assured of the fact."[18]

McFarland's subsequent reports revealed the impressive range of his responsibilities and expertise as he discussed with equal comfort medical aspects of insanity, yields on the asylum's farm, the comparative architectural design of asylum buildings, and details of needed improvements to the asylum's water, ventilation, and sewage systems. During his first six years as superintendent, the asylum's main building was completed, auxiliary buildings were enlarged, landscaping of the grounds began, and the farm was developed. McFarland aspired to make his institution a model for the state and the nation and appealed to the civic pride of the legislature and residents of the state to garner support for his efforts.[19]

By 1858 Jacksonville trustees could report that 1,017 patients had been treated since the first patient was admitted in November 1851 and 229 patients were then undergoing treatment. The yearly cost of treatment, at $144 per patient, was well below the range of $182 to $234 per patient reported by 8 comparable institutions. The trustees commended their own "systematic economy" in overseeing the institution's finances and praised McFarland's "energetic and skillful superintendency."[20]

McFarland was likewise satisfied with his institution's smooth operation, reporting that there was "nothing to record of especial interest." Indeed, he concluded, "If the perfection of machinery is to be judged in any sense by its noiseless action, we have reason to be satisfied."[21] Unfortunately, the harmony and "noiseless action" of McFarland's asylum was about to be disrupted.

Nevertheless, as Elizabeth Packard arrived at his institution in 1860, McFarland was literally at the top of his profession, serving as president of the AMSAII and leading debates on important professional issues of his day. These debates included heated discussions about the concepts of "moral insanity" and "monomania," the diagnosis given Elizabeth Packard. These terms, already controversial within the profession, would be debated and ultimately discarded from the vocabulary of psychiatry. Indeed, Packard's case provides an intimate snapshot of this debate and the development of the psychiatric profession in nineteenth-century America.

"Monomania" referred to cases of insanity in which the patient seemed rational on all but a single issue, typically a peculiar religious belief or irrational jealousy of a spouse. "Moral insanity" was used to describe cases in which an individual's moral (affective, or emotional) faculties were deranged without apparent impairment of intellectual ability. Asylum doctors contended that patients with this diagnosis often showed no intellectual impairment and that affective impairment was often distinguishable only by someone expert in dealing with cases of insanity. Thus, the general public might not recognize that the person was insane.

Packard's diagnosis of moral insanity with monomania on the subject of religion demonstrated how views of mental illness were infused with cultural attitudes involving religion and morality. Like many of his colleagues, McFarland believed that "religious excitement" produced in revivals and unorthodox religious practices offered evidence, if not cause, of insanity. The mind of the insane, he wrote, had "a natural affinity for the unseen and the mysterious [thus] the talk of the insane man is often of 'spirits,' 'heavenly telegraphs,' 'mesmerism,' 'magnetism,'—of subjects lying on that debatable ground where natural science loses itself in the mythical."[22]

However, McFarland was quick to add that he saw no evidence "that the truths of the Christian religion . . . ever produced insanity in a mind of healthy constitution." Here he offered as examples the heroes of Calvinism that Theophilus Packard so admired, writing, "If the conception of religious truth produced insanity, by itself, we should infer that those great, comprehensive and impassioned minds which, in Edwards and Whitefield, glowed with such religious fire, would supply cases in proof."[23] Conversely, McFarland observed that the religiosity of the insane tended to be dull and unimaginative.[24]

Historians of psychiatry such as David Rothman have suggested that the concept of moral insanity allowed asylum superintendents to describe "in the widest possible terms the kinds of behavior that might constitute evidence of insanity." As a result "the barrier between normality and deviance was very low."[25] Furthermore, asylum doctors also stressed that insanity "was not the special curse of one group" and that all elements of American society were vulnerable to it. Thus, Rothman explained, "The preconditions for individual pathology so pervaded the society and the manifestations of the disease were so broad that no one who stood on one side of it today could be sure he would not cross it tomorrow." He concluded that "official definitions did not limit insanity to a special style of behavior or restrict the range of possible symptoms . . . Any action could be a manifestation of insanity when placed in the context of the patient's life."[26]

This ambiguity in defining moral insanity created substantial anxiety in legal, religious, and professional circles, not to mention in the press and general public. Doctors who, like McFarland, were concerned that the mentally ill could be imprisoned or even executed for crimes committed because of derangement, found the term "moral insanity" useful in defending apparently lucid individuals who had committed appalling crimes. McFarland, in fact, was frequently called on to testify for the defense in such cases.[27]

But judges, juries, and lawyers, reluctant to concede their own good judgment, questioned psychiatrists' claim that they alone possessed the skill to discern whether a criminal act was committed willfully and knowingly or unwittingly due to insanity. Indeed, newspaper accounts of trials reveal "expert" psychiatric testimony often influenced judgments in criminal cases less than public opinion, the nature of the crime, or the race and class of the defendant.[28]

The concept of moral insanity caused anxiety in religious circles as well. While many clergymen were sympathetic to the efforts of psychiatrists in treating the insane and even served as chaplains in mental hospitals, some objected that moral insanity was simply "a new word for sin."[29] For evangelical Christianity, the psychiatric concept of moral insanity challenged the theological concepts of original sin and free will. Free will implied the inherent ability to choose between good and evil acts. Thus, the notion that mental illness, not evil, could cause immoral or illegal acts involved, as historian Norman Dain noted, "a basic disagreement about the nature of man."[30] The claim by some psychiatrists that the excessive religious expression encouraged by revivalism might be a trigger for insanity added further tension between religion and psychiatry.[31]

Still others, including woman's rights activists, were concerned that the diagnosis of moral insanity could become a catchall for cases in which there was little real evidence of insanity and certainly no need to isolate an individual from general society. Thus, the concept of moral insanity was troubling to many within and without the psychiatric profession. As Dain noted, it was an interpretation of mental illness "that abounded in social, legal, and moral implications" and opened psychiatrists to accusations of both ignorance and collusion in false commitments.[32] Packard's case would certainly prove his point.

While "moral insanity" was a controversial term, "moral treatment," the treatment mode McFarland practiced, was the accepted therapeutic model at that time. First articulated by Philippe Pinel in France, moral treatment emerged in America early in the nineteenth century. It was Pinel's enlightened philosophy that led European physicians to unlock lunatics from chains and treat them with "a regime based on kindness and sympathy," preferably in hospitals situated in a pastoral environment. Restraints, bloodletting, and drugs were, for the most part, exchanged for "a system of humane vigilance" in a calm, quiet atmosphere that would promote convalescence.[33] The attractiveness of this model helped fuel the movement to build publicly supported asylums in America.

However, like the term "moral insanity," the term "moral treatment" was problematic. As historian Gerald Grob noted, it was based in part on the theory that "disease was often a function of immoral or improper behavior as well as physical ailments or defects." The belief was that a change of environment could "help the individual change himself."[34] In this therapeutic environment, the therapist assumed the role of kindly benefactor or father figure. Ideally, both the therapist and the attendant modeled the proper behavior desired in the patient.

Lacking clear treatment standards, doctors differed widely in how they implemented moral therapy. For example, Dr. Samuel Woodward of the Worcester, Massachusetts, asylum believed the secret of managing the insane was: "Respect them and they will respect themselves, treat them as reasonable beings, and they will take every possible pains to show you that they are such."[35]

Just days before Elizabeth Packard was admitted to the Jacksonville asylum, Andrew McFarland elaborated his view of the therapist's role in moral treatment at the annual meeting of the AMSAII. His paper about "Attendants in Institutions for the Insane" emphasized the importance of the superintendent's control of both staff and patients.[36] Because asylum attendants of necessity filled a vital role as an "intermediate class between the superior [doctor] and the subject [patient]," McFarland believed it was imperative that they obey the superintendent's instructions unquestioningly, much as was required of military soldiers. He warned that "a troop of ill selected and ill disciplined hospital attendants [could] wreck the reputation of any institution."[37]

Of course, the superintendent should be thoroughly familiar with all aspects of the patient's care. Furthermore, McFarland continued, the superintendent should "require that the spirit of his own being should infuse itself . . . into the mental and moral life of his subject until the latter would become elevated by his smile, would bow at his reproof, and, in all respects, regard [the superintendent] as the dominant and good spirit from which the subject-mind was to catch all its motive forces."[38] Quoting Shakespeare to make his point, McFarland added: "Like . . . a benignant Prospero, the superior mind controls, for the best of purposes, the Caliban whom disease brings under his direction . . . The superior thus takes full possession of the subject; acts for him, thinks for him, involves within himself his responsibilities, and becomes accountable for him, both to the God who created him, and to society, which is formed to see him protected."[39] Undoubtedly, this was not a philosophy of treatment that Elizabeth Packard was likely to find therapeutic. Indeed, the stage was set for a contest of wills between doctor and patient.

On Thursday, 31 May 1860, two days after presenting this paper, McFarland called the morning session of the AMSAII to order and announced that he must leave due to a serious illness at home. He then startled colleagues by resigning as president of the Association. Proceedings published in the *American Journal of Insanity* reveal no dissention with other members of the Association; however, they imply that his resignation was probably due to an internal dispute. Several colleagues "expressed their deep regret that the President should have deemed such a step necessary, and could not think it possible to have been taken except upon some misconception or some mistake as to facts."[40]

Surprised that colleagues refused to accept his resignation, McFarland told them that his resignation "was intended to be peremptory." He entreated the Association to elect someone else to preside over the meeting and "relieve him from the embarrassment of the position in which he was placed." Still, the group refused his resignation, and the proceedings recorded that, "greatly embarrassed," McFarland yielded and "took his leave in a few words of deep feeling, and cordial good-wishes." Vice president Thomas Kirkbride of the Pennsylvania Hospital for the Insane took the chair and the meeting continued. Evidently, no comments regarding McFarland's departure were published subsequently.[41] Although listed officially as president of the AMSAII from 1859 to 1862 and active in the Association for years to come, he never again presided over the organization.

This was, perhaps, a portent of things to come. McFarland returned to Jacksonville 19 June 1860, in time to approve Packard's admission to the asylum the previous evening. Whatever difficulty had prompted his return home was about to be multiplied. Indeed, the summer of 1860 would mark a turning point in the lives of both Elizabeth Packard and Andrew McFarland.

7 "A World of Trouble"

ANDREW MCFARLAND WAS about to learn what Theophilus Packard knew: Elizabeth Packard could be a troublesome woman. It was impertinent for her to insist that the systematic theology of a noted theologian or minister was unreasonable in the light of common sense. Yet even when her ideas were clearly absurd, she defended them so ably that the average person found it difficult to contradict her. But, above all, she perversely refused to acquiesce to either her husband's or her doctor's view of proper thought and behavior. And she would cause, as McFarland later told her husband, "a world of trouble" for the doctor.

Elizabeth believed that McFarland recognized in this first interview that she was sane, but did not want to contradict the decision of the assistant who had admitted her. Nor, she suspected, did he want "to disappoint the wishes . . . of a very respectable and popular minister." She expected McFarland to keep her at the asylum a few days then send her home "to the satisfaction of all parties."[1] But she had once again seriously miscalculated her situation. McFarland was not only predisposed to accept the judgment of her reputable husband that she was insane, he shared Theophilus Packard's orthodox religious views and disdain for Spiritualism and other novel religious notions.

Packard wrote that she was initially treated like a guest at the asylum, which was not unusual for patients considered to be mildly deranged. She spent a good deal of time reading newspapers and magazines, such as the *Missionary Herald, Christian Freeman, Millennial Harbinger*, and, her favorite, *The Independent*.[2] She enjoyed considerable freedom and was permitted to take other patients for carriage rides on the hospital grounds. She wrote that she was even allowed to shop alone in Jacksonville.[3] Indeed, the relative freedom she enjoyed in these first weeks seems incompatible with her husband's claim that she was so deranged that she posed a threat to his family's lives.[4]

She also received visits from friends and family members, including her older sons, Theo and Isaac, who, she said, visited despite their father's objections.[5] Mr. and Mrs. William Blessing, friends from Manteno, also visited her, bringing with them Dr. G. T. Shirley from Jacksonville. Packard said that, after interviewing her, Dr. Shirley assured her friends that she was not insane. The Blessings subsequently convened a group in Manteno to discuss how they might obtain a writ of *habeas corpus* in her behalf. However, her husband evidently dissuaded the group by bringing in Reverend Ansel Eddy from the Chicago New School Presbytery along with a lawyer from the Chicago firm of Cooley & Farwell. Packard's friends settled for raising money for her defense, which they sent to her son, Theo.[6]

Nevertheless, she worried about her isolation from general society and the stigma she knew would accompany her institutionalization. "To be lost to reason," she wrote, "is a greater misfortune than to be lost to virtue; and the contumely and scorn which the world attaches to it are greater." She craved the daily support and validation of friends and worried that isolation from rational companionship would indeed drive her insane. "I so much needed," she recalled, to be lifted from the "awful vortex which this insanity scandal had plunged me."[7]

Thus, Packard said that she was both shocked and relieved to discover other women in the asylum that she was certain were quite sane. Her husband would have been dismayed to know that many of these new friends were Spiritualists who apparently taught her "many new ideas."[8] She believed some of these women were committed either because of their Spiritualist beliefs or by dissolute husbands. She wrote that "these sane wives" remained in the asylum "until they begged to be sent home" to their husbands.[9]

She viewed this as a conspiracy between their husbands and the doctor and suggested, in language that woman's rights advocates would recognize, that "the *subjection* of the wife was the cure the husband was seeking." She later accused McFarland of receiving women "on the simple verdict" of their husbands' opinions, rather than using his own professional judgment and added, "You do not seem to apprehend the glaring truth of the present day, that woman's most subtle foe is a tyrant husband."[10]

Packard differentiated these women from those she would encounter on the "maniac's ward" who were unkempt, violent, and irrational. Although she felt sympathy for those women, she clearly did not identify with them. Rather, she reported their behavior as an anthropologist might report observations of a foreign culture. She sought to understand the logic behind the seemingly illogical behavior of the nonviolent insane and was generous in accepting their versions of reality. She would contest the broad definitions of insanity offered by her doctor, insisting to him that irrational behavior, not unusual opinions, should be the "index of the mind." As writer Mary Elene Wood suggests, Packard both "distinguishe[d] herself from the 'maniacs' in the asylum" and questioned "the distinction between sanity and insanity" prevalent in contemporary thought.[11]

Nevertheless, Packard would recall the summer of 1860 as "the sunny-side of prison life" during which she was "the Doctor's favorite." McFarland, she said, treated her with "polite attentions and marked respect" in his eagerly anticipated visits to her room.[12] She recorded an incident in which she confessed to McFarland that she had let a male patient push a swing for her in the asylum courtyard, upsetting one of the other female patients. Packard wrote that a sympathetic McFarland told her not to worry about the incident, then "bestowed a kiss upon my forehead."[13] At first, Packard said she regarded the kiss "as a mere impulsive act, dictated by no corrupt motives." But she would later tell him she considered it "an indiscreet act for a man in his position."[14]

Clearly she related this incident to suggest that her doctor was attracted to her romantically. There is no evidence, apart from Packard's perception, that this was true. But, encouraged by his apparent attentiveness, she was increasingly attracted to him.[15] Indeed moral treatment, as McFarland described it, would have encouraged this admiration with the hope that the patient would then adopt the rational thoughts and behavior he modeled.

But Packard hoped to convince the superintendent that she was sane by her decorum and rationality, if not the reasonableness of her ideas. She tried to reason with him about what it meant to be insane, asking, "If one's opinions are not accompanied by irregular conduct, ought the opinions alone be treated as evidence of insanity?" McFarland, she recorded, replied that they indeed could, but declined to elaborate. She persisted, "But have we any right to restrain the personal liberty of any one whose conduct shows no irregularities?" To this, she said, McFarland "made no reply."[16]

In August 1860, McFarland wrote Theophilus, saying, "Mrs. Packard shows the advantages of separation from home and the scenes of her excitement in decided improvement. She seems contented with her situation." He remarked that her case was "indeed an interesting study," noting that she possessed a "fine mind and brilliant imagination" as well as "ingenuity in the use of specious reasonings." She could, he observed, play on the sympathy of others with an "artfulness . . . that few can resist."[17]

It is unlikely that McFarland would have engaged in genuine dialogue with his patient. The objective of moral therapy was to model, observe, and encourage patients to behave "properly" within the familial environment of asylum society with the hope that they could replicate that behavior outside the asylum. Packard was treated with the kindness and consideration a parent might give a sick child, not a rational adult.

Slowly, she came to believe that the "desired effect" of her treatment was "to break down" her conscience "in the first instance to my husband's will and, in the second, to yield it to Dr. McFarland's dictation." Her own reason was to be replaced by that of her doctor who, she wrote, "considered his judgment a safer guide for my actions than my own conscience was!" Not surprisingly, she objected strenuously to this "usurpation," declaring that she believed her "own conscience is a safer guide for my own actions than the judgment of any superintendent," including "the great Dr. McFarland."[18]

Indeed, she soon understood that her inferior position, as McFarland had described in his conference presentation, was like that of a Caliban—a slave denied both her rights and her reason. In later books, she described herself both as "a slave of the marriage union" and as "a slave, now imprisoned in Jacksonville Insane Asylum, placed there by her husband for THINKING."[19]

Thus, treatment Packard received in the asylum seemed to her merely a new manifestation of the same forces of authority and control that had failed to "normalize" her behavior outside the asylum. She later told readers, "I found that my personal liberty, and personal identity, were entirely at the mercy of Mr. Packard and Dr. McFarland; that no law of the Institution or of the State, recognized my identity while a married woman; therefore, no protection, not even the criminal's right of self-defence, could be extended to me."[20]

Indeed, for Packard the asylum became, as Michel Foucault depicted it—a place of imprisonment, punishment, and subjugation in which she was denied her own reason.[21] No demonstration of intellect or decorum could provide sufficient evidence of "cure" to obtain release. Instead, her defiant "perversity" toward her husband must be replaced with compliance to his judgment and will. McFarland, she said, made it clear that so long as she refused to yield "to these notions of duty respecting my husband, he considered the asylum as the most proper place for me to be in!"[22] She concluded that "both husbands and asylum superintendents [had] absolute, entire, irresponsible, despotic power."[23]

Understanding that submission could buy freedom and a return to her children, she later told her readers that she assumed responsibility for the consequences of resistance, stating firmly: "I have deliberately and intelligently suffered the loss of all things for conscience sake." She asked rhetorically whether she should have submitted "to oppression and spiritual bondage, rather than have attempted to break the fetters of marital and religious despotism?" Her answer was, "No . . . I have no recantations to make, and can give no pledges of future subjection to either of these powers, where their claims demand the surrender of my conscience to their dictation."[24]

In reality, Packard's naivety regarding her legal rights and ability to prove her sanity had placed her in a situation over which she now had little control. It is unlikely at this point that falsely acquiescing to her husband or recanting her beliefs would have obtained her release. By then, both her husband and doctor were determined to either correct her behavior or contain it within the walls of the asylum.

In a later book, she described a dream in which others looked on disapprovingly as she struggled to pull a heavy load across a bridge. She recounted, "I seemed to be alone upon the connecting link between the natural and spiritual worlds. The bridge connecting them is nearly completed. But who dares to step out beyond the limits of popular opinion and sentiment, and let himself be cut loose from all things tangible, to gain the hidden treasures of knowledge laid up in God's vast storehouse?"[25]

She interpreted this dream as affirmation of her struggle for private conscience and free expression, and answered her own question rhetorically: "Who dares to stand alone in his opinion, and face a frowning world? Mrs. Packard dares to do it . . . in spite of all the locks, bolts, bars, and keys of all the insane asylums of Christendom."[26]

By late autumn 1860, Packard's tactics had changed and she began to resist her confinement actively. She evidently wrote letters to McFarland and the hospital trustees defending her sanity and demanding her release. She also approached hospital visitors to ask for help. But complaints from patients about "conspiracies" against them were considered part of the persecution complex often exhibited by the insane. Thus, her efforts were futile.

Packard also began to criticize McFarland's management of the asylum and created discontent among the staff by pointing out the discrepancy between the wages of male and female attendants.[27] In addition, she began to document incidents of patient abuse in a journal that became the basis for her later books. She described in inflammatory detail how patients were plunged under water until nearly dead, dragged by their hair, and abused by striking and kicking. She acknowledged that McFarland tried to stop such abuse and had fired attendants for mistreating patients. Still, she reported, abuse was "most shamefully practiced still in secret."[28]

Asylum superintendents conceded that circumstances of asylum life made a degree of abuse inevitable, and despite the trend toward moral therapy restraints and treatments such as hydrotherapy were still used in American asylums.[29] While these were sometimes necessary and applied in the patients' best interests, in the hands of a frustrated or simply mean attendant their application could be terrifying.

McFarland was certainly aware of the difficulty of maintaining trustworthy staff. As he noted in his presentation to AMSAII, many attendants were inexperienced and lacked the maturity of character required to deal with difficult mental patients. Most, he noted, were in their early twenties and from the lower classes and, thus, were unlikely to understand the needs of his patients, many of whom were "men and women of age, intelligence, high self-respect, and pride of character, heightened in numerous instances by mental disease."[30]

McFarland's presentation only hinted at the extraordinary difficulty of recruiting, training, and retaining suitable attendants. In a study of two nineteenth-century New York asylums, historian Ellen Dwyer revealed the full complexity of asylum life and the role of attendants. Dwyer found that, despite their importance to the hospital's operation, attendants were usually hired by the asylum steward and supervised by assistant physicians, not the superintendent. Dwyer suggested that the stewards' "informal" (i.e., personal and political) hiring criteria did not assure high-quality attendants.[31]

Dwyer pointed out that at one New York asylum the list of attendants' duties and responsibilities was "five times longer" than the list for medical officers. Furthermore, rules for attendants often extended beyond the workplace to include conduct of their private lives. Despite such heavy responsibilities, attendants had little formal power over their work environment. All of these factors along with the arduous workload, poor wages, and low status led to a high turnover of attendants.[32] Indeed, historian Gerald Grob found that, in some areas, "the norm" was a turnover rate "between one-third and one-half of the staff annually." All of this left an asylum superintendent in the unenviable position of managing from a distance a treatment modality (moral treatment) that required his direct influence and fatherly persona.[33]

Packard believed that abuse was inherent in asylums despite a superintendent's best efforts. She observed, "An attendant very quickly becomes hardened by treating human beings as brutes merely, and this seared or hardened conscience very soon approves of horror from which he would at first have shrunk in disgust."[34] Likewise, even competent and kindhearted asylum superintendents could become hardened "despots." She would later argue that the best way to minimize abuse was to open asylums to public oversight and to permit patients both conduits of communication and redress for their complaints.[35]

Like most superintendents, Andrew McFarland was invested in his work to an extraordinary degree. Private and professional life intertwined, as the Mc-Farland family lived in the hospital complex and his wife and children assisted in patient care. His daughters, Mary and Harriett (Hattie), visited the wards and worked alongside Packard in the sewing room, where Mrs. McFarland served as matron.

In her efforts to discredit McFarland, Packard insinuated that his family perhaps benefited too much from their close association with the institution, suggesting that she had sewn items for the family. She complained, "When I found that the superintendent's interests meant the institution's interests, I determined my services should not go to support such claims." She recounted how she once sent Mrs. McFarland a bill for $5, but received in return only a "yard of calico worth twenty-five cents."[36]

By November 1860 Packard had accelerated her complaints and efforts to obtain freedom. She wrote McFarland a lengthy "Defense" of her sanity that both cajoled him with admiration of his "manliness" and demanded her immediate release. When he did not respond, she sent him a heated "reproof," threatening public exposure of abuse and mismanagement at his institution. It warned, "I have powerful friends of freedom who will help me to break the chains, with which you bring your slaves here in a slavery, worse than Southern slavery."[37]

This reproof railed that it was time "for downtrodden and oppressed women to have their rights" and warned that she would use "her voice and her pen [to] move the world." Foreshadowing her future crusade she wrote, "Let pure spiritual woman become exasperated beyond her powers of endurance . . . and I pity her adversary then." In a final jab, she reminded McFarland, "There was an eye-witness to that kiss which you bestowed upon me in your office, when you thought we were alone!" A postscript added, "Remember, Dr. McFarland, this is your last chance . . . Repentance or exposure!"[38]

This, Packard reported, received an immediate response. McFarland, she said, ignored everything except mention of the alleged kiss. "At that point," she told readers, "his feelings burst their confinement and he seemed determined . . . to either rule or ruin me!"[39]

The "sunny side" of asylum life ended as Packard was moved to the Eighth Ward, which housed the most seriously ill patients in the asylum. She reported that, now, most of her attempts to communicate with friends outside the asylum were blocked. She continued to record her observations of asylum life, ingeniously concealing her notes within her hatband, between the glass and back of her hand mirror, and in the linings of her band-box, satchel, and bonnet.[40]

She wondered why McFarland believed it necessary to keep her from writing friends. She hypothesized that he could tell from her writing that she was sane and feared she would indeed expose his "despotism." She observed, "I have read the letters and writings of the insane, here, and they are just like themselves—full of inconsistent, unreasonable utterances—a *fac simile* of the brain which manufactured them." Indeed, she suggested, a written document might be "the most infallible test" of one's mental ability.[41]

The tone of McFarland's December 1860 report suggested the difficulty of recent months at the Jacksonville asylum. In a melancholy reflection on the burdens of administration, he referred to care of the insane as "the most exhaustive pursuit beneath the sun." What made the job most difficult, he wrote, was not the "confinement, physical labor, the sights and sounds of deepest woe, nor the exercise of the ordinary firmness and vigilance incident to the trust." The heaviest weight was his singular responsibility for the patients. He soliloquized, "He who holds in his hands the liberty, and, to a large degree the happiness of his innocent but suffering fellow beings, conjures up the spectre *responsibility*—which, like the pursuing phantom of the Spanish dramatist, never leaves him for an hour. It starts up in the social circle, hovers around the disturbed pillow, makes home the habitation of unrelaxing care, and, rings its reproofs into the wearied ear during the few days of allotted annual absence."[42] Indeed, Packard's reproof would ring in his ears for years to come. After her release, she published it as a pamphlet that reportedly sold more than a thousand copies.[43]

Packard claimed that for several months following this incident she was strictly confined to the "maniac's ward," where she was exposed to the most uncivil environment she had ever experienced. Unlike her companions in the other ward, on this floor she found "scarcely a patient in the whole ward who could ask or answer a question in a rational manner." She added that "this ward was then considered the worst in the house . . . [and] contained some of the most dangerous class of patients."[44]

There, she said, unprotected by the oblivion of madness, her senses were assaulted by the odors, sounds, and images that enveloped her. The ward, she wrote, was "so filthy, that an eighth ward patient could be told" from afar by the odor. She helped bathe other patients and clean their rooms more in self-defense than from altruism. She added, "I smelled and tasted these stinks so much after I entered this stink-hole, that, for a time, I couldn't taste anything else."[45] But, paraphrasing scripture, she added, "I have found out that I can live, move, breathe, and have a being, where I once thought I could not!"[46]

As a defense against this completely foreign and personally invalidating environment, Packard developed a routine that was remarkably like that recommended for prevention of insanity by Dr. Pliny Earle in his essay for the U.S. Census published in 1864. Earle advised regular sleep and work habits, moderation in all things, and "living as near to nature as our multifold artificialities will permit."[47] This, of course, echoed popular wisdom offered in works such as Catharine Beecher's *Treatise on Domestic Economy,* Ralph Waldo Emerson's essay "Nature," and Henry David Thoreau's "Walden."

Packard described a routine of prayer, study, reading, and social activities balanced with chores such as cleaning and sewing. She ate lightly and did "gymnastic exercises" by an open window and ended each day with prayer and a good night's sleep which, she noted pointedly, was "indispensable to a happy, vigorous state of the intellect."[48]

During her confinement on the Eighth Ward her mail was restricted in what she considered a capricious manner. She recalled that, while she could not contact a friend, a lawyer, or anyone who might come to her defense, she was allowed to receive letters from her husband that sometimes contained disturbing news. Expressing incredulity, she wrote that in one letter he detailed his plan "to break up the family and put out the children" to other families. He asked her "to whom he shall give my babe, and to whom he shall give my daughter . . . and such like questions!" She called readers' attention to the irony, that although she was supposedly insane, "he could ask the counsel and advice of this *non compos* on these most important matters!"[49]

This letter apparently continued with the news that her daughter, Libby, had fallen and hurt her side, "so that it pains her most of the time." Yet Libby continued doing "all the work for the family." Packard told readers that she grieved at the thought of her eleven-year-old daughter burdened with the "cares of a woman." "Poor child!" she wrote. "How her mother longs to embrace her, and sympathize with her."[50]

Early in 1861, reformer Dorothea Dix visited the Jacksonville asylum on her way to Springfield to lobby for funding to improve the facility's water supply.[51] Packard claimed that during this visit she "had several pleasant interviews with Dix," whom she regarded "as a Christian, although honestly and conscientiously wrong, in sustaining our present system of Insane Asylums." Packard said that she later wrote Dix, telling her that asylums in general were "the curse of the age" and that the Jacksonville asylum in particular "caused a thousand fold more misery, agony and suffering, than it has alleviated."[52] Recounting this story later, Packard warned readers, "Be not deceived as Miss Dix has been, by the mock statute of *human* laws, by which these institutions are ostensibly governed. For, believe me, they are a dead letter in their practical application to the patient."[53]

Packard insisted that the system of asylums fostered by Dix "must be destroyed, to be constructed anew on a righteous basis."[54] She understood that her ideal of home care for the insane would not always be feasible. Her one attempt to create an organization during her later reform work involved an effort to establish a fund for state or private facilities to care for those who had no friends or family to watch over them or who were too ill to be kept at home. Despite her rhetoric about "destroying asylums," the laws that Packard would later propose were aimed at establishing external oversight of asylums and protecting a patient's basic civil rights within a more closely regulated management system.

Perhaps inspired by Dix, Packard wrote that she began to imagine a new calling for her life. She resolved "that henceforth, and forever" her occupation would be "to eradicate, expose, and destroy this sum of all human abominations"—the present insane asylum system. With an eye to this mission, she carefully documented her observations and experiences within the asylum in great detail.[55]

In February 1861, McFarland wrote Theophilus that time had, unfortunately, brought no improvement in his wife. "In the place of the usual emotions, that exist in the bosom of a wife, even of a wronged and injured wife, there appears only an unmitigated hate." McFarland continued, "The poison has infused itself through her moral nature, so that through its influence, truth itself is sacrificed."[56]

Meanwhile, Packard wrote that her fellow patients' indignation over her mistreatment led to "threats of mob action on at least two occasions."[57] Sophie Olsen, whose asylum narrative Packard later published as part of her own book, reported that "all the seventy patients in the Eighth ward who took the least interest in anything, sympathized with Mrs. Packard," and many of the attendants "defended and very highly respect Mrs. Packard."[58]

In response to these rumblings, McFarland apparently imposed tighter restrictions on Packard and the entire ward.[59] Olsen described the treatment on the ward at this time as a "reign of terror" during which patients were rarely allowed out of the building, dances were suspended, and patients were not permitted visitors. In addition, Olsen wrote, conversation among patients was discouraged and "all who did not render instant obedience were severely punished."[60]

The patients responded by plotting a revolt. Banding "together in little secret societies," the women decided to "make a general onslaught" against state property by destroying all they could "without discovery." They determined to make it clear to Superintendent McFarland that it was "his own extreme severity" and the "complete desperation" of the patients' circumstances that brought about this "military necessity."[61] The plan apparently worked. After "hundreds of dollars worth of property" was destroyed Olsen reported that "the Doctor saw his mistake in drawing our reins so tightly, and . . . saw it for his own interest and safety to relax them."[62]

Around this time McFarland wrote Theophilus, telling him that disease had "erased from Mrs. Packard's mind the sentiments or instincts of maternal as well as marital affection." In contradiction to Packard's accounts of grieving for her children, McFarland told Theophilus that he believed she was "at heart really indifferent to her children," and only used an apparent love for them "as a barb to inflict a wound on you."[63]

In the fall, perhaps as a further concession to the turmoil created by the patients, Packard was moved to the "new Seventh Ward." The patients on this ward were relatively quiet and less disturbed. She was once again permitted to eat in the dining room and talk with her old associates.

But these privileges were short-lived, as she apparently provoked yet another incident. Still searching for a sympathetic ear, she reportedly asked the asylum chaplain, Reverend Julian Sturtevant, to meet with her in the reception room after chapel services. However, according to Packard, McFarland forcibly blocked this meeting by seizing her arm and ordering her back to her ward. The feisty Packard refused and when McFarland let go of her arm, she fell to the floor.[64] Packard reported indignantly that McFarland then walked past her, conferred with the chaplain and an assistant, and the three men walked away. Packard was left on the floor much as a parent might leave a toddler who had thrown a tantrum. This incident evidently produced a moment of self-revelation in Packard. She told readers that at that instance, "I began to try my powers of self-dependence, and found I could not only raise myself, but could also stand alone, too, without a man to lean upon!"[65]

In a letter to Theophilus in April 1862, McFarland alluded to the difficulties Packard was causing. He told Theophilus that his wife was "as unyielding as ever . . . [and] shows rather the malignity of the fiend, than any natural sentiment." He added, "She gives us a world of trouble, which I only put up with under the thought that she would give you, if possible, still more."[66]

A few days later he wrote again, enclosing a paper written by Packard in which she referred to her husband as the head of a conspiracy against her and "the devil incarnate." Speaking of her adversaries, Packard had threatened, "I fear them not, but they may well fear me, for I shall be their destruction."[67]

Meanwhile, the incident on the staircase apparently prompted Packard's return to the Eighth Ward. Although it had been cleaned and remodeled since her last residency there and now housed "a quiet class" of maniacs, Packard was suspicious of this move. She refused to go willingly and insisted on being carried there "saddle seat" fashion as a demonstration of civil disobedience.

She complained about the lack of reading material on this ward and explained, "It was war time when daily events of the most thrilling kind were occurring, and I felt it to be a great privation to be deprived of the news."[68] She believed the Civil War was God's judgment on the nation "for the sin of oppression."[69] She counted herself among the oppressed and considered her government "the most oppressive government on earth, so far as the rights of the slave, the rights of women, and the rights of the insane are concerned." God, she wrote, was now settling with the nation "for these wrongs and outrages against these members of His family."[70]

He doctor's reflections on the war were more sanguine. Indeed, McFarland believed "war excitement" tended to have a "healthful . . . operation on the public mind" since "its influences come upon the individual mind from without, instead of being a feeling generated from within." Thus, it stood in "great contrast with those gales of popular delusion, such as 'Millerism,' 'Spiritualism,' etc., which have wrought such ruin in time past, and whose melancholy wrecks are still found strewn among all our institutions for the insane."[71] Whether he considered Packard among those "melancholy wrecks" can only be surmised.

To her great surprise, upon arrival on the newly renovated Eighth Ward she was given a pleasant room by herself with the liberty of closing the door for privacy. This room, she said, became her "*sanctum sanctorum.*" She recalled how she had once longed "for the *rest* of the Sabbath" since Sunday was, for a minister's wife and mother of six children, "the hardest working-day of the whole week."[72]

Now, the Illinois Hospital for the Insane became for her a genuine asylum—a safe haven. There, cloistered "from intruders, by God's providence" she found opportunity to rest, freely explore her religious notions, and formulate a plan for her future.[73]

Thus, Packard's commitment to an insane asylum would ultimately "cure" neither her demand for her rights nor her theological exploration. Having lost all that was dear to her—family, home, reputation—she had little else to lose in pursuing autonomous ideas and goals. In her words: "The worst that my enemies can do to defame my character, they have done, and I fear them no more. I am now free to be true and honest, for this persecution for opinion and conscience's sake, has so strengthened and confirmed me in the free exercise of these inalienable rights in the future, that no opposition can overcome me . . . I feel that I am born into a new element—freedom, spiritual freedom."[74]

8 "An Unendurable Annoyance"

AFTER TWO YEARS OF EXTRAORDINARY difficulty with Elizabeth Packard, Andrew McFarland was anxious to see her leave his institution. At the September 1862 meeting of the asylum's board of trustees, he recommended they discharge her "for reasons of general expediency."[1] However, Theophilus attended the meeting and urged that she be kept at the asylum.[2]

He evidently presented sworn statements from a doctor, a neighbor, and members of his church regarding his wife's conduct just prior to her commitment. The doctor offered examples of what he considered insane behavior, including "her almost incessant talking about her husband and the doctrines of Spiritualism," "her great neglect of her family and household duties," [and] her hatred of all persons who believed her insane.[3] An elder from the church reported that when Packard's request to read a paper to the congregation during a Sabbath service was declined, she took her "two little children by the hand . . . went directly to the Methodist church" and asked to join their society.[4]

After Theophilus presented these statements, Packard was introduced to the trustees and read a prepared essay, entitled "Calvinism and Christianity Compared," which McFarland had approved beforehand. The lengthy essay, which Packard later published, explained why she opposed teaching Calvinism to her children.[5]

In it she attacked Calvinism as "the devil's authority" in contrast to true Christianity. Using arguments taken, in part, from the Unitarianism and Universalism that her husband abhorred, she continued: "Christ taught there is but one God. Calvin taught there are three Gods . . . Christ taught that every sin would receive its just punishment . . . Calvin taught that the favorites in God's family would be exonerated from this law."[6]

Packard told the trustees that her incarceration was the result of a "notorious family rebellion" brought on by "the Calvinistic law of marriage, which enslaves the wife." Her husband had her imprisoned in the asylum in an "impious, Calvinistic attempt to chain my thought, by calling me 'insane.'" Furthermore, she said, the law by which she was committed had deprived her of the right of self-defense. This was, she told them, "a crime against the constitution . . . and also a crime against civilization and human progress." "Who," she asked, "will dare to be true to the inspirations of the divinity within them, if the pioneers of truth are thus liable to lose their personal liberty?"[7]

In summary, she asserted that such "kidnapping [of] intelligent moral agents of their accountability" was the "climax of all human wrongs, to which Calvinism gravitates." It was, she said, an "impious attempt to place the divinity within me, a spiritual woman—a 'temple of the Holy Ghost'— upon a level with the brutes" and, thus, it constituted "blasphemy against the Holy Ghost."[8]

Packard then asked to read a second document, which McFarland had not screened. This second essay, which Packard also later published, accused her husband and doctor of colluding to keep her at the asylum. "You say, Dr. McFarland, that my abuses must be balanced by my children's abuses." Why, she asked, did she not have "a right to teach them what I think is God's revealed will? . . . Must I yield my own convictions of truth and duty to [my husband's] dictation?"[9]

She then compared her husband's ideas with her own in a parable of two teachers. The female teacher, who taught Copernican science, was favored by the students due to her "fidelity and kindness." The male teacher, who taught Ptolemaic science, was "chagrined and crest-fallen . . . at being . . . outshone by a woman's virtues and corresponding success." The male teacher attempted "to remedy this state of things" by forcing her from the school-room "and placing her in a prison on the false charge of insanity." She continued: "Suppose the appeals of the injured teacher . . . were met by the response . . . that the good of the pupils required that the male teacher's wishes be carried out respecting her, for she was alienating the heart of the pupils from their male teacher, and from his system of astronomy!!!"[10]

This, she explained, was comparable to the conflict in her family. She simply wanted her children to embrace new, more enlightened notions of religion, while her husband insisted she must teach them a Calvinism that, in her view, was as outmoded as the Ptolemaic universe.[11]

Packard believed the trustees were sympathetic to her views and willing to send her to live with one of her older children or her father.[12] But, she startled everyone by asking to stay at the asylum as a paid boarder. As much as Packard wanted her freedom, she realized that neither her older sons nor her father could support her, and she had no means of supporting herself. Her "*sanctum sanctorum*" at the asylum would buy her time to come up with a plan for supporting herself. The astonished trustees promptly denied her request and her release was "indefinitely postponed."[13]

Theophilus recorded none of this in his diary. He noted briefly that he had attended the meeting to give the trustees "a more full view of [his wife's] singular and peculiar case." His wife, he said, then "appeared and stated her case" with "the result was she was retained in the hospital." He then described his pleasant visit in Jacksonville during which he had preached the Sunday service at the local Congregational church.[14]

Meanwhile, Packard retreated to her room to consider how she might support herself when released from the asylum. Writing and selling books seemed a logical choice. Other women had succeeded as writers, and her asylum notes provided plenty of material to draw on.[15] She wrote that "the vision of a big book began to dawn" in her mind. She decided to write it as an allegory rather than as "an ordinary book in the style of common language." She would frame it as the story of two trains—one representing Christianity and the other Calvinism. The Christian train would reflect all that was good "in our family institutions, our Church and State institutions, and our laws" while the Calvinist train would represent all that was evil.[16] According to Packard, she described her plan to McFarland and was surprised when he encouraged her to proceed, even hinting that he might help publish her book.[17] Her anger with him melted, temporarily.

In his December 1862 report, McFarland did not mention Packard directly, but perhaps had her appeals for her freedom in mind as he ruminated on the reality that incarceration in an asylum required "a deprivation of personal liberty." That was, he conceded, "an abrogation of the first right of a human being: a denying of his competent agency in all that man was created for." Comparing involuntary commitment with Abraham Lincoln's wartime suspension of the writ of *habeas corpus*, McFarland remarked that such "an absolute seizure of the rights of man" could only be justified by "the gravest necessities."[18] He concluded with the observation that in most cases when former asylum patients complained about the institution in which they had been confined those individuals likely still showed "evidences of mental unsoundness."[19]

In the same report, McFarland advised that, with more than three hundred patients, his asylum had reached its "extreme limit" and must therefore "exercise the law for the discharge of incurables."[20] This was contrary to McFarland's personal view that keeping incurable and curable patients together was more cost effective and assured better care for the incurably insane, especially since Illinois had no facilities for state care of incurable patients. However, the

Jacksonville asylum had been established primarily as a hospital for treatment of curable cases, and the trustees were obligated to discharge "incurable and harmless cases" to make room for more "hopeful" cases.[21]

At the trustees' meeting that month, McFarland urged Packard's release as an incurable. But his request was again denied, possibly due to continued pressure from Theophilus. The trustees voted that "further consideration of the case be indefinitely postponed."[22]

Meanwhile, Packard drafted "the substance" of her "Great Drama," sharing portions of it with other patients, asylum staff, and McFarland. The first feverishly composed chapters rambled in no apparent order through Packard's life story. In the process, she elaborated the unconventional theological views that McFarland placed among the current "gales of popular delusion" that might predispose one to insanity.[23]

But, at the same time, the manuscript contained a clear denunciation of despotism, in both marriages and asylums that rang with the popular rhetoric of personal liberty.[24] It was for the superintendent a two-edged sword that might convince some she was insane while garnering the sympathy of others. He reneged on what she considered his promise to publish it.

Packard had by then placed all her hopes for an independent future on publication of this book. Desperately disappointed, she poured out her heart in a letter to McFarland in which she expressed love and respect for him.[25] She told him that, while she loved his spirit and manliness, she could not love his person, "so long as that love is justly claimed by another woman— your legal wife." She offered her heart to McFarland, confiding somewhat disingenuously that he was "the first true man" she had ever met.[26]

Packard told McFarland "the only response" she asked of him was to vindicate her "assailed character" by helping her publish at least twenty-five copies of her book and promised to pay him back within three months after her release. She told him she would regard his help as his seal of engagement "until death parts us." She then expressed her desire to leave the asylum in March with her son, Theo, "as my protector [to] take charge of my children at that time." Finally, she urged McFarland to burn this letter "since exposure of it might imperil my virtue." The note was signed, "Yours, in the best of bonds, Elizabeth."[27]

According to Packard, the letter received an immediate response as McFarland confronted her with what he deemed an "unladylike" love-letter. She recorded that he personally locked her in a screen-room used for isolating problem patients. According to Packard, he then searched her room and took her book manuscript before escorting her back to her room. When he unexpectedly returned the manuscript a few weeks later, Packard was certain her "charming powers" had influenced him.[28] More likely, it took him that long to evaluate the lengthy manuscript and determine that it, along with her "love-letter" to him, now demonstrated clear evidence of insanity.

In February, Packard's cousin, Angeline Field, visited her, bringing money and an invitation to stay at their home, which was now in Granville, Illinois. Field urged her to divorce Theophilus before he could send her to another asylum. But Packard rejected a divorce that she was certain would cut her off "from children and home—all my rightful claims." Furthermore, she refused to leave the asylum until her "character was vindicated." She told Angeline that she "preferred to die here" rather than "to go into the world to be looked upon as an insane person." Packard wrote that Angeline left in tears, but agreed to help find a way to publish the book that Packard believed would affirm her sanity.[29]

At the March 1863 meeting of the trustees, McFarland again recommended Packard's release. This time the trustees agreed and she was "ordered to be discharged after June 19, 1863." The trustees approved, giving three months' notice for discharge rather than the normal thirty days at the "remonstrance" of friends and relatives.[30] The intent was evidently to give her husband ample time to make other arrangements for her.

In a letter to Theophilus dated 14 April 1863, McFarland advised him of the trustees' decision. He explained that the "cause of this step" was the "amount of trouble, which Mrs. Packard causes us, and the disastrous influence which she exerts on the other patients."[31] Theophilus, who had maintained a steady correspondence with McFarland, later noted that the doctor had in "40 or 50 letters" described the "extraordinary, unique" and truly "marvelous *peculiarities*" of his wife's case. She was, McFarland told him, an extraordinarily troublesome patient, who "stirr[ed] up the other patients to discontent and insubordination."[32]

McFarland also told Theophilus that for six months his wife had been "writing a farrago of stuff, which she calls a book." He continued: "The mass of it is simply silly—the talk of a not very bright child of six or eight years. Much of the remainder is scurrilous and some of it decidedly vulgar and mischievous." He noted that there would always be "some even of fair intelligence in other things, who will be led away, either by prejudice or ignorance of such cases, to believe that she is not insane." He advised that she be allowed to "write out her insanity" suggesting that the resulting book should be "enough to convince the most incredulous."[33]

Meanwhile, in May 1863, McFarland traveled to Philadelphia to attend the annual gathering of the AMSAII, where he presented a paper entitled "Minor Mental Maladies."[34] Discussions at this meeting illustrated the doctors' parallel struggles to construct etiologies and treatments for mental illness and to establish their professional authority in the public eye. Particularly at issue was the need to agree upon consistent definitions of insanity that could support a doctor's expert legal testimony. In connection with this, the doctors debated classifications, shared case studies, and attempted to arrive at consensus regarding the controversial category of moral insanity.

McFarland's paper addressed many of these concerns. His wide-ranging observations covered hypochondria, "secret vices," and ailments now recognized as anorexia and Munchhausen Syndrome. He purposely omitted discussion of hysteria and "the whole class of quasi mental disorders" connected with it. However, he devoted much attention to postpartum insanity, which he believed was a chronic and little recognized disease that provided "the most plausible instances of what has unfortunately been styled *moral insanity*."[35]

McFarland described his understanding of this malady, noting that this disease usually did not involve actual immoral acts such as lying, dishonesty, or moral impurity. He described its more typical symptoms, saying: "A lady, affected by this form of disease, is found to have suffered a remarkable change, dating from some previous confinement. Traits of character appear, hitherto unknown by those most in her intimacy. She becomes irritable, subject to causeless fits of passion, and . . . estranged from those in whom she had before invested fullest confidence."[36]

McFarland observed that, although both the subtle nature of moral insanity and the ambiguity of the term created "perplexities," he believed it represented a genuine form of insanity. Indeed, he was impressed by the number of cases in which insanity bore "the aspect of mere moral perversity" such as an inclination to cause trouble for others and an "apparent delight in contemplating the mischief and destruction which their own hands have wrought." Such individuals lacked any vestige of sentiments of "gratitude, affection, or of the instinct of love as found even in the lower orders of animals." Instead, they demonstrated "a general hardness of the whole moral nature," even while retaining full power of their memory, perception, judgment, and all that constituted reason.[37]

"All insane asylums," McFarland continued, "abound[ed] in cases of unquestionable mental disease" that were "so obscure that the unskilled observer" would not discern it. He described the behavioral clues that accompanied this type of insanity: "A certain suspicious reserve, a mysterious shyness of manner, some haughtiness of bearing, or something marked and singular in tone of voice and manner of utterance, some strange attachment to some particular position or seat, or special stress applied to the doing of some act, may be all that distinguishes the individual from other men."[38] Nevertheless, McFarland continued, the experienced physician would recognize "latent delusion" in such cases and would be "prepared for the sudden exhibition of extreme or violent acts" that sometimes evolved from an apparently mild disorder.[39]

McFarland concluded with comments about "minor mental maladies" whose leading feature was "a love for the extreme, the eccentric, and the general opposite to the received opinions, practices and fashions of the rest of mankind." This was evident, for example, in the individual who "follows a side track" in "opposition to everything established by the concurrence of the rest of mankind." In politics, such an individual believed himself "far advanced from everybody else." In literature, he chooses "something, part medical, part religious, and part politico-economical." Typically, such individuals were "loners" who kept the rest of society "at arm's length."[40]

McFarland's paper sparked vigorous debate and it was clear that leading psychiatrists were divided on the usefulness of moral insanity in diagnosing mental disorder. The ensuing discussion consumed thirty-five pages of the Association's proceedings for that year and was directly relevant to Packard's case.

Some of those present recommended clarifying the nomenclature by calling the phenomenon "emotional insanity" instead of "moral insanity." Dr. John E. Tyler (McLean Asylum for the Insane, Somerville, Massachusetts) worried that "the very term 'moral insanity' seems to convey the impression . . . that it is an excuse for crime or wrong action of some sort." He believed that derangement likely began as a physical disorder that then progressed to involve the moral and, finally, the intellectual faculties.[41]

Dr. John P. Gray (New York State Lunatic Asylum, Utica) rejected "emotional insanity" as an equally misleading term and argued that insanity was "something more than the perturbed emotions and the loss of self-control." Gray declared that in the thousands of cases he had observed, he "had never seen a case at all corresponding with the description of moral insanity, given by any of the medical writers on the subject."[42]

Complimenting McFarland's "very able and interesting paper," Dr. Isaac Ray (Butler Hospital for the Insane, Providence, Rhode Island) agreed that "mental aberration . . . which we do not discern" might very well be present. But, he cautioned colleagues not to insist (particularly in court testimony) that there was a latent or unseen intellectual delusion, adding, "[If] all we see is moral impairment [then] that is all we have a right to affirm the existence of."[43] Asked to provide his definition of moral insanity, Ray, a founding father of the AMSAII and an expert on the jurisprudence of insanity, defined it as "that form of mania in which the moral powers are affected, without there being any intellectual disturbance appreciable."[44]

Dr. W. S. Chipley (Eastern Kentucky Lunatic Asylum, Lexington) disagreed, insisting that "insanity does not exist where the intellectual faculties are intact and healthy." He continued, "To constitute this disease, I think there must be defective development, aberration or enfeeblement of the reasoning faculties." It was Chipley's opinion that the "older writers" on the subject simply erred.[45]

At this point McFarland restated his belief that intellectual derangement was always the underlying cause of what might seem only moral deviance. Then, without mentioning Packard by name, he detailed her case as an example of moral insanity. He told colleagues about a patient who, over the period of five or six years, "began to manifest a disposition to thwart her husband in little matters, and throw checks in his way—question the propriety of what he was doing in regard to . . . his church and in regard to his family." "Yet," he continued, "during all this time she showed no sort of intellectual impairment. She was the centre of a great circle of friends, which she [gathered] about her wherever she was."[46]

"Matters became so troublesome" because of this woman's conduct that her minister-husband was forced to move from parish to parish. Along the way, he continued, the woman "began gradually to absorb all the erroneous ideas of that sort of half medical and half theological stuff, unfortunately too current in certain circles, and she got her mind filled with them." Despite her "extraordinary powers of mind," her character gradually changed "into a general 'devilishness' in regard to everything about her."[47]

McFarland told his colleagues that, at the time of the woman's admission to his institution, a diagnosis was elusive. He acknowledged, "Up to this time, I do not think any one would have discovered in that lady any intellectual impairment at all. There were extraordinary mental capacity and power, great charm of manner, and taste in dress, and good judgment. But with those qualities there was a disposition to make everybody miserable about her." The woman, he continued, opposed her husband in "matters of religious belief—tore his church all to pieces, and created great dissensions in the family."[48]

McFarland confessed to colleagues that, "for two years of the closest study," he could not "discover any intellectual impairment at all—certainly nothing that deserved the name." Nevertheless, he continued, her behavior toward her husband "had something diabolical about it. Every instinct of love was banished from her." Still, McFarland said, he could not discover any intellectual impairment.[49]

McFarland reported that he had only recently uncovered her true intellectual delusion. From her book he determined that the source of "all this perversity" in her conduct "arose out of one single delusion; and the delusion was, that, in the Trinity, distinctions of sex had to exist . . . That there was God the Father, Jesus Christ the son, and she was the female Holy Ghost."[50] Thus, McFarland concluded, he could now see how the case was "perfectly consistent with the idea of an originally intellectual delusion, underlying and producing all the so-called phenomena of moral insanity."[51]

In the course of these comments, McFarland expressed his exasperation with Packard and, in a remarkably cavalier statement, told colleagues: "She gave me infinite trouble, and after having her about two and a half years, I got tired of her, and I proposed to the board of Trustees to discharge her as the only means of getting rid of an intolerable and unendurable source of annoyance."[52]

McFarland concluded with the suggestion that if others had difficulty accepting the term "moral insanity" "then let us banish that obnoxious adjective from the language." He urged the Association to seek consensus on credible definitions and nomenclature for such maladies that would be acceptable both to the general public and in courts of law.

However, the debate continued as many of the doctors present questioned McFarland's conclusion in this particular case. Dr. Tyler asked pointedly if McFarland believed "the lady . . . was insane before he ascertained the existence of delusion." McFarland's remarkable response was, "Yes, sir, I believed that delusion existed, and that I should find it."[53]

Dr. C. H. Nichols (Government Hospital for the Insane, Washington, D.C.) expressed difficulty believing that this "lady was led to the petty, tireless persecution of her husband, and to the unwearied pursuit of every ill purpose, by the belief that she was the 'female Holy Ghost.'" He questioned how such a delusion could remain latent for eighteen years and stated flatly, "I see no natural connection between such delusion and the perversion of her moral faculties."[54]

McFarland responded that he had no hesitation making a diagnosis of insanity in an individual who exhibited "strange moral perversities, inconsistent with the previous character, conduct, education and habits of life of the person." However, rather than arguing the point further, McFarland suggested that they were "differing not so much in regard to the facts" as they were on the "propriety" of using the term "moral insanity."[55]

Now Isaac Ray pressed McFarland, saying, "I fail now to see where you have made the issue. Is the issue one of things or merely of words?" McFarland replied that it was not merely a matter of words, although he believed "much of the evil would be done away with by a change of words."[56]

The discussion rambled on, but ultimately ended inconclusively. The superintendents would not, in fact, resolve their conundrum over moral insanity for many decades. But that issue and others related to the jurisprudence of insanity weighed heavily on their minds. They noted cases in Europe in which psychiatrists had been sent to prison for giving affidavits of insanity with which a court later disagreed.[57]

Thus, before adjourning, the AMSAII appointed a committee to survey state laws related to commitment, admission, discharge, appointment of guardians, and the general legal process connected with declarations of insanity. Isaac Ray was appointed chair and McFarland as the representative from Illinois.[58]

The superintendents hoped the resulting report would assist them in shaping laws that would protect the best interests of both patient and doctor. These laws were critical not only for the profession, but for the individual doctor who was asked to testify in court—or called into court to defend his professional decisions.

Elizabeth Packard's case would amplify the difficulties within the psychiatric profession. Her doctor was undoubtedly aware of his professional vulnerability in such an ambiguous case. The fact that colleagues did not universally support his conclusions regarding this case must have been troubling. Thus, it is likely that McFarland anticipated Packard's impending release from his institution with both relief and trepidation.

On 18 June 1863, three years to the day after being admitted, Packard was released into her husband's custody, despite her indignant protest. Employing her now customary act of nonviolent resistance, she was carried from the asylum poised on a "saddle seat" formed by the arms of two attendants. Thus, she reported, "Like as I entered the Asylum against my will, and in spite of my protest, so I was put out of it into the absolute power of my persecutor."[59]

To her surprise and relief, Theophilus took her to the Granville, Illinois, home of Angeline and David Field. Apparently Theo, who was employed as a clerk at Farwell, Field and Company in Chicago, agreed to pay $100 for her to board at the Fields for the next year.[60]

While in Granville Packard continued work on her book, but had difficulty finding money to publish it. She lamented, "I find it very hard for a woman who has lost her reputation as well as property, by the cruel defamation of insanity, to do anything alone."[61] Only then, she wrote, did she fully realize "what an unpardonable offense" McFarland had committed against her and her children by diagnosing her as incurably insane.

In October, she paid an apparently unwelcome visit to Theo in Chicago.[62] Theo wrote his father that she was at the Adams House Hotel "running up a debt of two dollars a day." He told him he intended to send his mother home and added, "There will of course be a scene at Manteno when she gets there, and I am glad I will not be there to witness it. You can live with her a short time—probably a few days." He suggested that Theophilus then take her back to Granville. Theo's letter, later published by his father, ended with a plea "not to let her come here again. I do not want to see her here again, and I have told her so."[63]

Packard apparently returned to Granville for a time, but recorded that on a "cold morning in November" she finally boarded the train to Manteno. She recalled that several friends met her at the depot and offered to escort her home; however, she decided to go alone with only William Blessing to drive the wagon and assist with her trunk.[64]

Community opinion in Manteno—divided from the outset—had apparently turned dramatically against Theophilus Packard in the three years since his jury of townspeople supported his decision to put his wife away. He had resigned as pastor of the Manteno Presbyterian church in July 1862, recording in his diary no reason other than his usual assertion that he "thought it best."[65]

Packard, of course, had her opinion on the matter. She believed he was asked to resign and described the change in his circumstances: "When I returned, he preached nowhere. He was closeted at his own domicile on the Sabbath, cooking the family dinner, while his children were at church and Sabbath school." His congregation, by her account (and substantiated by the church history), was "almost entirely broken up."[66]

During her absence her husband's financial difficulties had worsened and Packard found her family living "on charity."[67] Theophilus explained that, "after relinquishing preaching at Manteno," he stayed there and "took care of my young family" with no salary and "a debt of nearly $4,000 pressing upon me." He was grateful that, "through the great mercy of God operating thro' the kindness of beloved friends, my family lived and we had a house, food & clothes."[68]

By the time Packard returned home, both Theo and Isaac were working in Chicago and living independently.[69] Samuel left home soon after his mother's return. Although only sixteen years old, he began studying law that winter at the Chicago firm of Barker and Tuley.[70] The younger children, George and

Arthur, eleven and five, barely remembered their mother. Thirteen-year-old Libby, who was evidently most adversely affected by her mother's absence, would suffer from mental disability much of her life. Thus, Packard's return home was bittersweet at best.

She wrote that she tried to rejoin the family as "mother and housekeeper" (but not wife) and resolutely set about reclaiming her place in the household. It quickly became clear, however, that even a partial restoration of family life was impossible. Packard recorded that soon after her return, her husband confiscated her trunk and papers, restricted her access to her children and friends, and locked her in a room at night.

Theophilus disputed this assertion, insisting that she was always free to move in and out of the house as she pleased. However, once again, he began collecting letters of support from friends and family, including the children. Theo and Isaac, who had objected to their mother's commitment, now seemed to support their father. Isaac wrote his father saying he "did not sympathize" with his mother's treatment of his father and added, "I thought you knew my views of the case had undergone a change lately."[71]

About the same time, Samuel, Lizzie, and George signed a statement regarding their "dear mother's derangement." It read, "By her refusing to speak to our father or to have anything to do with him, and by teaching us that he is the devil, and also by saying all who call her deranged blaspheme against the Holy Ghost, and by other things also, we are sure that she is not in her right mind."[72]

In early January, Packard evidently discovered letters discussing her husband's plans to send her to the asylum in Northampton, Massachusetts.[73] She recorded that, alarmed, she immediately sought assistance by dropping a note out her bedroom window to a passerby with a request that it be delivered to Mrs. William Haslett, "the most efficient friend I knew of in Manteno."[74]

The Hasletts responded by leading a group to the Packard home with the intention of freeing her by force if necessary. Recalling the incident, Theophilus recorded indignantly that "a Manteno mob assembled to attend to her case & sent a couple of men to me, to regulate my family affairs! O what scenes were these! I cannot <u>here</u> describe them."[75]

On 11 January 1864, William Haslett, Daniel Beedy, Zalmon Hanford, and J. Younglove filed a petition with the circuit court in Kankakee County, Illinois, stating their belief that Elizabeth Packard was "unlawfully restrained of her liberty" and that her husband "cruelly abuse[d]" her by confining her in a cold room without adequate clothing. The writ stated that she had been denied visits to or from friends without "just cause or ground for restraining said wife of her liberty." The men attested to their belief "that said wife is a mild and amiable woman" and requested a writ of *habeas corpus* in her behalf.[76] As a result, Circuit Court Judge Charles Starr ordered Theophilus to present his wife to the court and to show cause for his treatment of her.

Outraged, Theophilus recorded, "Four intermeddlers in town got out a writ of habeas corpus, requiring me to take her before Judge Starr of Kankakee, as though I was falsely imprisoning her!"[77] When the parties involved assembled in the courtroom, Judge Starr ordered a trial, not on the question of spousal mistreatment, but on the question of Packard's sanity. Elizabeth Packard had finally obtained the trial at which she could defend her sanity.

9 From Courtroom to Activism

TESTIMONY IN PACKARD'S trial began on 12 January 1864 and caused an immediate sensation. A noisy crowd packed the courtroom, and it was clear the predominantly female assemblage favored Packard as the heroine of the drama unfolding before them.

Theophilus hired attorneys Thomas P. Bonfield, Mason B. Loomis, and C. A. Lake to represent him. Bonfield, a well-known Kankakee County pioneer, wrote later that he was astonished that the case was not immediately dismissed. He objected to a jury trial and pointed out that it was customary for the judge to rule in *habeas corpus* cases. He believed, too, that it would be impossible to seat an impartial jury. When those motions were denied, he decided not to bother requesting a change of venue, which he understood would also be refused.[1]

Figure 5. Judge Charles R. Starr. *Source: Portrait and Biographical Record of Kankakee County, Illinois* (1893), 209.

Bonfield later pointed to sectarian strife in the community as the cause of the sentiment against Theophilus. However, the partisanship of the principals in the case was mixed. Bonfield was a Universalist, although he was also a liberal contributor to the Episcopal church that his wife attended.[2] The judge, Charles R. Starr, was a member of the Congregational church in Kankakee, but his wife was previously Unitarian and they were married in a Unitarian ceremony.[3] Five of the twelve jurymen were Presbyterians, though not members of Theophilus's church.[4]

To present her case, Elizabeth hired Stephen R. Moore, John Orr, and Harrison Loring. Moore, a Methodist, was ranked as "one of the foremost lawyers of the state."[5] His account would become the unofficial record of Packard's trial after the official documents were lost in a courthouse fire.

Moore argued that Theophilus, not Elizabeth, carried their "differences of opinion" over religious matters "from fireside to the pulpit" and made them "a matter of inquiry by the church." This, he said, "resulted in open warfare" in which her views were "misrepresented . . . from the pulpit" and she was made "the subject of unjust criticism."[6]

As one might suspect, Moore's version of the proceedings received injured criticism from Theophilus and his supporters. Even Elizabeth admitted that Moore purposely left out some testimony, explaining that her brother-in-law and deacon Josephus Smith from her husband's church "perjured themselves openly . . . [in] *manufactured* testimony against my moral character, which, when tested by cross-examination, would not hold together."[7]

Theophilus's attorneys called as witnesses three doctors, two members of his church, and his sister and brother-in-law. Each of the doctors had examined Packard at her husband's request prior to her incarceration. Christopher Knott of Kankakee stated that he met with Packard on two occasions for thirty minutes each, after which he signed a certificate saying she was a monomaniac "partially deranged on religious matters." Under cross-examination, Knott suggested that she was insane as was "three-fourths of the religious community" and named as comparable examples Henry Ward Beecher, Horace Greeley, "and like persons."[8]

Dr. J. W. Brown cited multiple reasons for his judgment that Packard was insane, including her claim that she was "in advance of the age thirty or forty years" and her objection to being called insane. Part of Brown's testimony was delivered in multisyllabic terms that apparently evoked uproarious laughter from onlookers. Moore recounted that it took several minutes to restore order in the court. Packard later wrote, disdainfully, that Brown was a wheelwright who had "studied medicine just long enough" to believe "his

Figure 6. Attorney Stephen R. Moore. *Source:* Palmer, *Bench and Bar of Illinois* (1899), vol. II, 978.

opinions would be entitled to infallibility, especially if given in the high-flown language of an expert."[9]

The third doctor, Joseph H. Way of Kankakee, testified that he had at first believed Packard was "somewhat deranged or excited" in matters relating to religion. But, conceding that he was "not much posted on disputed points in theology," he admitted that he had since found other (presumably sane) people who held ideas similar to those of Packard.[10]

Abijah Dole, Theophilus Packard's brother-in-law, testified that in frequent visits to the Packard home he had on several occasions found Packard "in an excited state of mind." In tearful testimony, Dole seemed to hint of witchcraft. He recounted that he had been called to the house early one morning and observed Packard in a disheveled state still in her nightclothes looking "very wild and very much excited." Her daughter, Libby, "was lying in bed, moaning and moving her head." Dole testified that when he first saw Libby he believed Packard "had exerted some mesmeric or other influence over the child that caused it to moan and toss its head."[11] Under cross-examination, however, Dole admitted that Libby was ill with "brain fever" at the time and that he supposed Packard's anxiety was caused by concern for the child, whom she had been watching over all night.[12]

Moore reported that Sybil Dole's arrival in the courtroom with Packard's daughter created "quite a stir." According to Moore, Libby went straight to her mother and was "clinging to her with all child-like fervor" as Dole pulled her away. Once again, Moore said, the sheriff had to restore order to the courtroom.[13]

When called to the stand, Sybil Dole testified that she had known Packard for twenty-five years during which time Packard's "natural disposition" was "very kind and sweet [and] her morals without a stain or blemish." She said that Packard was "weeping and sick" as she left for her trip to New York and that "from her voice, and the manner she talked, I formed an opinion of her insanity."[14]

Sybil Dole apparently spoke about difficulties involving Abner Baker. However, if she testified specifically to a romantic relationship between Baker and Packard, Moore omitted it from the record. In her reported testimony, Dole said Baker came to Manteno to settle a disagreement over whether or not Theo could continue working in his store. According to Dole, Packard was wildly "excited about her son remaining at Marshall."

Dole reported that Packard "acted strangely" when Baker first arrived, but was calmer by the following day. Contradicting the charge that Packard had neglected her family, Dole stated under cross-examination that she "was a good, neat, thrifty, and careful housekeeper" who "kept the children clean and neatly dressed."[15]

Evidently, Andrew McFarland was away on a trip to Zanesville, Ohio, at the time of the trial and would not return for ten days, despite an urgent telegraph from Theophilus requesting his testimony. The judge refused to delay the trial, but allowed a recent letter from McFarland and a copy of Packard's hospital dismissal record to be read to the jury. Moore reported that both documents declared her incurably insane.[16]

In Packard's defense, Moore reported testimony of two doctors who had evidently refused to sign certificates of insanity for Packard. Both J. D. Mann and I. L. Simington testified that they had interviewed Packard before her institutionalization and found no evidence of derangement. Simington was the doctor Theophilus called a "quack" for not signing the petition supporting his wife's institutionalization.[17]

In other testimony, Joseph E. La Brie, a justice of the peace and member of the local Catholic church, swore that if Packard was insane "no common-sense man could find it out." He testified that, at Theophilus Packard's request, he had notarized Elizabeth's signature on a deed just before she was taken to the asylum. Moore's implication, of course, was that both her husband and a justice of the peace apparently considered her competent enough to execute a legal document at the time of her commitment. Packard later made much

Figure 7. Kankakee County Court House.
Source: Atlas of Kankakee County, Ill. (1883), 25.

of this fact in her books, observing ironically that she was apparently sane when it suited her husband's purposes, but insane when it did not.[18]

Evidently, Moore then invited Packard to read to the court the essay, "How Godliness is Profitable," which she had presented to the Bible class. He reported that when she finished reading, the court was disrupted by applause, "which was promptly suppressed by the sheriff."[19]

Testimony resumed with the Blessings, Packard's friends from the Methodist church. William Blessing explained that, although Packard had always seemed sane to him, he did not intervene to help her initially because he "did not like to interfere between man and wife." Mrs. Blessing stated that when they first visited Packard at the asylum, she had the keys to the ward and freely showed them around the hospital. She testified that she had also visited Packard at home a few days after her return home and found her at work cleaning the house.[20]

Another friend, Mrs. Haslett, testified that she, too, had visited Packard at home. "I was let into her room by Mr. Packard; she had no fire in it; we sat there in the cold," Haslett told the court. "Before this, Mrs. Hanford and myself went there to see her; he [Theophilus] would not let us see her; he shook his hand at me, and threatened to put me out."[21]

Perhaps the most articulate witness in Packard's behalf was a Dr. Duncanson from Kankakee, who had been educated in Scotland at Anderson University and the University of Glasgow. According to Moore, Duncanson testified that he believed Packard was not only sane, but "the most intelligent lady I have talked with in many years."[22]

Declaring Packard "an expert in both . . . Old School and New School theology," Duncanson noted that many of her ideas were "embraced in Swedenborgianism, and many are found only in the New School theology." Perhaps most significant, he stated that Packard's "explanation of woman representing the Holy Ghost [was] a very ancient theological dogma and entertained by many of our most eminent men." He assured jurors that "the best and most learned men of both Europe and this country are advocates of these doctrines, in one shape or the other."[23]

On 18 January 1864, the case went to the jury. According to Moore, they returned in seven minutes with the verdict that Elizabeth Packard was sane. Moore reported that this announcement brought cheers throughout the courtroom as "the ladies waved their handkerchiefs, and pressed around Mrs. Packard" to extend their congratulations.[24] When order was restored, the judge ordered that Packard "be relieved from all restraint incompatible with her condition as a sane woman."[25]

Theophilus Packard characterized his wife's trial as the "reign of mobocracy, insult, partiality, prejudice, injustice, and malignity." He reported that, after attending for five days, he feared "the mob spirit was so diabolical" that his life was in danger. Thus, he said, "I quit the sham court, and packed up my goods, and with two of my young children left for the East, January 18, 1864 and arrived at South Deerfield, Mass. Jan. 22, 1864." Before leaving, he placed five-year-old Arthur in the care of his sister, Sybil, and stored the family's furniture along with Elizabeth's clothing and personal effects with the Doles.[26]

Elizabeth reported that, as he fled Manteno, Theophilus left a note inviting her to follow him to Massachusetts with the promise that he would provide her "a suitable home." This was perhaps intended to protect him from any accusation of desertion. Packard wrote that she declined his offer, trusting neither "his humanity [n]or judgment in providing [her] another home."[27] She knew that Massachusetts's law, as in Illinois, gave her husband complete authority over her and that her "suitable home" in Massachusetts would likely be another insane asylum.

Packard's joy over the verdict in her trial was quickly submerged by the realization that she was homeless, penniless, and childless. She described her plight in a manner guaranteed to inspire sympathy, writing, "After this life of faithful service for others, I am thrown adrift, at fifty years of age, upon the cold world, with no place on earth I can call home, and not a penny to supply my wants with, except what my own exertion secures to me."[28]

Packard recorded that she was turned away from the Doles when she tried to see young Arthur. Soon after her attempt the child was sent to his father in Massachusetts. There, Theophilus placed all three children in the care of another sister, Marian Severance, in Sunderland.

Packard recorded that six men from the community went with her to the Doles to recover some of her property. However, Abijah Dole apparently returned home as they finished loading their wagons. An argument broke out and a window was broken. Dole evidently called in the local sheriff and charged the would-be Samaritans with riot and trespass.[29]

Despite her entreaties to them to "stand their ground like men," they evidently returned the furniture and paid Dole $200 in damages to avoid a trial. Packard was disappointed by their "lack of manliness." She explained to her readers that she had intended to use their trial as a test case for married women's property rights in Illinois, adding that she had already enlisted the aid of "two of the most influential lawyers in Illinois."[30] She did not name the lawyers, but may have been referring to woman's rights activists James and Myra Bradwell.

Packard recorded that Judge Starr and her attorneys strongly advised her to seek a divorce as the only means of protecting her liberty and the only hope of regaining her children and property. For the record, she refused, saying the only "Bible reason" for divorce was infidelity. She certainly had no cause to doubt her husband's fidelity and, she added not quite truthfully, he had never "had cause to doubt hers."[31]

Nevertheless, surviving court records indicate that Packard did sue for divorce shortly after her trial. The complaint, dated 8 February 1864, accused Theophilus Packard of "repeated and extreme acts of cruelty," including confining his wife to her house and room, not permitting "neighboring women to visit or call upon her, as is customary among good society," preventing her from visiting neighbors, confining her at the Jacksonville asylum "without any reasonable cause," and of "personally using violence" toward her "by striking, dragging [her] by the hair of her head and by diverse and sundry other acts of cruelty not above specifically set forth." The complaint did not mention property or child custody, requesting only that both parties might be "freed from the obligation" of their marriage bonds and that she might have such "relief as shall be agreeable to equity."[32]

The summons to Theophilus was returned by Sheriff Jacob Obrecht, 2 April 1864, with a note saying the "defendant not found in my county."[33] However, Theophilus apparently learned about the summons and directed his lawyer to respond in his behalf. He noted in his diary that when his "counsel appeared to oppose it [the divorce], she at once abandoned the case."[34] Later, he made sure that the contradiction between this legal action and his wife's published statements on divorce was publicized as evidence of "the lack of truthfulness which characterizes" her books.[35]

Packard mentioned none of this in her books, maintaining her stance that she was opposed to divorce. She wrote that she did "not want to be a divorced woman." She explained that she wished "to be a married woman, and have my husband for my protector; for I do not like this being divorced from my own home . . . Neither do I like this being divorced from my own children. I want to live with my dear children, whom I have borne and nursed, reared and educated, almost entirely by my own unwearied indefatigable exertions; and I love them, with all the fondness of a mother's undying love." She argued further that divorce was a "Secession principle" that undermined "the very vital principle of our Union, and saps the very foundation of our social and civil obligations."[36]

Certainly, Packard also realized that, even apart from any allegation by her husband of "wanton behavior," a court was unlikely to grant her custody of her children since she had no means of supporting them.[37] Thus she would seek legal recourse other than divorce. She knew that before she could "reasonably hope to succeed" in getting the children, laws must be changed and her "poverty must be supplanted by plenty."[38]

Toward this end, she evidently used money given her by friends in Granville to print a thousand copies of a letter entitled "An Appeal in Behalf of the Insane" written by Mr. and Mrs. James Coe who had been employed at the Jacksonville asylum. The documents offered a vivid account of abuse at the Jacksonville asylum. According to Packard, this 10 cent circular sold well enough to become "the nucleus of my publishing business."[39]

In the meantime, she continued work on her book. Concerned that its substantial size would "frighten away the *practical* reader," she decided to publish it in several small volumes. After paring the first volume down to 158 pages, she borrowed $10 from Zalmon Hanford, the husband of a friend, and traveled to Chicago to obtain estimates from printers.

Her activities during this time caused considerable consternation in the family. Theo wrote his Grandfather Ware that his mother had "changed her hotel four times since coming [to Chicago] on the 17th of March." He implored his grandfather to confer with his father "and adopt some plan to get her into proper keeping." He offered to help put her on a train to Massachusetts if someone else could travel with her.[40]

However, Packard apparently conducted her business in Chicago without interruption. She hired a printer to publish her book and over the next several months sold advance subscription "tickets" to it, "mostly in country villages on the railroads" in Illinois.[41] Motivated by "an invincible determination" to demonstrate that she could support herself, she sold enough tickets to pay for printing the book.[42]

Meanwhile, she capitalized on publicity from her trial by writing and selling other "small books" at 10 to 25 cents. She reported that these pamphlets helped cover travel expenses as she canvassed for her forthcoming book. Undoubtedly with her husband in mind, she told her later readers, "Never in these days of struggle did I ask for charity."[43]

Among the first of her smaller publications was *Mrs. Packard's Reproof of Dr. McFarland,* a thirty-two-page booklet featuring the note of reproof that had provoked McFarland to confine her to the "maniac's ward." In addition to letters of support from former asylum employees, it included McFarland's rebuttal to her reproof, which had been published in the *Chicago Tribune* following her trial. Packard called McFarland a "despot and a liar" and shamed him for his lack of "manliness" and honesty. In response to his statement that she exhibited insanity "in the form of intensity of hatred toward her husband," she declared that, considering her husband's treatment of her, she believed she "hate[d] him with just and sufficient cause."[44]

The pamphlet concluded with a denunciation of Illinois's unjust commitment law, which, Packard reported, had deprived her "of every means of self-defence, with no sort of jury trial," and permitted her to be kept for "an indefinitely long term of imprisonment." She asked rhetorically whether taxpayers could afford to keep sane women hospitalized for three years. She also questioned McFarland's professional competence, noting that hers was not the first case in which a jury had disagreed with his judgment. She added that it would be no surprise to her if courts, juries, voters, and taxpayers came to realize that "the fallible Dr. McFarland does not himself know a *sane* from an *insane* person."[45]

Apparently, during much of 1864 Packard focused on managing her budding publishing business. When published, her first book bore the lengthy title *Exposure on Board the Atlantic & Pacific Car of Emancipation for the Slaves of Old Columbia, Engineered by the Lightning Express, Or Christianity and Calvinism Compared, With an Appeal to the Government to Emancipate the Slaves of the Marriage Union.* Packard claimed that profits from this book enabled her to pay her three lawyers in full within six months after her trial. Noting with satisfaction the success of this initial venture, she boasted that she had accomplished this completely "without a partner."[46]

She dedicated the book to her children and declared her love for them, writing, "Death and a living tomb cannot separate us. We are one in Christ." But she then explained that all her "earthly love" had died and "the death agonies of the maternal love well nigh rent soul and body asunder." "Yes," she continued, "the mother has died! But she has risen again—the mother of her country—and her sons and daughters are—*The American Republic.*"[47]

With those words, Packard seems to have accepted the loss of her role as mother and claimed the new role of reformer. Nevertheless, her reform work would begin with efforts in Illinois and Massachusetts to pass legislation that would enable her to gain custody of the children. She clearly now viewed her reform work as essential not only for the welfare of her own children, but all children.

Most of Packard's first book was written in normal, if emphatic, prose. However, the introduction was written in the "allegorical style" initially intended for the entire work. An asterisk near the beginning alerts the reader to that fact. In the introduction, she drew images from abolitionist literature to urge readers to get aboard the "lightning express" to emancipation for married women and declared, "I already have one Uncle Tom Cabin's full of material ready [for publication]."[48]

After the introduction, Packard for the most part abandoned allegory in favor of her own voice. The tone remained urgent and melodramatic, and the text was peppered with exclamation points and emphasized by italics. She included reproductions of her statements before the trustees, her essay on "Calvinism and Christianity Compared," copies of letters written during her stay at Jacksonville, and the defense of her sanity written to McFarland while she was still a patient.

Succeeding chapters consist of essays and parables advocating religious tolerance, liberty of conscience, freedom of speech, and women's rights. In an essay on tolerance, for example, she depicted a pilgrimage in which Christians from all sects and denominations were arrayed on a large hill. "All and each," she said, held "a distinctly different view of the same landscape below." However, upon reaching the summit, the pilgrims were amazed to learn they were all right. "Each, and all, from your own stand-point have reported correctly." She continued, "Each being true to himself, has safely arrived at his destined goal. But no one can see just as he did; for his angle of vision, his organization, differs from each and all others, and yet he is true to himself— and true to God."[49]

Throughout this book, Packard presented herself as a "true woman," but also as a reformer who was intellectually "ahead of her time." She freely confessed her "advanced" religious and social ideas. She argued, for example, for the plausibility of transmigration of souls, reasoning that "matter and mind always existed, although in different forms or bodies." Once these bodies were perfected over the "long transplanting process," she believed they would no longer die "or sink into a state of oblivion or forgetfulness of our past existences, as we now do."[50] She also suggested that clairvoyance ("second sight") was a gift of "spiritual illumination," comparable to the gifts of the spirit spoken of in the Bible in I Corinthians 12, for example, speaking in tongues, gifts of prophecy, and gifts of healing.[51]

Details of her life, including the cruelties of the asylum, are interspersed thematically within each of these chapters rather than in chronological order. She compared her marital conflict with the Civil War, writing that, as the North had borne with the South, so she had borne with her husband "long after forbearance ceased to be a virtue."[52] And throughout the book one point rings clear: she was an intelligent, competent woman who had been "cruelly wronged and abused" by the very men who should have protected her.

In this first book, Packard consciously portrayed her struggle for personal liberty as "a woman's rights struggle." Like woman's rights advocates, she considered the common law the root of women's legal disabilities, referring to it as the "nonentity principle" since it completely subsumed a married woman's legal identity within that of her husband.

However, Packard's dynamic woman's rights rhetoric was accompanied by conflicted and essentially paternalistic objectives. She wanted the law to require her husband to treat her as a "true woman" and to acknowledge her rightful authority within the domestic sphere. It was unfortunate, she said, that such stipulations were necessary. But, she continued, "Where neither love nor reason will hold a man to be the protector of these, his wife's rights, what can the wife of such a man do, without some such stipulation, or laws, by which her identity, as a woman, can be maintained?" She declared, "The law says I am a non-existent being after marriage, but God says I am an existent and accountable one still; therefore I claim the recognition of this higher law principle."[53]

These arguments were borrowed directly from woman's rights documents such as the Declaration of Sentiments produced at the Woman's Rights Convention at Seneca Falls in 1848. That document spoke of the "long train of abuses and usurpations" that subjected women to "absolute despotism." It was the duty of women "to throw off such government and to provide new guards for their future security." Women must forgo their patient suffering and "demand the equal station to which they are entitled."[54]

One of the Declaration's best-known tenets was that "the history of mankind is a history of repeated injuries and usurpations on the part of man toward woman, having in direct object the establishment of an absolute tyranny over her." Packard adopted terms such as "usurpation," "tyranny," "despotism," and "oppression" to describe her relationship with her husband and her position within their marriage. She also echoed many of the complaints expressed in the Declaration, which pointed out that upon marriage a woman became "civilly dead," forfeiting "all right in property, even to the wages she earns." A married woman, the Declaration continued, was "compelled to promise obedience to her husband, he becoming, to all intents and purposes, her master—the law giving him power to deprive her of her liberty, and to administer chastisement."[55]

Indeed, the language of Packard's first book demonstrates the elements of what historian Gerda Lerner called "feminist consciousness." According to Lerner, this includes the awareness that women are part of a subordinate and oppressed group; recognition that this subordination is not natural but determined by law and society; realization that women must join together to right these wrongs; and a vision of a new, more equitable, society for both men and women.[56]

Packard identified married women as a particularly oppressed class and declared herself "a martyr for the rights of opinion in woman."[57] She claimed to speak for this "whole class of slaves" in petitioning the government to protect married women "in the homes Providence has placed us in."[58] She joined rhetorically with other women to demand redress for the wrongs to married women, declaring, "Tis *freedom,* or *natural liberty* that we want, and it is all we ask of our country to bestow upon us . . . We ask our government for our *freedom to do right,* where God has placed us, and protection from the abuse of our inalienable rights."[59]

Finally, she envisioned a society improved by women's active participation, declaring, "What a sight better government we'll have, when we, women, get back . . . where *God* put us, in rank and file with our husbands, instead of being separated." In the society she envisioned, women's "seats would not have been vacant in our legislative halls, and in our Congress sessions and our female power, *joined with* the male power, would have saved our government from corruption."[60]

But while she seemed at times to advocate women's full political participation, in other statements she maintained allegiance to the doctrine of separate spheres. She believed—and indeed would soon demonstrate—that women could wield substantial political power without voting or holding public office.[61] Like other women who believed "moral suasion" was a more powerful tool than suffrage, she used the doctrines of separate spheres and domesticity to elevate woman's role and to place man in the position of servant-protector rather than sovereign-ruler. Thus, she wrote that the home was "woman's proper sphere" and the "husband is the God-appointed agent to guard and protect woman in her God-appointed orbit."[62]

She argued, however, that giving married women legal rights at least equal to those of single women would strengthen marriage and thus serve the greater good of society. She believed that present laws encouraged infidelity and divorce and argued, "The best interests of society demand that the sacred institution of marriage be based on the principle of right and justice to both parties, so that neither party can ignore or usurp the inalienable rights of the other."[63]

Like woman's rights advocates, she argued that women deserved the same consideration given free men. To male legislators she declared, "You have emancipated the Negro slave and we think our claim to 'life, liberty, and the pursuit of happiness' is equal, at least, to that of the colored men."[64]

The Seneca Falls Declaration of Sentiments declared that women's choice of a sphere of action was a matter of conscience rightfully left between her and her God.[65] This was also a standard argument of Garrisonian abolitionists who argued that, because "all human beings were moral beings, created free by God to determine their own salvation, no person could rightfully deprive others the freedom to make moral choices. To do so was a sinful abomination."[66]

Packard likewise employed moral government theory to defend herself as an accountable, moral being. Her insistence on her democratic right to private conscience echoed that of early woman's rights advocates such as Quaker Lucretia Mott. In fact, Packard's declaration that she "had just as good a right to her opinion as Beecher, Barnes, or Scott" paraphrased Mott's claim that she had "the same right to be guided by my own convictions as Luther, Calvin, and Knox had to be guided by theirs."[67]

The rights to freedom of religion, free speech, and personal liberty were sacred national values encapsulated historically in the rhetoric of revolution and contemporarily in debates over slavery and woman's rights. Packard's masterful appeal to these values resonated with many in Jacksonian America who were both jealous of those rights and suspicious of any authority that might attempt to usurp them. She would prevail upon the men in government to make laws that "guarantee[d] to married woman a right to her own home, and a right to be mistress of her own house-hold, and a right to the guardianship of her own minor children."[68]

Packard was careful, however, to reassure her readers that she was not among the radicals who demanded rights for women fully equal to those of men. She explained: "By no means; we do not want the man's rights, but simply our own, natural, womanly rights. There are man's rights and woman's rights. Both different, yet both equally inalienable. There must be a head in every firm; and the head in the Marriage Firm or Union is the man, as the Bible and nature both plainly teach."[69]

Packard reasoned that, if home was "the appropriate sphere of woman," woman should have rights there "secured to her by statute laws" to shield her from an unmanly husband who failed to honor and protect her rights. "In short," she explained, "woman needs legal protection *as a married woman. She has a right to be a married woman, therefore she has a right to be protected as a married woman.*" Otherwise, she concluded, "it is not safe for her to marry."[70]

Legal historian Hendrick Hartog has suggested that Packard's unique demand for legal protection in her role as a married woman was in effect a call for a "legalization of domestic feminism." She sought to use the power of law to change a husband's behavior, thereby interjecting legal control into what was universally considered a private domain. While such intrusion by government, even if desirable, would be impossible to enforce, it provided Packard a useful stance in lobbying legislators. As Hartog noted, Packard's demand for her rights as a married woman served as "a strategic tool that allowed her to appeal to male legislators for relief and change, using a rhetoric that flattered them and did not challenge their paternalistic male authority."[71] Thus, Packard would combine the rhetoric of woman's rights, republicanism, and true womanhood to devise a masterfully politic position from which to argue her case. Throughout her career as a writer and reformer she would return repeatedly to these themes, emphasizing one or the other as the situation required.

10 "My Pen Shall Rage"

IN HER ASYLUM NOTES, Packard recorded that she understood that angry words—"the utterances of my natural indignation"—would likely be construed, literally, as madness. Thus, she said, "Reason taught me to be quiet while in the asylum, that I might rage all the more vehemently when I got out." Now she declared, "My pen shall rage if my tongue didn't . . . It shall rage, and it will rage, until he, whose right it is, shall rule over humanity."[1] Now she began to deliver on that promise.

Her campaign would be fueled not only by her writing and legislative lobbying but also by heightened public concern about insanity and asylums. Indeed, by the mid-nineteenth century, the asylum narratives of former patients comprised a unique genre of literature.[2] Among the more notable of these was *Hard Cash,* an exposé by English novelist Charles Reade. Successive editions of this book were released in England and the United States just as Packard's books and pamphlets began to circulate. While her works echoed the melodramatic titles and sentiments of such narratives, she would prove significantly more effective in moving public opinion and spurring legislative action. Indeed, as one historian suggested, these critiques were "fleabites" compared with Packard's books.[3]

Packard's first book appeared amid increased national anxiety about causes and cures for insanity. The U.S. Census report published in 1864 declared insanity "a subject not only of general interest, but of no small political and social importance." The Census included a detailed report on American asylums with commentary by Dr. Pliny Earle, a founding father of the AMSAII. At that time, Earle was superintendent of the Massachusetts State Lunatic Hospital at Northampton—the asylum to which Packard's husband had hoped to send her only a few months earlier.[4]

Earle's essay reflected the preeminent, though by no means unanimous, thought on causes, classifications, and treatment of insanity.[5] Reflecting debates of the AMSAII, Earle questioned whether monomania and moral insanity were valid terms. He noted that monomania was rare, "if indeed it ever exists," and declared that moral insanity was "treated as a nonentity" by most lawyers, doctors, and all but "a very few of the many physicians" experienced in treating the insane.[6]

Despite Earle's assertion that it was a "nonentity," the concept of moral insanity continued to be applied and debated by psychiatrists for the remainder of the nineteenth century. However, this equivocation within the profession only added to public confusion over definitions and diagnoses of insanity. Clearly, Packard's complaints against asylums and the psychiatric profession were about to fall on ground fertile for reform.

The AMSAII, meeting in Washington, D.C., in May 1864 debated the recommendations of the committee appointed the previous year to investigate insanity laws. The report, written by Isaac Ray and entitled "American Legislation on Insanity," was published in the July 1864 issue of the *American Journal of Insanity*, six months after Packard's well-publicized trial, and reflected many of the concerns raised by her case.[7]

Ray's report demonstrated that leaders of the AMSAII were predisposed to a defensive posture aimed as much at securing their professional integrity as at addressing the issues underlying complaints about their practices and institutions. Indeed, they believed general acknowledgment of their unique expertise was essential to establishing both the best treatment and the laws necessary to enable prompt treatment of mental illness.

Ray's report was critical of legislation that restricted asylum superintendents' primary authority to judge whether an individual was insane and in need of treatment. In particular, he questioned the need for "personal liberty laws" (such as those Packard advocated). He granted that if "governed by abstract principles of the sacredness attached to personal liberty," one would agree that laws depriving anyone of liberty should be limited "by a multitude of restrictions."[8]

But, Ray continued, abstract principles were a "poor foundation" for "repressive laws" that would make commitment of the insane more difficult. "Stern necessities," he asserted, made it necessary "to deprive the insane of their liberty," and interference with the law on this matter was "unnecessary and impertinent." It seemed that Ray might have had the Packard case in mind as he suggested, for example, that no one would question the right of a husband to confine a wife in his own house "if she is bent on self-destruction, or disposed to wander about, or impelled to acts of mischief." Indeed, he noted, failure to do so "would be justly regarded a most reprehensible neglect of duty."[9]

Ray went on to say that some patients were both unfit to remain in a private family and problematic if institutionalized. Such individuals might seem models of "propriety and injured innocence," but could completely destroy home life by "their bursts of passion, their irregular ways, their disregard of domestic proprieties."[10] Ray's comments again bring Packard to mind as he added, "A woman who might be endured in a family composed of only two or three discreet, phlegmatic adults, would be intolerable" in a family with children.[11] Yet, Ray continued, when placed in an institution, such individuals were "often regarded by the world as victims of domestic cruelty, and the popular wrath is kindled by charges against faithless husbands." The unfortunate result was often misguided legislation aimed at securing their "liberty" and punishing those who had confined them.[12]

Noting the embarrassment that family and friends of the insane often suffered, Ray argued that "the sacredness of private grief" demanded the "least formality necessary" in authorizing "isolation of an insane person." Thus, he recommended that, "public clamor to the contrary," the only protections necessary should include a certificate signed by one or two doctors, an application by friends or family, and concurrence of the hospital superintendent. These were, of course, precisely the documents provided in Packard's case.[13] Noting that the writ of *habeas corpus* was always available to those concerned that their personal liberty was in danger, Ray concluded that the legislation currently in effect in most states was sufficient.[14]

Ray's report also recommended against establishing state commissions to monitor insane asylums, arguing that authority must remain in the hands of the expert physician responsible for the patient's care. "One can scarcely exaggerate," he stated, "the amount of mischief [commissions] would accomplish." Certainly, he insisted, an institution's board of trustees provided adequate oversight.[15]

The report ended with twenty-one recommendations called "Project of a General Law for Determining the Legal Relations of the Insane." Perhaps anticipating the contentious discussion that followed, he recommended that the Association not publish this report or subsequent discussion concerning it.

Indeed, there were many objections to the report's wording and content. One superintendent thought it unwise "to open this subject in advance, as we might thus excite the suspicion that we feared investigation."[16] Another disagreed, noting that investigative commissions had already been appointed in Massachusetts and New York, and it was time for the AMSAII to take a stand. The superintendents voted to accept Ray's report without endorsing it. They also unanimously passed a resolution against lunacy commissions.[17]

Despite Ray's call for discretion, the October 1864 issue of the *American Journal of Insanity* contained a trenchant dissenting report from Dr. J. Parigot of New York. Parigot urged colleagues to reject Ray's recommendations and challenged the AMSAII to behave as a scientific body and act to reform itself, "calling to its assistance eminent lawyers and savants in the highest branches of philosophy."[18]

One by one, Parigot rebutted Ray's assertions. Chiding Ray's comment that personal liberty was an "abstract principle," Parigot argued there was "no abstraction in civil liberty," and society had a "special obligation to protect the rights of the insane." Indeed, the proper purpose of legislation on insanity should be "to secure individual liberty against error, ignorance or crime."[19]

Parigot ridiculed the contention that some types of insanity might be apparent only to the trained eye. Calling them "the shame of the professions, and a mockery and contempt of justice," he condemned the typical certificates of insanity that required only a single sentence from a general practitioner stating that an individual was insane, without documenting symptoms or recommending treatment.[20]

Instead, cases of insanity should be scientifically diagnosed and documented to indicate the nature of the insanity as well as to provide a treatment plan and prognosis. Parigot added that proper registration of patients upon hospital admission and detailed case records should be the *sine qua non* of a well-managed institution. These safeguards would not only secure the patient's civil liberties, but also protect physicians from accusations of malpractice, thus putting an end to "all the accumulated difficulties" in Ray's report.[21]

Parigot also challenged the logic of Ray's "extraordinary assertion" that one could "scarcely exaggerate the amount of mischief" that might be caused by oversight commissions. Lunacy commissioners, he wrote eloquently, should "be living *habeas corpuses*" that would "satisfy that natural desire of prisoners for obtaining their liberty" and listen with sympathy to "real or imaginary complaints." He suggested the hope thus transmitted to patients would be therapeutic, not disruptive.[22] Parigot admonished that, if asylum superintendents were indeed beyond reproach, they should not object to oversight commissions, protective legislation, or more detailed record keeping.[23]

It was against this maelstrom in the psychiatric profession that Packard launched her crusade for "personal liberty" for asylum patients and married women. If Dorothea Dix was the "angel voice for the insane," Packard would become the gadfly of the psychiatric profession, goading it toward the change that younger members, such as Parigot, believed would benefit both patients and the profession.[24]

Packard recorded that by the fall of 1864 she had earned enough from book sales to pay her way to Massachusetts to visit family members she had not seen in more than a decade. She went first to her brother Austin's home in South Deerfield, then traveled with him the few miles to Sunderland to visit her father. Concerned that Theophilus, who lived nearby, would again exercise his legal authority to commit her, she recorded that she stayed only a few days at her father's home then proceeded to Boston to "seek some protection of the Legislature of Massachusetts."[25]

Packard's work in legislatures would be facilitated not only by a groundswell of public support for her plight, but also by the amorphous nature of the state legislatures of her time. Historian Gerald Grob noted that the structure of these "pre-bureaucratic" legislatures was extremely fluid, with many legislators serving only one term. Legislators and legislative committees lacked substantial staff support to assist in analyzing policy decisions and considering long-term implications. Indeed, there was little useful data or developed theory to assist them in policy development. Grob suggests that these factors fostered passage of laws "that reflected only individual and immediate concerns," rather than well thought-out public policy.[26]

Before approaching Massachusetts legislators, Packard apparently secured letters of introduction from two well-placed acquaintants in Illinois. She recorded that state representative S. S. Jones of St. Charles provided a testimonial letter, dated 2 December 1864, stating that he knew her personally and certifying that, after full investigation "before an eminent Judge of our State" she had been pronounced sane. Judge William A. Boardman of Waukegan likewise attested to personal knowledge of her case and vouched for her sanity based on his years of experience in medical jurisprudence. Calling her "a person of strict integrity and truthfulness," he pronounced her a "victim of religious bigotry, purely so."[27]

Theophilus later countered these testimonials with letters from Illinois clergymen who stated that Jones and Boardman were Spiritualists who favored free love. According to Reverend J. Lyman Morton of Waukegan, Boardman was "the brooding hen of Spiritualism" in that community and spoke "against the Bible, the Institution of Christianity and the marriage relation." Reverend Elbridge G. Howe of Waukegan noted that Boardman's first wife was a Spiritualist who succumbed to insanity and that Boardman was divorced from his second wife.[28] Jones was similarly castigated as a Spiritualist and a Universalist whose views "concerning marriage, free love, affinity, etc." were condemned even by other Spiritualists.[29]

Meanwhile, Packard arranged for a Boston printer to produce another six thousand copies of her first book under the new title *Great Disclosure of Spiritual Wickedness!! In High Places.* This, she said, was "a preparatory step . . . to get up an agitation" for her proposed legislation.[30] By January 1865, a copy of this book was in the hands of Boston reformer, Samuel E. Sewall, who reviewed it in an article for the *Boston Daily Advertiser* headlined "Defects in the Law Respecting Insanity."[31]

Sewall took up Packard's cause, declaring that her trial illustrated "the reckless manner in which some physicians give certificates of insanity" and "the danger which surrounds persons, especially married women who hold obnoxious opinions." Sewall noted that Massachusetts law was no better than that in Illinois in this regard. "It is monstrous," he concluded, "that any person should be liable to imprisonment for life by the sentence of two physicians . . . selected . . . not by the public, but by interested parties."[32]

Packard apparently supported the efforts of Sewall and another well-known reformer, Wendell Phillips, to draft a petition to the Massachusetts legislature proposing two laws related to commitment of the insane. Both were veteran abolitionists and ardent supporters of women's rights. Both were also Harvard-educated lawyers. Phillips's famed oratorical skill and Sewall's connections in the legislature made them formidable friends for an aspiring reformer. As Packard joined the fray in Massachusetts, Sewall was already assisting two Boston women, a Mrs. Denny and a Mrs. Phelps, who, like Packard, claimed they had been wrongly imprisoned in an asylum.[33]

Packard reported that she collected signatures on the petition in support of their bills, which Sewall then presented to the legislature. The first bill specified that "No person shall be regarded or treated as an Insane person, or a Monomaniac, simply for the expression of opinions, no matter how absurd these opinions may appear to others."[34] Capturing the intellectual climate of the time, Packard explained, "We are living in a Progressive Age. Everything is in a state of transmutation, and as our laws now are, the Reformer, the Pioneer, the Originator of any new idea is liable to be treated as a Monomaniac." This law, she declared, would protect "the personal safety of Reformers."[35]

The second bill recalled her argument to McFarland that "conduct should be the index of the mind." According to Packard, it stated that "No person shall be imprisoned and treated as an insane person except for irregularities of conduct, such as indicate that the individual is so lost to reason as to render him an unaccountable moral agent."[36]

This law seemed to address the anxiety evoked in society by broad definitions of insanity. Packard observed, "Many contend that every person is insane on some point, [thus] all persons are liable to be legally imprisoned under

Figure 8. Elizabeth Packard. Courtesy of The Abraham
Lincoln Presidential Library and Museum, Springfield,
Illinois.

our present system." This law, she noted, would guard personal liberty "as an
inalienable right."[37]

Packard reported that as Sewall and Phillips argued in favor of these proposed laws, three representatives from the AMSAII, Drs. Clement Walker
(Boston Lunatic Hospital), Edward Jarvis (superintendent of a private asylum
in Dorchester, Massachusetts), and John E. Tyler (McLean Asylum for the
Insane, Somerville, Massachusetts), arrived to present the Association's opposition to such legislation. Both Walker and Tyler had participated in the lively
discussion that followed McFarland's presentation (including his discussion
of Packard's case), and Jarvis was a personal friend of McFarland. Packard
recorded that the men told legislators that those who signed Packard's petition probably did so "out of compliment to the lady" without understanding
what the petition sought.[38]

Massachusetts's lawmakers, however, were apparently convinced otherwise.
While the two bills did not pass as written, the legislature did add protection
for married women to the commitment procedure. This law (passed in March

1865) required asylum superintendents, upon admitting a married woman, to notify ten near relatives of the woman. It further provided that the patient must be permitted unrestricted communication with those ten relatives and any two other persons designated by the patient.[39]

Packard wrote that, with these changes to Massachusetts law, she felt "comparatively safe" in that state. Essentially homeless since leaving the asylum, she returned to Sunderland to stay with her aged father and stepmother, who now believed that Theophilus had misled the family regarding her supposed derangement. Her father and brother, Austin, now gave her notarized depositions attesting to their belief that she was sane. Her father also changed his will to leave Packard her inheritance directly rather than in trust through her brother.[40]

Her father also interceded with Theophilus, asking him to return some of Packard's belongings and permit her to visit her children. She wrote that Theophilus at first refused but capitulated when public remonstrations from her respected father raised the ire of townspeople. According to Packard, she was permitted a brief, chaperoned visit with Libby, George, and Arthur at her father's home.[41]

Meanwhile, Sewall's review of Packard's book in the *Boston Daily Advertiser* evoked a heated response from Theophilus. In a letter-to-the-editor published in the 4 April 1865 edition of the paper, he castigated Sewall for accusing him of "despotic caprice" and suggested he should seek a more reliable source of information than a woman known to be insane. He questioned whether Sewall had actually read Packard's book and pointed to the chapter on transmigration of souls as clear evidence of derangement. Perhaps, he suggested, Sewall's mind, too, had "swung away from its proper moorings." He swore on his reputation "as a Christian clergyman" that the facts of his wife's case proved her insane. Furthermore, he said, "our family physician warned us that our lives were in danger [and] for weeks before her removal the sleeping rooms of some of the family were secured at night to avert this danger."[42]

Theophilus insisted that the judge at his wife's trial had "yielded to . . . mob pressure, and [acted] without law, precedent, or authority." Thus, the case was not dismissed, as it should have been, because that "would exonerate a clergyman that a mob was determined to wound." He described an appalling scene in which "an enraged, seething mob filled the court room," and "hisses even from females, threats and outrageous language pervaded the atmosphere." Confirming Stephen Moore's account, Theophilus told how the verdict had been greeted "with shouts, cheers, and waving of handkerchiefs!"[43]

Now, Theophilus complained, his wife was "roving from town to town here in Massachusetts," stirring up trouble and peddling her pamphlet.[44]

Sewall responded with a relatively brief "Rejoinder to Rev. Mr. Packard" in which he suggested that the minister made "rather a bad case for himself" by admitting the "indignation of his neighbors" toward him in contrast to their strong support for his wife. Furthermore, said Sewall, the reported testimony from the trial clearly showed that Packard was sane.[45]

The exchange raged on as Theophilus countered with a "Reply to Mr. Sewall's Rejoinder," declaring that Stephen Moore falsified facts of the trial. He appended five letters to support his claim.[46] Moore responded in defense, saying, "It would be very unlikely that I should make an incorrect report of an important case which I knew would be read by my friends and business acquaintances, which (if incorrect) would work a personal injury. Policy and selfish motives would prevent me from making an incorrect report, if I was guided by nothing higher."[47]

Moore discounted the letters Theophilus published as nothing more than the opinions of his "co-conspirators," whose testimony had been rejected by a jury of twelve men. Finally, Moore declared that Bonfield's claim that the courthouse was filled with a disorderly crowd "very well calculated to prevent a fair trial" was "simply bosh." The "furious populace," Moore chided, consisted of "about 200 ladies . . . who visited the trial until it was completed because they felt a sympathy for one of their own sex whose treatment had become notorious in our city."[48] Moore concluded, "The published report of the trial is made. It no doubt presents Mr. Packard and his confederates in a very unfavorable light, but it is just as they presented themselves. If they do not like the picture they should not have presented the original."[49]

As Packard stirred populace, press, and politicians with calls for asylum reform, the AMSAII convened in Philadelphia for its 1866 conference. Though seemingly resigned to ongoing criticism, they were clearly concerned about the reputation of their increasingly embattled profession. More and more frequently, individual doctors were facing legal action by former patients or their guardians.

The superintendents reminded one another to document cases in a manner that could withstand a legal contest. A. H. Van Nostrand called for laws that "would relieve us from liability to these infernal prosecutions." Others present suggested the Association could minimize adverse public impressions by being more judicious in reporting its proceedings. Tilden Brown, superintendent of New York City's Bloomingdale Asylum, reminded colleagues that discussions about moral insanity in particular had fueled criticism from without and created strife within the profession. Moral insanity, he suggested, was "rapidly becoming a bug-bear" at Association meetings. He proposed that they "pass a resolution never to discuss this subject again."[50]

The venerable Pliny Earle agreed, recalling that discussions on moral insanity a few years earlier "did no good to the reputation of this Association."[51] Earle also suggested that Association members should tone down the language of their published reports and discussions and cease *ad hominem* public attacks on their critics. Perhaps it was the stature of those such as Sewall and Phillips in Massachusetts that led Earle to caution, "I think it would be wiser to leave out such expressions as, 'our unprincipled assailants.' Let us give due credit to those who complain, for honesty of purpose, even if they do make us trouble."[52]

As the superintendents stewed, Packard remained at her father's home in Massachusetts working on another book, entitled *Marital Power Exemplified,* in anticipation of her next legislative foray. In this book, she explained to readers that the purpose of her writing was not "merely to tickle the fancy" or to achieve "notoriety or popularity."[53] Rather, her purpose was "to defend the cause of human rights" by bringing the "usurpation" of these rights into public view.

Packard knew very well that to advance her objectives she must sell books profitably and sway public opinion in her favor. "Reforms," she understood, "succeed just in proportion as the need of them is apprehended by the public mind."[54] Thus, to attract readers and gain sympathy, she deliberately chose the sensational, melodramatic style used in contemporary romance novels as well as in other asylum narratives.

But her writing bore the additional burden of having to demonstrate her sanity, and Packard was clearly aware that her first book had not satisfactorily met that objective. Thus, *Marital Power Exemplified,* published in 1866, was a defense of both her sanity and her writing. In this book Packard insisted not on the rightness of her ideas, but on her right to hold them.[55] She acknowledged that "many things" in her first book may have been difficult to understand and begged readers not to "judge her harshly."[56] Aware that some might construe her emphatic language and frank expression of emotion not only as a lapse of ladylike comportment, but also as madness, she asked readers to forgive her use of strong language. It was, she said, "the only suitable and appropriate drapery for a reformer."[57]

Nevertheless, Packard reined in her "adamantine pen" in *Marital Power Exemplified.* Although she often experimented with genres and styles, her writing in this book was measured and reasoned with minimal use of italics or emphatic punctuation. Nor did this book contain any allegories, parables, or exposition of religious ideas. Perhaps the most straightforward of her books, it was clearly aimed at establishing her credibility with lawmakers and the general public. Interspersed throughout were testimonials, either in the form of namedropping, as in her mention of Gerrit Smith, or in reproduced letters, including one from Samuel Sewall, who, she said, considered her his "friend and fellow laborer."[58]

Sewall's letter described Packard as a "person of great religious feeling, high moral principle, and warm philanthropy." Sewall noted that she had invited his words of recommendation, but added, "I do not think them at all necessary, for she can recommend herself, far better than I can."[59]

Marital Power Exemplified contained Stephen Moore's record of her trial and a brief narrative of events in the two years afterward. But it focused on answering the questions doubters most frequently asked about her case. For example, one query was, "Is your husband's real reason for treating you as he has, merely a difference in your religious belief, or is there not something back of all this?"

Packard devoted nearly eight pages to her answer. She again assured readers that infidelity was not the underlying issue and explained that she and her husband had simply grown apart in their ideas. "He was dwindling, dying," while she "was living, growing, expanding." She told readers that in her candid opinion, her husband became "a *monomaniac* on the subject of woman's rights."[60] This, she believed, was the root of their problem.

Meanwhile, Theophilus fumed in his diary that, to his injury, his wife had in 1866 published another of her books "containing falsehoods and slanders" about him and sold it "extensively East and West" to his detriment. He complained that newspapers often published her "false story" while refusing "to publish the testimony" from his supporters.[61]

This, however, was not true. Newspapers in Illinois, Massachusetts, and Connecticut did publish his letters. Indeed, during the spring of 1866 the *Northampton Free Press* published a series of eight lengthy articles from Theophilus refuting the "atrocious charge" made against him.[62] In these articles, Theophilus also defended Andrew McFarland, noting that trustees of the Jacksonville asylum had in June 1864 unanimously reappointed him to another ten-year term as superintendent. If McFarland were part of a "foul conspiracy," Theophilus asked, "Why has not the Superintendent been removed?" Furthermore, he continued, "If this Board of Trustees has been in the alleged conspiracy, why has not the Illinois Legislature removed them? Is that Legislature itself in the conspiracy?"[63]

By May 1866, Packard's focus was on the Connecticut legislature. There, rather than changes to insanity law, she proposed legislation to improve the legal position of married women. Packard recorded that she worked with "prominent members of the bar" in New Haven as well as with lawyer Francis Fellowes in Hartford to draw up a petition to the legislature. An article in the 18 May edition of the *New Haven Daily Morning Journal and Courier* reported that "between 300 and 400 of our leading citizens" had purchased Packard's newest book and invited "all who desire to aid this estimable lady in her laudable efforts" to sign her petition and buy her book at Judd & White's bookstore on Chapel Street.[64]

Packard's petition explained that although society now assigned a married woman the "place of companion" and "joint partner" with her husband, the law had lagged behind this social progress. Again invoking rhetoric of the woman's rights movement, she argued that, under existing law, marriage was little more than "licensed oppression" based on "the spirit of the common law of the dark ages." She explained that, at present, a wife's only legal means of self-defense was divorce.[65] "No lady," she confided to the men, "wants to be a divorced woman," and a woman shouldn't "be driven into a divorced state in order to secure the protection of her natural rights."[66]

Packard wrote that newly elected Connecticut Governor Joseph R. Hawley invited her to defend the petition before a joint meeting of legislative committees, where she spoke publicly to a large crowd for the first time. She assured her readers she "did not seek or even anticipate" such a position, but added that her experience as a teacher had prepared her to speak in public comfortably.[67]

Packard's speech to Connecticut legislators was a model of flattery and moral suasion, aimed to prick the conscience of any "true man" as she espoused the ideology of domestic feminism. Praising their "manliness," Packard invited her "gallant brothers" of the legislature to bear with her as she revealed to them the fact that married women were no more than slaves under the common law.[68]

"Gentlemen," she said, "in securing our emancipation you will have to encounter the same pro-slavery argument and spirit" that Lincoln met.[69] The opposition will tell you, she continued, "that the slaves are better off as they now are—that they are taken better care of by their masters than they could take of themselves—that the interest of the master demands the good treatment of his slave—that public sentiment is a sufficient law of protection to the slave's interest—that the subjection of the wife is the Bible law of marriage—and besides, there is not one married woman in a thousand who even knows that she is a slave."[70] These arguments, she declared, must again fall before the truth that all "slavery is wrong, and the principle of freedom is right."[71]

Packard assured legislators that granting married women rights equal to those of their husbands would not diminish male authority. The man would certainly, she said, remain "the responsible head of the family." But, she added, "A man is less than a man who will not be influenced by his wife through his affection and reason, if her reasons are sound and logical, and her affections pure and chaste." She concluded by reassuring the legislators that women did not hold them responsible for the "antiquarian" laws that enslaved married women. But, she said, they now had the opportunity to correct the errors of bygone days.[72]

Packard reported that she offered three bills to the judiciary committee in Connecticut. The first, drafted by Francis Fellowes, entitled married women to institute suits "for injury to their persons, to their liberty, or to their property in the same manner and to the same extent as if unmarried." The second bill, evidently drafted by Packard, provided that a married woman should "retain the same legal existence which she possessed before marriage, and shall receive the same legal protection of her rights as a woman, which her husband does as a man." A third bill, also drafted by Packard and apparently later folded into the first bill, gave a woman the "same right to appeal to the Government for redress and protection that the husband has."[73]

According to Packard, these bills seemed destined for passage when Theophilus "unleashed an avalanche of scandal" against her in letters to Connecticut lawmakers, clergy, and newspapers.[74] In a letter to the *New Haven Daily Morning Journal and Courier,* for example, he repeated what had virtually become his mantra that "more than fifty competent and credible witnesses" concurred that his wife should be removed to a "hospital for the cure of the insane." He reiterated his declaration published in Boston newspapers that her trial was "*illegal, oppressive and mobocratic*" and that the account by Stephen Moore was "to a great extent *false and calumnious.*"[75]

The New Haven paper also published a letter that Andrew McFarland had written to Mrs. Alma Eaton, wife of a physician acquaintance of McFarland. McFarland wrote that Packard had created a furor in "a hundred places before" and warned: "I know it is very difficult to convince people, who are under the first fascination of Mrs. Packard's eloquence—who are under the spell of her marvelous power in enlisting sympathy—who are led captive by a tale of woe such as she can weave—who witness the perfection of her mind in all its ordinary manifestations, that she is, and has been for some years . . . insane to a very high degree."[76]

In contradiction to his published statement to colleagues of the AMSAII in 1863 that it had taken more than two years of "the closest study" to detect evidence of "intellectual impairment" in Packard, McFarland now told Eaton that anyone who observed Packard for more than a week would be convinced she was deranged.[77]

McFarland also discounted her claims of religious persecution, saying religion had "nothing to do with the mass of disconnected, diseased and anomalous sentiments to which she gives utterance." He added that although there was "a gloss of piety" in her words, the religious views of Tom Paine were "high morality" in comparison to hers.[78]

This letter-writing campaign evidently succeeded in derailing Packard's efforts there. The 14 June 1866 edition of the *New Haven Daily Morning Journal and Courier* reported that the judiciary committee returned an adverse recommendation on her petition. The newspaper included a polite note from Packard thanking the legislature and the citizens of New Haven "for the respectful sympathy and manly courtesy" extended to her along with her hope that the statutes would be revised in the near future.[79]

Packard would recall the failure of her Connecticut campaign as "one of the severest strokes" ever received against her "precious cause." She held her husband and McFarland responsible, and her antipathy toward both men deepened.[80]

FOLLOWING HER DEFEAT in Connecticut in June 1866, Packard returned to her father's home to ponder her next move. In late August, Samuel Ware died, having "repented of the wrongs . . . innocently done" to his daughter.[1] He bequeathed $2,000 to charity, but left most of his $14,211 estate to his three children in equal parts.[2] Dispersal of the money was delayed when Packard's stepmother contested the will.[3] Thus, Packard returned to Chicago in late 1866 without her share of the inheritance, but apparently with substantial profits from sales of her books.

She recorded that she sent her husband "a Christmas letter" that year saying that by "kind Providence" and her own diligent efforts she had been "so abundantly rewarded and successful" that she was in a position to assume "pecuniary responsibilities" for her family. She offered a home to both him and the children—with the condition that the property must be in her name. The family, she said, could choose the location for the home, except that it must be near a college that accepted both males and females.[4]

Packard recorded that Theophilus refused her offer "with indignant scorn," but that she, nevertheless, began sending him "board money for the children" so that they could be kept together and not dispersed among family members. She reportedly also sent gifts and money directly to the children. To further ease his financial woes, she agreed to sign away her right of dower to their property in Mount Pleasant.[5]

Theophilus mentioned nothing about assistance from his wife, but recorded that he had "received liberal aid" from friends in the community. He also noted in his diary that "through the great mercy of God and in his wonderful Providence," he was finally able to pay off the nearly $4,000 debt he had incurred a decade earlier.[6]

Andrew McFarland, likely with Packard in mind, had once reported that one patient with moral insanity could "cause more annoyance than scores of ordinary cases." It was fortunate, he suggested, "if some imaginary call" sent such persons "abroad . . . as peripatetic reformers." Such "a vagrant life,"

= BPD !

he noted, tended to "dissipate . . . any intensities of feelings" and the sad individual would "eventually sink out of sight."[7]

Unfortunately for McFarland, Elizabeth Packard's career as a "peripatetic reformer" was only beginning, and she was not about to sink out of sight. Indeed, McFarland now stood in the crosshairs of her agenda for justice and reform as she prepared to carry her accusations of "foul conspiracy" to the Illinois state legislature.

While Packard was in New England, Illinois had amended its commitment law, largely in reaction to publicity stirred by her case. The new law, approved in February 1865, required a jury trial for "women and infants" as it always had for men. It also provided that the person alleged to be insane must be present at any hearing or trial regarding his or her case.[8]

McFarland, of course, opposed this law and immediately called for its repeal.[9] Packard, however, believed the new law was flawed because it included no penalties for noncompliance. She now turned to Cook County Judge James Bradwell for assistance.

Both Bradwell and his wife, Myra, were not only woman's rights advocates but were, like Sewall and Phillips in Massachusetts, politically astute lawyers

Figure 9. Attorney James B. Bradwell. Courtesy of The Abraham Lincoln Presidential Library and Museum, Springfield, Illinois.

capable of exploiting legal and legislative channels. Within a few years, Myra Bradwell would earn recognition as founding editor of the influential *Chicago Legal News* and, later, as the first woman admitted to the bar.[10]

However, in the winter of 1866 it was apparently James, not Myra, Bradwell that Packard sought out for help in amending the law. Judge Bradwell was already concerned about irregularities in admissions at the Jacksonville asylum. In reviewing bills for support of indigent patients from Cook County, Bradwell evidently discovered that even some male patients had been admitted to the asylum without a trial.[11] It appeared to him that McFarland had not altered procedures at the asylum to comply with the 1865 jury trial law.[12]

Employing the method she had used in Massachusetts and Connecticut, Packard reported that she worked with Bradwell and "other legal advisors" to draft a petition, which she then circulated among "the most prominent and influential men" in Chicago.[13]

In January 1867, as the legislature convened, Packard apparently delivered her petition to Governor Richard J. Oglesby. She wrote that, despite his per-

Figure 10.
Attorney Myra
Colby Bradwell.
Courtesy of The
Abraham Lincoln
Presidential Library
and Museum,
Springfield, Illinois.

sonal friendship with Andrew McFarland, Oglesby was persuaded by the names on the petition to refer her to legislators who might assist her. These, she wrote, included Elmer Baldwin and Moses Leavitt in the House and Jasper D. Ward in the Senate.

Meanwhile, Packard distributed her books to local newspapers and began to repay in kind the "avalanche of scandal" loosed on her in Connecticut. Any ambivalence she had once entertained about the character of her doctor was gone. Given his "cruel slanders" against her integrity, virtue, and sanity, she conceded that she "felt under no obligation to shield his reputation."[14]

Indeed, she declared, "Mr. Packard is a *fool* in calling me insane, because he don't know any better. Dr. McFarland is a *villain* in calling me insane, because he does know better . . . and still, for policy's sake and to save himself and the institution trouble . . . he denies the truth and tries to defend a lie knowingly and deliberately." She then added venomously: "But of the comparative merits of these two mates—the fool and villain—I make no estimate. It's enough for me to shoot these rattlesnakes, and then drag their lifeless bodies before the public, for exhibition on the public gallows of the printed page."[15]

In dramatic letters-to-the-editor to various newspapers, Packard described abuse and corruption at the asylum and pointed blame directly at McFarland. She challenged his assertion that there had never been a serious question regarding an irregularity in admissions at his asylum. "Has the Doctor forgotten," she asked in the *Jacksonville Sentinel,* "that the question had been once, at least, seriously raised by the Court at Kankakee City in the case of one whom that Court decided had been falsely imprisoned for three years at that Hospital?"[16]

Packard apparently enjoyed significant backing from many Illinois newspapers and was especially gratified that both the *Chicago Tribune* and the *Chicago Times* gave her valuable support. This demonstrated, she noted, "the pleasing fact, that both of the political parties of this State can unite in this cause of common philanthropy."[17] The *Illinois State Register* in Springfield, a Democratic paper, especially championed her cause and, she said, "very kindly allowed me the use of their columns to portray facts of the most startling character for the perusal of the members [of the legislature]."[18]

On 3 January 1867, for example, the *Register* reported that "an intelligent lady, whose appearance and manners indicate education and heart" had left with the editor "a volume containing the history of her misfortune and persecution." The brief article indicated her intention "to bring the subject matter of complaint before the general assembly."[19] The *Illinois State Journal* in Springfield also noted its receipt of a book from "the well-known Mrs.

E. P. W. Packard of Kankakee" and commended it "to the members of the Legislature."[20]

Jacksonville newspapers, not surprisingly, staunchly defended Andrew McFarland. The editor of the *Jacksonville Journal,* noting McFarland's call for repeal of the 1865 jury trial law, urged the legislature to amend the law to relieve its "oppressive features." The editor cited the Illinois Supreme Court decision in *Eddy v. the People,* which stated that an individual must be given "reasonable notice" that he or she was about to be committed.[21] In his opinion, that ruling "afforded ample protection" in the commitment procedure.[22]

On 24 January 1867, as a torrent of articles continued in area newspapers, Moses Leavitt of Cook County introduced Packard's bill, H.B. 608, "An Act for the Protection of Personal Liberty," in the Illinois House. On 12 February, Packard addressed the legislature in an emotional plea for passage of the bill. Describing her incarceration, she explained that efforts to protect her from incarceration in an asylum had been "overpowered by the majesty of the law, added to the dignity of the pulpit." She told legislators that "the claims of humanity and the honor" of the state of Illinois demanded that they establish legal safeguards against false commitment.[23]

Packard's account of her bill's progress over the next five weeks was considerably more dramatic than the neat record published in the House and Senate *Journals.* She detailed how her Personal Liberty Bill was stalled in committee by friends of McFarland, shouted down in debates, nearly tabled,

Figure 11. Illinois Senate debating Packard's Personal Liberty Bill, 1867. *Source:* Packard, *Modern Persecution* (1875), vol. II, 205.

and at times literally lost in the shuffle of legislation.[24] However, in the end, her bill was passed unanimously.[25]

Packard's Personal Liberty Law, approved 5 March 1867, reaffirmed the 1865 law's requirement of a jury trial for commitment and, in addition, stipulated that patients confined at the Jacksonville asylum prior to the 1865 law must be given a jury trial within two months of the effective date of the new law. Failure to comply was made a misdemeanor punishable by imprisonment of not less than three months or more than one year as well as a fine of not less than $500 or exceeding $1,000.[26] "Thus it was," wrote Packard, "that the barbarities of the law of 1851 were wiped out by this act of legislative justice."[27]

Andrew McFarland was outraged by the Personal Liberty Law, which he considered—as it indeed was—a direct affront to him. He told colleagues at the Chicago Medical Society that the bill was "conceived to annoy and punish" him and was "clearly intended as a stinging insult imputing [to him] a disposition to commit a high crime against the liberty of the innocent unfortunate, and appending the most degrading penalties known to the law for the offence." McFarland fumed: "An act to prevent John Brown, of a particular city, street and number, from stealing sheep, could be no more justly offensive to the John Brown indicated, than is this enactment to myself."[28]

Even worse than this personal affront, McFarland continued, was the cruel effect the law would have on his patients, subjecting "them to the mockery of a new inquisition—a measure full of disaster." McFarland offered what became his profession's standard objection to jury trial laws: "What should be decided by a county judge, in the privacy of his chambers, and upon the certificates of medical men, is made to depend upon the haphazard opinions and caprices of men grossly ignorant of the subject before them."[29]

But, even as the Personal Liberty Bill was passed, McFarland's woes with the Illinois legislature were growing. In response to the furor of accusations in the press, the legislature was preparing to investigate the Jacksonville asylum. Funding for all of the state's charitable institutions in Jacksonville was temporarily blocked as legislators considered resolutions calling for a formal probe.[30]

Jacksonville civic leaders, hoping to quell calls for an investigation, invited members of the press and legislature to tour Jacksonville and its various institutions. In January 1867 newspaper editors attending a convention in Springfield were brought by train to Jacksonville and taken by carriage to visit the community's charitable institutions. At the asylum, they viewed the main building and grounds, including the farm, stables, cow sheds, and pig yards.[31]

Afterward, they returned to the main building to enjoy a sumptuous dinner. Reporting on the fine time enjoyed by the reporters and their guests at the asylum, the *Illinois State Journal* enthused that the dinner included oysters, turkey, chicken, Madeira, and all "dainties and luxuries of the season." After dinner, the group toasted the good health of Dr. Andrew McFarland "with hearty applause" then adjourned to the asylum's reception room to enjoy "some fine Havanas."[32]

A committee from the Illinois House and Senate also visited Jacksonville and, the *Illinois State Journal* reported optimistically, "We understand the committee expressed much gratification at the condition and management of these several charities and will recommend the usual liberal appropriations for their maintenance during the next two years."[33] Additional legislators were invited to Jacksonville in February, and the *Illinois State Journal* reported that McFarland "and his efficient corps of assistants exhibited to them the capacities and uses of that Institution." This group was "feasted" at a local establishment and entertained with a concert.[34]

When it became clear that a formal investigation was inevitable, Jacksonville newspapers "welcomed" it as an opportunity to defend the honor of the community and its institutions. But exchanges between Jacksonville newspapers and others around the state were becoming heated.

The *Illinois State Register* for 22 February carried a front-page article head-lined "Insanity a Crime!" Packard later revealed that she was the anonymous author of this article. The article included a letter from a former attendant, Mrs. S. A. Kain, describing scenes of "brutal and heart-rending" abuse at the asylum.[35] Kain claimed that sane individuals were harbored at the asylum and suggested that the superintendent would take in any patient "provided sufficient bribe" was paid.[36]

Declaring that such accusations were "fabrications, springing from motives of jealousy, revenge, or a wanton spirit," the *Jacksonville Journal* now called for a timely investigation to clear the good name of the doctor. The *Journal* hoped McFarland would take his accusers to court if the legislature failed to act promptly to resolve the matter.[37]

But on the same day, the *Illinois State Register* reported further allegations against the asylum. In one letter, Mrs. P. L. Hosmer Graf, a former director of the asylum's sewing room, accused the trustees of failing to exercise proper oversight of the asylum and giving the superintendent "absolute power for the weal or woe of hundreds." Graf also criticized the recent legislative jun-kets to the asylum: "You spend a day . . . in the mere mock visiting [of] the institution—partake of bounties spread—see nice barns [and] fat pigs." Then, she continued, "You walk through the humane part which is dressed for the occasion, take the superintendent's word and pronounce him 'just the man.'"[38]

On February 25, the *Illinois State Journal* reported prematurely that a thorough investigation led by Senator Jasper D. Ward of the finance committee "found no irregularities at the asylum."[39] The next day, however, legislators reached agreement on wording for a joint resolution calling for a full investigation of all state institutions at Jacksonville, with emphasis on the Hospital for the Insane. The resolution called for a joint legislative committee "with power to send for persons and papers, and to examine witnesses." Members of the committee were Allen C. Fuller (chairman)[40] and Andrew J. Hunter from the Senate, and Elmer Baldwin, T. B. Wakeman, and John B. Ricks from the House.[41]

This committee was charged with examining the financial and sanitary management of the institution, determining whether any patients were improperly admitted or retained and "whether the inmates are humanely and kindly treated." The committee was instructed to work with trustees to correct "any abuses found" and "report to the Governor from time to time at their discretion."[42]

In April 1867, as the investigation was about to begin, Packard purchased a house in Springfield at a cost of $1,850.[43] The house, located in Whitney's Addition, was only a few blocks from the capitol building. However, although she retained the property until her death, there is no indication that she ever lived there. She perhaps preferred to board in Springfield in order to mingle more easily with legislators and other lobbyists.

In preparation for the investigation, Packard evidently organized a campaign of letters-to-the-editor reprinted in newspapers from Iowa to New England. It was clear from this onslaught and the response from McFarland's supporters that the investigation would be salacious.[44]

Early in May, Morgan County Judge H. G. Whitlock and six jurors held court at the asylum to hear the cases of patients who had requested a trial and reported that they found no "case of illegal confinement."[45] Later that month, the Illinois Supreme Court ruled that all persons in the asylum at Jacksonville must be given a trial whether or not they requested it.[46] As Judge Whitlock and a jury returned to the asylum to try the remainder of the patients, the *Jacksonville Sentinel* complained of the "unnecessary trouble and expense involved in carrying out Mrs. Packard's law," while the *Jacksonville Journal* asked, "How long must this farce go on?"[47]

The investigating committee held its first meeting on 14 May at Dunlap

House in Jacksonville. The committee agreed to keep a verbatim transcript of its proceedings but to keep all testimony private until submission of its final report to the governor.[48] McFarland's supporters immediately objected to the decision to keep testimony private, and the Jacksonville press promptly reported claims of a "star chamber" taking "ex parte testimony." Demurring to these complaints, the committee agreed to permit McFarland and Henry E. Dummer, attorney for the asylum trustees, to hear testimony and question witnesses.[49]

As the investigation began, McFarland traveled to Philadelphia to attend the AMSAII's annual meeting. This year the Association hired its own recorder and voted not to publish its proceedings in the *American Journal of Insanity*, as was customary.[50] Nevertheless, the *Journal* carried an unofficial account of the meeting in which editor John Gray noted that Andrew McFarland had given account of his "recent troubles" in Illinois. The superintendents sympathized with his "trying circumstance" and agreed that such problems were not "peculiar to him" but were "equally liable to befall any one who is engaged in our thankless profession."[51]

When the report of the investigating committee was finally released in December 1867, it revealed no evidence of fiscal impropriety and, in fact, found that the Jacksonville asylum was well managed financially. It also found no fault with management of the asylum's physical plant or sanitation, noting that McFarland and the trustees had continually sought solutions and funds to improve plumbing and ventilation in the main building.[52]

Despite Judge James Bradwell's allegations that paupers from Cook County were regularly admitted to the Jacksonville asylum without trials, the committee determined that all those committed after passage of the 1865 jury trial law had received trials.[53] The investigation also showed that no sane persons were confined in the asylum at the time of the committee's inspections in 1867.[54]

However, the committee noted that a disproportionate number of patients seemed to have been discharged during the five months between appointment of the investigating committee and the beginning of the investigation. While this apparent "increase in the rate of *recovery* [was] a little noticeable," the committee conceded it had no hard evidence that patients were discharged to avoid their examination.[55]

More problematic was the revelation that, of the 205 patients in the asylum on 3 April 1867, more than half had been admitted "without the proper *legal evidence* of their insanity, and the security required by law." Such legal evidence should have included certificates of insanity from two physicians plus documentation of the patient's legal status on arrival at the asylum.[56]

Most damaging, however, was evidence of mistreatment and improper classification of patients, which the committee received from numerous former employees and patients. One attendant, Mrs. S. A. Kain, reported she had personally witnessed plunge baths in which a patient was "generally plunged three or four times, until quite prostrate and unable to resist." According to Kain, the baths were sometimes used as a method of "breaking in" a new patient or eliciting compliance from unruly patients. She reported that an assistant physician had taught her "how long it was safe to keep [a patient] under water" without killing the patient.[57]

John Henry, a steward McFarland had fired in 1854, testified to "cases of cruelty and inhumane treatment." Henry claimed that, on at least one occasion, he had gone to the chairman of the board of trustees to report a case of abuse after McFarland failed to investigate his earlier complaint. Henry concluded that McFarland "was destitute of common sympathy" for patients, dismissed their complaints, did not give close attention to the conduct of attendants, and seemed "indifferent when complaints of cruelty were made to him."[58]

Witness after witness presented similar examples of abuse to specific patients.[59] In all, the committee identified eighteen attendants who had abused patients. While most witnesses did not believe McFarland approved such behavior, the implication was that he, nevertheless, tended to overlook it. Others, however, reported that they had observed McFarland himself abuse patients.[60]

The investigating committee gave special attention to Packard's case, noting that, due to her notoriety as an advocate for change in commitment laws, it seemed "proper" that her case should be included. They denied charges that their report was based primarily on her testimony and insisted that their findings could stand apart from her allegations.[61]

Nevertheless, Packard's written testimony occupied forty pages of the committee's unpublished journal and nine pages of its published report. Her initial testimony was taken 4 June 1867 in Jacksonville, with McFarland and Dummer present. To Packard's mortification, McFarland promptly introduced into evidence the love-letter she had given him while a patient. According to Packard, Chairman Fuller, observing her distress, adjourned the hearings for the day to give her time to prepare a response.

The next day, with her composure restored, Packard read a written defense of the love-letter in which she described her attraction to McFarland as an intellectual union of minds and admitted that she had once wished he could be her husband and protector. She confessed that "not one word of sentimental love ever passed between" them. Nevertheless, she said, McFarland was "the first and only man . . . to whom my whole soul could pay the homage of my womanly nature."[62]

This was, of course, not exactly true. Her defense of her attraction to McFarland, couched in the language of Spiritualism, sounded much like her defense of her feelings for Abner Baker. She wrote of McFarland, "I simply loved him because I could not help it. Neither did I try to prevent it, for there is no sin in these magnetic laws of attraction . . . [since] the act is not one of our own volition."[63] She told the investigating committee that she could not "pretend to explain the philosophy of the phenomena" that evoked her feelings for McFarland. She added that she merely presented "the simple facts . . . for the metaphysician to analyze and explain."[64]

The committee conceded that the letter was, at the very least, "an indiscreet and foolish letter—open to severe criticisms, if not condemnation."[65] But, while they found the letter to be "a curious medley," they decided it did not provide evidence that she was insane at the time she wrote it four years earlier. Based on her "character as a lady" and the "entire absence of any intimation from any source against her integrity," they agreed she was undoubtedly "a virtuous lady," despite the "unfortunate and foolish letter." Furthermore, the report continued, "the question of her sanity or insanity" was irrelevant to the investigation.[66]

The committee, however, was convinced of the "culpable impropriety" of introducing the letter as evidence against Packard. They condemned McFarland for his "unnecessary and wanton attack upon a defenseless lady, because she had become identified with complaints made" against him. Furthermore, the committee believed that, in making the letter public, McFarland had breached his own rule requiring confidentiality regarding patients. He had, thus, broken "the sacred seal of confidence in him as a gentleman."[67]

Astounded by this response, McFarland then produced copies of the initial manuscript for *The Great Drama* in which Packard claimed to be God's writing medium as well as the medium for truths expressed by "earth's noblest thinkers," including Shakespeare and Washington. Again, Packard was called upon to explain her extraordinary assertions. Under cross-examination by McFarland and Dummer, she explained that she was "God's medium" in the sense that she was a reporter of truth. God was the author of all truth; "I only report it—am only the medium of it—simply tell it." Denying direct revelations from God or other spirits, she said that inspirations of truth came to her primarily from books and it was in that manner that the ideas of great men quickened her own thought.[68]

The committee reported that "the prompt and plausible manner" in which Mrs. Packard defended and explained her views "increase[d] the probability of her sanity, and afforded a striking instance of the danger of pronouncing a person insane simply because of their belief upon such subjects."[69] It was the committee's opinion that the "charge of insanity [against Packard] was based wholly upon a change in her religious views, from the Calvinistic to the more modern and more liberal views, as taught by Rev. Henry Ward Beecher."[70]

During the investigation, the committee was strongly criticized for giving credence to the testimony of former patients, including Packard. Altogether, they interviewed twenty-two former patients. Most, they reported, demonstrated "more than ordinary intelligence, and appeared candid and eminently worthy of the fullest credit."[71] After consulting experts, such as superintendent John Fonerden of the Maryland Hospital for the Insane, they decided "the statements of those who are fully recovered may generally be believed, provided they are honest and their memory not defective."[72]

Furthermore, the committee believed that even the complaints of current patients and those who were clearly insane deserved some degree of credence. "To totally reject their statements as never worthy of credit, and especially in an investigation of this kind, would be to leave them not only defenseless, but a prey to every brutal lust and passion."[73]

To bolster their defense, McFarland and the trustees invited testimony from experts in the field of psychiatry, including Drs. Henry K. Jones and Charles C. Cornett, former assistant physicians at the asylum; Dr. R. J. Patterson, president of the faculty of the Chicago Medical College; and his colleague, Dr. H. A. Johnson. The testimony of these men, which was immediately leaked to the press, attested to McFarland's professional skill and moral character.[74]

But the investigating committee also cited published statements by other asylum superintendents that appeared to sustain the charge that McFarland improperly classified patients. This charge was clearly based on Packard's testimony that as "punishment" for her reproof of the superintendent she was placed in a ward with violent maniacs where she was physically attacked. They noted especially Isaac Ray's statement that "in every well-regulated" institution, rules of classification required placing together those patients who were "least likely to offend or disturb one another." Accordingly, "a refined, cultivated person" should be "placed where he will not be annoyed by the vulgar and profane."[75] W. P. Jones, superintendent of the Tennessee Hospital for the Insane, was even more explicit, saying that "to permit the unrestrained association of homicidal patients with others, would indeed be most culpable and cruel conduct on the part of any superintendent."[76]

In defense of his methods attached to the committee's report, McFarland explained his view "that patients of opposite character and tendencies" frequently benefited when placed together. He explained that "the violent and noisy would sometimes be restrained by the quiet and orderly," while the "sedative and melancholy would be profitably aroused by the boisterous." Thus, both types of patients might benefit from these "counteracting influences."[77]

The committee found McFarland's explanation wholly unacceptable and agreed that his classification of patients was "fundamentally wrong."[78] Furthermore, although McFarland had posted written regulations governing care of patients, the committee believed he had "failed to adopt vigilant means to prevent or detect or punish" abuse of patients by attendants. The report continued: "He [McFarland] assumes that insane patients are never to be believed, and therefore does not listen with favor to their complaints. He substantially denies the right of petition and investigation, and like all public officers who do this, he finds himself, too late, surrounded by difficulties, and imposed upon." In general, the committee determined that McFarland's management of patients was "too severe, and his discipline of attendants too mild."[79]

The committee acknowledged the "overwhelming testimony" to McFarland's good moral character received from his associates. However, they concluded, "testimony of character cannot prevail against such unquestionable proof of facts." Concluding that McFarland had failed the public trust, the investigating committee unanimously recommended his dismissal.[80]

12   Vindication and "Virtuous Action"

THE *REPORT OF THE INVESTIGATING COMMITTEE* appeared in the 6 December 1867 edition of the *Chicago Tribune* even before reaching the hands of Governor Oglesby, who was touring in Europe. As might be expected, it reignited the furor that had simmered throughout the investigation.

The *Illinois State Register* applauded itself for supporting Packard who, they said, had "tried in vain to get the attention of politicians and presses of the dominant party." Now, they reported, "Mrs. Packard's statements appear to be true."[1]

Meanwhile, the *Jacksonville Journal* "refuse[d] to believe a word against" McFarland and insisted he was "wrongfully accused . . . of crimes that *every honest man in the city of Jacksonville knows he never dreamed of committing.*" The *Journal* attacked committee chairman Allen C. Fuller as "the inquisitor would-be governor of Illinois, and renowned follower of Grandmother Packard."[2]

McFarland and his supporters immediately complained that the report was published before they could read and respond to it, and reasserted their argument that most of those testifying were disgruntled former employees and patients, motivated by either revenge, politics, or insanity.

On 12 December 1867 a large group of Jacksonville's "best and most prominent citizens" gathered at the court house to express their views on the report. Among those present were Senator Murray McConnell, Judge Henry Dummer, the Reverend Dr. Julian Sturtevant, and Professor Jonathan Baldwin Turner.[3] Turner, a former asylum trustee, suggested that it was actually a credit to McFarland that only twenty instances of abuse could be found, given the fact that some 2,500 patients were treated during his twelve-year tenure. The group agreed that any testimony that might impeach the committee's "pet witness"—Mrs. Packard—had been cut short, while testimony that might "exculpate" McFarland had been suppressed. The meeting concluded as the group approved a set of resolutions affirming their faith in McFarland and called on the trustees to rebut the investigating committee's report as soon as possible.[4]

Beyond the expected pro-Packard and pro-McFarland divisions, the investigation exposed deeper political rivalries and also ideological wounds from the recent Civil War. The *Chicago Tribune,* for example, chided Jacksonville for its pecuniary motives in supporting McFarland. The *Tribune* editorialized, "The good people of Jacksonville, many of whom live on the crumbs dropped from the tables of the charitable institutions in the place," seemed to view the *Report of the Investigating Committee* "as a direct attack on their bread and butter."[5]

A week later, in a front-page editorial, the *Illinois State Register* (a Democratic Party paper) reminded readers that committee chairman Fuller along with a majority of the investigating committee and officers of the asylum were all "radical [Republican] politicians, who had been using the patronage and influence of their institutions in support of radical men and radical measures." The editorial concluded that, as far as Democrats were concerned, all of the "radicals" involved in both the investigation and the institution had "proved themselves equally corrupt."[6]

The Jacksonville correspondent for the *Register*, writing under the pseudonym "Nemesis," agreed. He railed that while a good crowd of McFarland's "Jacobin" supporters had met, the group hardly represented all of the "good people of Jacksonville." Clearly relishing the Republican infighting, Nemesis declared, "Democrats care very little about it" since they can wait a year until "the next election numbers the days of Dr. McFarland."[7]

Then, dredging up raw wounds from the war, Nemesis declared: "Democrats, don't forget these men who during the war refused to celebrate the 4th of July with 'democrats' . . . who publicly declared that all those who dared to differ in opinion with them 'must be put down and trampled underfoot like serpents,' who used the epithets copperhead, traitor, rebel, etc." Concluding the diatribe, Nemesis declared, "All these things did Dr. McFarland, and does he expect support from democrats now? . . . That revenge is sweet that sees the sworn friends of that conclave destroying one another with the virus of their own throats. It ain't our funeral, and we wear no crepe."[8]

Meanwhile, McFarland's friends agreed he was "a badly treated and persecuted gentleman."[9] In an open letter to "ministers of the gospel in Illinois," Reverend Ludwig M. Glover, pastor of Jacksonville's First Presbyterian Church (of which McFarland was a member), declared that his "confidence in the ability, skill and faithfulness of Dr. McFarland . . . remains high and unimpaired."[10]

In this letter, Glover described Packard as "a woman of considerable talent, shrewd but crafty, and malignant," whose animus toward the doctor was inspired by spurned love. Convinced that Packard "had directed [the committee's] movements to suit her wicked if not insane purpose," Glover remarked that it was "with some propriety that the papers speak of it as the 'Packard investigating committee.'"[11]

To Packard's chagrin, many newspapers reprinted her love-letter to McFarland, which had appeared in the *Chicago Tribune* as part of the investigating committee's report. The *Jacksonville Journal* suggested that the investigating committee, by claiming Packard was sane, exposed her "to the public gaze as a strumpet," while McFarland and the trustees held Packard "guiltless because she was insane." The article concluded, "It has been said that a woman's revenge is terrible, but it must now be admitted that a crazy woman's revenge is terrific."[12]

On 27 December 1867 the *Jacksonville Journal* noted that Andrew McFarland was so ill that his life was threatened and that he had been staying with relatives in Ohio for the past three weeks.[13] In a later book, Packard wrote that McFarland fled to his sister's home in Zanesville, Ohio, shortly after publication of the investigating committee's report. The book included an illustration of a distraught McFarland standing in his sister's parlor crying, "I am ruined! I am ruined! Mrs. Packard has ruined me!" In the book Packard wrote with irony, "His friends thought he was insane, that trouble had dethroned his reason and driven him mad, as insanity was hereditary in his family."[14]

Although he was, in fact, not ruined professionally, there is no question that McFarland was personally devastated by the investigation. In January 1868, he wrote his colleague, Edward Jarvis, that the situation in Jacksonville had "all the worst points of a hospital imbroglio, in which a pretty able committee is, as you will perceive, determined to make the largest possible draughts upon popular ignorance, credulity, and prejudice." McFarland said that his greatest fears were not for himself, but "that this Packard—who is a sort of Joan D'Arc in the matter of stirring up the popular prejudices—may carry her crusade against institutions for the insane into other States."[15]

In a second letter several months later, McFarland poured out his distress, telling Jarvis: "You are supposing . . . that you have some reputation for science, humanity, skill in your profession, etc., etc., throughout a State. Yet here comes in a crazy woman, whose influence, compared with yours, you, at first sight, think as nothing; but when the balance comes to be struck between your reputation and her industrious efforts, and her powers of misinformation, you find yourself so much at a discount that your pride, your conception of public reputation, and your self love are all scattered at a blow."[16] McFarland confided, "I have drunk at the very deepest wells of humiliation and am humiliated."[17]

Not surprisingly, Packard was the focus of the asylum trustees' counterattack. In their published response to the *Report of the Investigating Committee,* the trustees attributed "this entire investigation, and all the agitation that has led to it" to Packard's "unparalleled efforts." They acknowledged that Packard had an "agreeable personal appearance" and was "extremely fluent in conversation." However, they reported that during her stay in their institution she was also "untruthful and ceaseless in her efforts to spread jealousy, discontent and disaffection among all with whom she associated."[18]

The trustees suggested that investigators were more interested in making a case against McFarland personally than in ascertaining present conditions at the asylum. They noted, too, that members of the investigating committee were predisposed to favor Packard and that many on the committee had voted in favor of her Personal Liberty Bill after she "plied them with pamphlets, affidavits, and personal appeals."[19]

The special report of the trustees granted that abuses had undoubtedly occurred at the Jacksonville asylum, but insisted they did not result from "unhumane regulation" or "laxity of supervision." They noted that the constant turnover in employees, many of whom were discharged for incompetence or misconduct, ensured that "an army of witnesses, often ignorant, unfriendly, and even hostile" could always be mustered by anyone "disposed to make an attack." If, in addition, "the statements of the insane are taken without a question, as it is quite natural for the unreflecting to do, how wide a door is opened for mistake, misrepresentation and false clamor."[20]

In conclusion, the trustees reaffirmed their full support for McFarland, stating that he was "eminently qualified for the position of Superintendent" and his "removal or retirement would be a great loss to the State." They were convinced that he was not "guilty of abuses, or neglect of duty," but rather had "been honest, vigilant, humane, and intelligent" in his management of the Jacksonville asylum. They noted, too, that applications for admission had not diminished and suggested that was noteworthy evidence of continued public trust in the asylum.[21]

McFarland's defense, appended to the trustees' report, began by suggesting, rather imprudently, that the investigating committee apparently had not "quite comprehended" the "exact relations which the insane sustain toward an institution in which they are gathered for treatment." Such understanding would, he believed, have restrained the "boldness" of the opinions offered by the committee regarding "subjects that have not yet been mastered by the science, skill, and experience that have been lavished upon them by some of the best minds of the last half century."[22]

McFarland then suggested that some of the apparent difficulties observed by the investigating committee actually resulted from the "excitements fomented" by their visits at the asylum. The intrusion into the wards by a "party of strangers" carrying notebooks and asking questions had, he accused, disrupted order and upset patients.[23]

Reiterating remarks regarding asylum attendants made in his earlier presentation to AMSAII colleagues, McFarland noted that because of a superintendent's "wide range of duties," he could "at best be merely an inspector" who spent "only a very small fraction of the day in the present of each of his patients." He must, therefore, depend on the "agents" under him to carry out his instructions and rules of the institution. He conceded that his efforts "to supply the Institution with intelligent, educated, and, at the same time, humane, attendants, were without success."[24] He, too, granted that "abuses do exist, in a qualified sense, in this, as in all other places where the insane are provided for." Often this occurred when attendants were attacked or found it necessary to restrain a violent patient. In cases of outright cruelty, he said, the attendant was fired. He noted that Mrs. Kain, who had testified before the committee, was an example of such a cruel attendant and believed her testimony revealed "the ingrained tyrant she really was."[25]

McFarland then returned to his recurring theme regarding the great difficulty that a patient suffering from moral insanity could cause within the asylum community. Such patients, he admitted, "tax[ed] to the utmost the vigilance of those assigned to [their] care."[26] In a reference to Packard, he noted that the "impression" that he classified patients improperly "doubtless arose from the representation of a notable case of this form of insanity." He explained that, after extreme forbearance toward the "evil influences" of this patient, she was "removed to the class next below the one in which it was first attempted to domiciliate her, not—bear in mind—for her 'punishment,' as has been industriously bruited," but to protect less troubled patients from her "ceaseless endeavor."[27]

Elaborating, he explained that the classification of patients required "a nice and exact understanding of what . . . may benefit the individual and yet not be detrimental to the well-being of the whole." Indeed, it might "be compared to the art of the designer, who matches his different colors to produce the general effect most pleasing to the eye." He continued, "To say that classification consists simply in putting the noisy with the noisy, the silent with the silent, and the filthy with the filthy, would be the lowest exercise of this, the most exalted function of the physician to the insane. If it were so, the management of an asylum might be left to almost any man possessed of the three leading senses."[28]

McFarland concluded his defense by declaring, "If the writer of this had any revenges to gratify, he would desire no completer satisfaction than the perpetuity of those passages of the committee's report wherein are commended the merits and mental soundness of the grand originator of this entire agitation—Mrs. Packard."[29]

The *American Journal of Insanity* responded to news of McFarland's censure by the Illinois legislature with a bitter editorial. Editor John P. Gray noted that, "for the last two or three years, or more, the State of Illinois has been singularly under the influence and dictation of a handsome and talkative crazy woman, and of a Legislature prompted by her to be crazy on at least one point—that of the State Hospital for the Insane."[30]

Gray concluded that, in the end, the investigating committee chose to sacrifice "a victim to a popular clamor, rather than vindicating the truth." Thus, McFarland and the trustees were "criminated" on specious evidence "to gratify a woman's spleen, a partisan purpose, or a popular frenzy, and perhaps all three."[31]

After more than a year of public turmoil, Andrew McFarland tendered his resignation as superintendent of the Jacksonville asylum on 30 November 1868 at the conclusion of his biennial report. Noting the improvements and progress of the institution during his tenure, McFarland concluded that a trust once borne "with ease and comparative pleasure" had now become "a burden gladly to be laid down."[32]

Reporting his resignation in the *American Journal of Insanity,* editor John Gray railed that the Illinois legislature had been fooled "by a fascinating crazy woman, who managed to seduce partisan prejudice and ignorance for her allies." Gray noted that McFarland had announced himself a candidate for the Illinois state legislature "with a hope, if elected, of enlightening the people of that State on the subject of their public charities."[33]

Neither fool nor villain, Andrew McFarland seemed more a Shakespearean hero trapped in a conflict from which no one would emerge unscathed. Sympathizing with Theophilus Packard, he was doggedly determined to find the insanity that he believed must necessarily underlie Elizabeth Packard's religious ideas, anger toward her husband, and outspoken resistance to his authority. However, his insistence that "perversity of behavior" and a "latent delusion" regarding religion were evidence of insanity was simply too broad a definition to withstand the scrutiny of public, if not professional, opinion.

Making matters worse, McFarland defended himself in elitist terms and demanded deference based on his superior status, upright character, and good intentions. Such arguments did not mollify the ordinary citizens of nineteenth-century Illinois, nor their legislative representatives. This enabled Packard, aided by local and state politics, to replace the "noiseless" operation of McFarland's asylum with a cacophony of public recrimination, calling into question both his professional and personal reputation.

McFarland apparently did not follow through on his threat to enter politics. Instead, two years after leaving the state asylum, he filed a certificate of incorporation with twenty-five stockholders to establish Oaklawn Retreat, a private asylum constructed on land that McFarland owned just outside Jacksonville. The Retreat initially accommodated thirty patients and, for more than a decade, accepted only male patients.[34]

Packard for her part believed she was fully vindicated by the *Report of the Investigating Committee*. In May 1868, a month after the publication of the trustees' special report, she released *The Prisoner's Hidden Life, or Insane Asylums Unveiled*. She declared that the facts in this book had been "authenticated and corroborated" by the Illinois investigating committee, which had attested to the "intelligence, character and credibility" of witnesses, including herself. Appended to this work was the testimony of several of those witnesses, including that of her friend, Sophia Olsen. Packard later published *Mrs. Olsen's Narrative of Her One Year's Imprisonment at Jacksonville Insane* as a separate pamphlet.

The Prisoner's Hidden Life, one of Packard's most popular publications, was a typical asylum narrative, containing both the horror and romance of the Gothic fiction popular with American readers since the late eighteenth century. Packard's writing in this work, in particular, revealed elements of what has been called "female Gothic."[35] Author Kari J. Winter observed that, while male Gothic novelists focused on "horrible spectacles of sexual violence, gore, and death" and identified evil with the "other"—women Catholics, Jews, and ultimately the devil—in contrast, female Gothic novelists "uncovered the terror of the familiar: the routine brutality and injustice of the patriarchal family, conventional religion, and classist social structures."[36]

Writer Eugenia DeLamotte concluded that female Gothic writing was inherently feminist in its theme of heroines who escape oppressive fathers and husbands and wander through dark labyrinths, either physical or psychological, in search of liberation.[37] Particularly in *Prisoner's Hidden Life*, Packard's writing exemplifies female Gothic as a metaphor for transgression of "boundaries of the self."[38] Her story is one of internal struggle between her desire for domesticity and true womanhood and her passion for personal liberty. She thus challenged social, spiritual, and sexual boundaries only to become ensnared within the boundaries on her reason and freedom imposed by her diagnosis of insanity.

Similarly, Winter suggested that the Gothic genre exemplified women's need to subvert patriarchal society in order to achieve some element of personal freedom. Winter observed that female Gothic writers "focused on the terrifying injustices at the foundation of the Western social order." Thus, the objective of the Gothic heroine was "to uncover and name the horrors that fill her world."[39]

The Prisoner's Hidden Life abounds in Gothic images of villains, tyrants, ghostly images, dark forebodings, fear, anxiety, suspense, and imprisonment couched within themes of oppression and liberation. Packard told readers that she "penned [her] narrative" under a "dark cloud of adverse events, whose silver lining" was yet to be seen by her "physical vision."[40]

She then named the horrors of her entrapment, first in a spiritually abusive marriage and then in the dark wards of an insane asylum patrolled by a heartless doctor and ill-tempered attendants. This book is replete with images of dungeons, "secret cells," and attacks by furious maniacs that left her and other inmates bruised and bloodied. Reflecting on the terrible treatment she observed, Packard wrote, "The black tale of wrongs and cruel tortures . . . experienced at the hand of this giant like tyrant no tongue or pen can ever describe!"[41]

Packard described her "presentiment of coming evil" as she confronted her doctor with demands for better treatment of patients, despite warnings of other patients that she would be sent to the dungeon.[42] She recalled her horror at being moved to the "maniac ward." "Here," she wrote, "I am literally entombed alive by fraudulent means, for a wicked purpose. The walls of my sepulcher are the walls of this Asylum."[43]

Against this darkness, Packard portrayed herself as the struggling heroine who rose above her situation. She professed a higher authority than the husband and doctor who oppressed her and thanked God for protecting her sanity as He had protected Daniel in the lions' den. Thus empowered, she claimed personal liberty as both her right as a human being and her responsibility as one obligated to answer only to her God.

Although determined to obtain her freedom, she nevertheless found meaning in her suffering, writing that "as the dyer uses mordants to set his colors, so my Heavenly Father has employed the mordant of adversity to individualize my sentiments of morality and virtuous action. And, by my experiences, it would seem, that my Father intended to so capacitate me, that I should be daunted and discouraged by nothing."[44] To the extent that she succeeded in surmounting both these societally imposed limits and those within her own psyche, Packard indeed emerges as the heroine of her story.

Packard's writing struck a popular cord. Hers, it seemed, was a true story that bore out all the clichés of evil male tyrants and oppressed but powerful heroines that populated the popular novels of the time. Her book business blossomed. She reported that, by 1868, she had sold more than 18,000 books.[45] An advertisement in the first edition of *The Prisoner's Hidden Life* (1868) offered that title, containing "450 pages large 12 vo. bound in cloth," for sale at $1.50. *Three Years Imprisonment for Religious Belief* (elsewhere titled *Marital Power Exemplified*), "bound in cloth back, enameled sides, gilt letters and lines, flexible" and containing "158 royal octavo pages," sold for $1. *Mrs. Olsen's Prison Life,* containing 140 pages, sold for 50 cents and *Mrs. Packard's Address to the Legislature of Illinois,* "a pamphlet bound in paper cover," was priced at 25 cents.

The advertisement included a few lines of description of each publication and directed buyers to Clarke & Co. Publishers at No. 8 Custom House Place in Chicago. Successive editions of *The Prisoner's Hidden Life* were released in 1869 and 1870, indicating there was demand for the book, and it appears Packard was indeed able to support herself with this income.

Packard reported that, in her "extensive travels" promoting her books and legislation, she had met thousands who shared her view that insane asylums, in "their present corrupt basis," must be overthrown.[46] Convinced that the institution at Jacksonville was not an anomaly, but was instead representative of the entire American "asylum system," Packard pointed to "the need of a universal and radical reconstruction" in care of the insane.[47]

She ended *The Prisoner's Hidden Life* with a call for establishment of an Anti-Insane Asylum Society and presented a constitution for the organization. The preamble to this constitution stated that it was "self-evident . . . our present system of treating the Insane, is a gross violation of the principles of Christianity, and of mental pathology, and therefore, can not receive the sanction of the enlightened and conscientious."[48]

Acknowledging, "It takes a long time to revolutionize such popular institutions, sustained by the State's power," she asked supporters to join her protest by pledging never to allow themselves or any relative or friend to be admitted to an asylum or hospital for the insane. Instead, they must promise to care for any friend or relative who became insane in their own home.[49]

Through this Society, Packard also sought to establish a fund to provide for care of persons whose relatives were unable to care for them. Investigation of such cases and distribution of funds was to be managed by a committee appointed by the Society. Packard invited readers to circulate the constitution in their communities and send the names of those pledging support to her address in Chicago. In this manner she hoped "to form a nucleus of a humanitarian reform in this most needed department of human rights."[50]

Evidently, Packard's effort to form an Anti-Insane Asylum organization was not successful, and she did not mention it in her later books. Nevertheless, based on her attempt and her success in promoting legislation in behalf of the insane, the modern ex-patients movement traces its beginning to Packard in the nineteenth century and Clifford Beers in the early twentieth century.[51]

Although Packard would be most remembered for her influence on legislation related to insane asylums and commitment law, her underlying concern was always for the rights of married women, whether in protecting them from false commitment or assuring them rights equal to those of their husbands in regard to earnings, property, and child custody.

In *The Prisoner's Hidden Life*, Packard was able to claim partial victory. However, she had not yet obtained custody of her minor children. Nor had she achieved her larger political objective of reforming the laws that made women "nonentities" subject to false incarceration in insane asylums. Now, with her husband and doctor essentially vanquished, she turned her attention to equal rights legislation, in part, as a step toward gaining custody of her children.

This involved not only proving her mental fitness, but also proving her ability to support the children. She believed the "facts of [her] experience proved that a married woman is as capable of self-support as a married man."[52] However, Illinois laws did not protect a married woman's right to her own income or property. Thus, in *The Prisoner's Hidden Life*, Packard signaled her intention to bring legislation for married women's rights to the 1869 session of the Illinois legislature.

BY 1869 PACKARD HAD "sold enough [books] to purchase a nice little cottage and a lot in Chicago, free from all encumbrances."[1] The property, valued at $5,000, was located at 1496 Prairie Avenue, several blocks from the district that would, within a few decades, be home to wealthy businessmen such as Marshall Field, George Pullman, Philip Armour, William Kimball, and Joseph Sears.[2]

Packard perhaps chose to settle in Chicago because her three oldest sons were living there. *Edwards City Directories* for the 1860s show Theo and Isaac boarding at 245 W. Monroe and Samuel renting at 122 Cottage Grove Avenue. Despite the acrimony between Packard and her husband, each of the Packard children now apparently maintained respectful relationships with both parents. How much, if any, economic support they provided their mother is not clear. In his diary, Samuel, who by 1869 was a partner at the

Figure 12. Samuel Ware Packard.
Source: Chicagoans As We See 'Em (1904), 195.

law office of Packard and Cooper, mentioned helping to support his father, but not his mother.[3]

However, Samuel did assist his mother in legal matters related to her book business and legislation. Packard noted with "a mother's pride" that she was indebted to Samuel, "more than any one person," for help in drafting a "bill to equalize the rights and responsibilities of husband and wife."[4] She wrote that Samuel, through his work as an attorney, had come to recognize "how absolutely helpless married women" were under the law. Now, Packard wrote, "This dear son, who once in his childish ignorance sustained his father in his wicked course, had now become his mother's real and efficient defender and protector."[5]

Packard understood that "almost insurmountable" obstacles still remained between her and custody of her three minor children. Thus, she recorded that in the winter of 1868–69 she and Samuel drafted a comprehensive bill covering a married woman's right to property, earnings, and child custody as well as the right for a woman to press legal suits in her own name.[6]

Illinois had by 1869 made some progress toward improving the legal rights of married women. Suffragists Frances Gage and Hannah Tracy Cutler had toured the state in 1860 after which Cutler drafted a bill for married women's property rights.[7] Cutler's "Act to Protect Married Women in their Separate Property," effective 24 February 1861, gave a married woman in Illinois the right to any real or personal property she owned at the time of her marriage or acquired "from any person, other than her husband, by descent, devise or otherwise." Such property was exempt from a husband's control and could not be attached for his debts.[8] However, the Illinois Supreme Court ruled in 1864 that the law did not cover wages or earnings of married women; therefore, a woman's earnings could be taken to pay her husband's debts.[9]

An attempt to repeal the Separate Property Act in 1865 apparently failed. But for several years there was considerable confusion regarding the status of the law. Cutler believed that the laws had been left out of "a codification a year or two after" its passage.[10]

Now that Packard was supporting herself with a successful publishing enterprise and had purchased property with that income, she feared her husband might attempt to claim her earnings.[11] Thus, as the Illinois General Assembly convened in early January 1869, Packard returned to Springfield to lobby for the bill she and Samuel had drafted. The *Illinois House Journal* shows that H.B. 696, "An Act to Establish and Protect the Maternal Rights of Married Women," was introduced on 26 January by Representative Samuel Wiley.[12]

Following her usual method, Packard sent articles supporting the bill to the *Chicago Tribune* and *Springfield State Journal.* "The Mother's Legal Rights," dated 29 January 1869 and signed "A Female Parent," insisted that mothers should be given "equal responsibilities with the father in the training of the children." In this article Packard called on legislators to "try the experiment and test us by endowing married woman with her natural rights as a woman." If this were accomplished, she suggested in an oblique reference to the suffrage movement, legislators "need not be surprised if woman's clamor for the rights of men should cease."[13]

A second article, dated 2 February 1869 and headlined "The Rights of Children," pointed to the ironic fact that, under present laws, unmarried mothers had legal custody of their illegitimate children, "while the legitimate offspring of the married woman have no legal right to the care and training of their own mothers!"[14]

Packard noted with amusement that she was honored to learn that one of her anonymous articles in the *Tribune* had been attributed to Chicago woman's rights leader Mary Livermore. But, she added, "This compliment, flattering as it was, did not supersede the need of direct personal effort for the success of the cause."[15] In fact, as Packard lobbied Illinois legislators, Livermore, Myra Bradwell, and other woman's rights leaders had initiated similar woman's rights legislation. In February 1869 they convened a woman's suffrage convention at Library Hall in Chicago.[16] Immediately after the convention, the Illinois Woman Suffrage Association appointed a committee to lobby for woman's rights laws. This committee included Myra and James Bradwell, Kate N. Doggett, Reverend E. Goodspeed, the Honorable C. B. Waite, and Rebecca Mott.[17]

The objectives of this committee paralleled those of Packard's bill to equalize spousal rights, which had already been introduced in the legislature. The suffragists' charge was to "change the laws [so] that the earnings of a married woman may be secured to her own use; that married women may have the same right to their own property that married men have; and the mother may have an equal right with the father to the custody of the children."[18]

Packard wrote that she defended her bill seeking maternal rights for married women before a crowded meeting of the Illinois House judiciary committee at the Leland House in Springfield.[19] However, she said that Representative Lester L. Bond, chair of the judiciary committee, advised her that they would not recommend passage of her bill. Although the committee favored many of its provisions, the bill evidently called for "too many radical changes at once."

Thus, H.B. 696 was tabled at the recommendation of the House Judiciary Committee, and Packard "concluded not to urge the bill any farther in its present comprehensive character."[20]

Following this setback, Packard said that she "wrote at once to Judge Bradwell," asking his advice and assistance. According to Packard, James and Myra Bradwell met with her at the Leland House, where he advised her to lay her bill aside for this session in favor of a bill that simply secured a married woman's right to her own earnings. Packard agreed and wrote that she "also accepted his kind offer to draft the bill, which he promptly did."[21]

Packard reported that Bradwell's bill read: "A married woman shall be entitled to receive, use, and possess her own earnings, and sue for the same in her own name, free from the interference of her husband or his creditors: Provided, this act shall not be construed to give to the wife any right to compensation for any labor performed for her minor children or husband."[22] The Illinois House *Journal* shows that this bill, H.B. 1536, "An Act in Relation to the Earnings of Married Women," was introduced in the House by Lester L. Bond on 2 March and signed into law by the governor 14 April 1869.[23]

Accounts written by suffragists make no mention of Packard in regard to this bill. *The History of Woman Suffrage*, compiled by Elizabeth Cady Stanton, Susan B. Anthony, and Frances Gage, credited passage of the Married Women's Earnings Act to the Illinois Woman Suffrage Committee without special note of Bradwell or any mention of Packard. Bradwell was acknowledged only as a member of the committee.[24]

According to Myra Bradwell's biographer, Jane Friedman, the committee of the Illinois Woman Suffrage Association discovered that, with only ten days remaining in the 1869 session of the legislature, there was no viable bill regarding women's property rights before the legislature. Friedman wrote that Myra Bradwell drafted the bill granting a married woman the right to her own earnings as well as the right to bring suit in her own name. According to Friedman, Bradwell "hand-carried her bill to Springfield and lobbied it through both houses of the legislature."[25]

Packard, who usually named her supporters (and detractors), made no mention of any role by Myra Bradwell or the Illinois Woman Suffrage Committee in passage of the 1869 Married Woman's Earnings Act. She noted passage of the bill briefly in a later book, saying that it was "presented, referred to the Judiciary, recommended, and passed without opposition." She added, "Now I, in common with other married women in Illinois, am . . . protected by law in my right to my home, bought with my own earnings."[26]

Noting that "modesty was not one of Myra's virtues," Friedman suggested that Bradwell was slighted in the *History of Woman Suffrage* because of "ambivalent" feelings between radical suffragist Susan B. Anthony and Bradwell, who was considered a moderate.[27] If national woman's rights leaders were put off by Bradwell's moderation, it would not be surprising for them to completely ignore Packard, who publicly opposed woman's suffrage and, despite her ventures into business and politics, continued to voice allegiance to traditional views of woman's sphere.

Furthermore, Packard may have distanced herself from the organized woman's rights movement for personal and pragmatic reasons. The backlash against woman's suffrage had evoked misogynistic ridicule of suffragists as mannish, beaked-nosed, querulous hens. Despite Packard's assertion that, having lost all she valued in life, she had little to fear from public opinion, she was indeed compelled to curry public opinion, particularly that of male legislators, in order to advance her objectives. Thus, she worked hard to maintain her public persona as a "true woman," who favored female suffrage only as a last resort if male legislators refused to "protect" married women's rights.

However, despite her best efforts, Packard was described in misogynistic terms and lumped with Illinois suffragists. For example, John Gray, editor of the *American Journal of Insanity,* described Packard as a "handsome and talkative crazy woman" who by her "double-springed tongue gave force and persuasion" to her allegations and managed "to bewitch a whole legislature."[28] Gray poked fun at Packard's references to "man's rightful lordship and woman's natural submissiveness," which he thought "might well astonish her Chicago sisters, who claim very strenuously that the superiority, if any, is quite the other way."[29]

Packard would never identify herself with her "Chicago sisters." Indeed, she avoided affiliation with any woman's rights organization or any "particular party," declaring that hers was "strictly a humanitarian—not a sectarian or a political reform." She continued to direct her appeals "almost exclusively" to men because men were "the government as yet." Thus, it was men who wielded the power necessary to advance her immediate objectives.[30]

That same year, Illinois established a permanent Board of Public Charities to oversee all of the state's public charitable institutions, including the asylum at Jacksonville.[31] Though there is no evidence Packard was directly involved in this legislation, it certainly was in keeping with her calls for external oversight of asylums. The Board oversaw transfer of individuals from jails and almshouses to state asylums and supervised plans for new asylums.[32] The law also authorized construction of two new asylums in Illinois.[33]

The Board advocated the cottage plan for these new institutions rather than construction of large structures such as the one at Jacksonville. The cottage plan, recommended by Andrew McFarland in an article a year earlier, called for a central campus surrounded by separate units housing small groups of patients.[34] Although Packard did not comment on this change, it would seem that this move away from the large, unwieldy facilities of earlier decades would have satisfied, in part, her call for destruction of the "asylum system" as she experienced it.

In the spring of 1869, as the Illinois legislature adjourned, Packard looked again to Massachusetts and the possibility of regaining custody of her children. She sent Samuel E. Sewall a draft of an equal rights bill for women, which she asked him to present to the Massachusetts legislature. Sewall, a Boston attorney, was a noted supporter of woman's rights and abolition of slavery. Packard was surprised to learn from Sewall that Massachusetts had just amended its law to give mothers an equal right to custody of their children. For parents who were separated, the state supreme court determined on a case-by-case basis which parent should have custody of minor children.[35]

Packard wrote that she left for Massachusetts immediately upon learning this, taking with her depositions from her two oldest sons, James Bradwell, and other supporters certifying that she was emotionally and financially capable of caring for her children. Evidently Theo and Isaac, who had once supported their father, now attested to their mother's competency and stated their belief that she was never insane. They also indicated their intention to live with her in her Chicago home.[36]

James Bradwell's letter of support (reproduced in Packard's book) stated that he had known Packard for many years and considered her "a superior lady" with "wonderful business capacity." Bradwell noted that Packard was now in comfortable circumstance and owned "quite an amount" of personal and real property. She was, he continued, "an able and ready writer, an energetic, capable, and worthy woman and mother . . . capable of bringing up her minor children in a proper manner."[37] Publisher W. H. Rand of the Chicago Tribune Company also provided Packard a letter testifying to her business acumen and noting that she was invariably prompt and "accurate in the details of business affairs."[38]

In contrast, it is clear that Theophilus Packard's fortunes continued to decline upon his return to Massachusetts. By 1865 he had relinquished his pastorate in Sunderland and moved to his sister's home in South Deerfield. Though he continued to preach occasionally at local churches, according to the *Congregational Year-Book* (1887) he never again served as pastor of a congregation. Without a steady income, he was barely able to support the children and was again dependent upon the charity of family and friends. In February 1869, he moved with the children from his sister's home to a rented house in Greenfield, Massachusetts. By May, when Packard threatened suit, Theophilus admitted that he was subsisting on "but a small income" with his means "largely exhausted."[39]

Upon arriving in Boston, Packard recorded that she engaged Samuel Sewall and T. Currier to sue for custody of her children.[40] She was startled when Theophilus capitulated without legal action. He recorded in his diary that "having been reduced in prosperity in supporting my children during the 9 years of <u>severe trials</u>, having evidence she possessed some $10,000, having consulted with friends, I thought it best to give up the three children to her on certain conditions, without having the case tried."[41] The conditions were that he always be given access to the children and that, if "they should be unable to live with her," he would provide a home for them with his sister and brother-in-law in Manteno.[42]

In June 1869, Packard returned to Chicago in triumph with Libby, George, and Arthur. Once again honoring the cult of domesticity, she declared that her public duties must now be "secondary . . . to those of maternity." Thus, she "most cheerfully laid aside all public duties, except the sale of books sufficient to support [her] family comfortably." She explained that her book business required her to be away for about three months per year. Otherwise, she intended to devote her time "almost exclusively to my family, refusing all the calls of social life and its varied responsibilities."[43]

Theophilus Packard followed the family to Chicago and boarded at the Douglas House approximately a mile from his wife's Prairie Avenue home. Theo and Isaac, as promised, moved in with her and assisted with the younger children. Samuel paid his father's board at the Douglas House and lived there with him for a few months after which he, too, moved to his mother's home.[44]

Packard wrote that her husband never "repented in the slightest degree of the course" he had pursued toward her, adding that "since he does not repent he will not allow me to forgive him." She believed Christian scripture taught that repentance must necessarily precede forgiveness.[45] Nevertheless, in accordance with their agreement, she permitted Theophilus to visit the children at her home, showing him "the respectful treatment of a stranger gentleman." She recorded that 3 July 1869 was the first time she, her husband, and all six children had ever been together "under the same roof" as a family. (Theo was already working away from home when Arthur was born.) She recalled that, on that "memorable Sabbath evening," they went together "in one solemn company to a Methodist church service" near her home.[46]

Theophilus noted in his diary that "the children got along living with their mother at her house comfortably well" and added that he "took pains to have them attend Evangelical meetings and Sabbath Schools." He added that they usually "attended Rev. Dr. Hague's meeting at the Baptist University." He stayed in Chicago until he determined it was "safe to leave my children as they were situated." In April 1870 he moved to Manteno, where he boarded for a while with the Wright family then moved to the home of Sybil and Abijah Dole.[47]

Packard could not resist gloating at the ironic reversal of fortune her husband, whom she had indeed hung on the "gallows of public opinion," had suffered. "Here," she wrote in a later book, "I would pause in the narrative, just to note the principle of retribution and compensation at this point so very conspicuous." She continued: "Five years previous, Mr. Packard, by his legal usurpation of all my rights, had made me a homeless wanderer, without a right to a child or one dollar of our common property, which then amounted to several thousand dollars, mostly in real estate . . . Now while I have a home, property, and children, he is homeless, penniless, and childless!"[48]

But Packard's triumph and enjoyment of her reunited family would be short-lived. In January 1870, Isaac left home to marry Mary Penfield of Penfield, Ohio. Theo would leave in November to marry Sarah M. Janes of Galena, Illinois. Both couples settled in Iowa.[49] Restless, lovelorn, and depressed, Samuel moved out of his mother's home to several Chicago area locations during 1870 and 1871, and considered relocating in the West for his health.[50]

More disheartening, twenty-year-old Libby apparently began to show evidence of mental illness. Theophilus recorded that in April his daughter "was taken deranged" and remained in "a sad state of mind and of ill health." He wrote that he visited her in Chicago and found her "greatly emaciated" and taking "little or no interest in any thing." Describing what may have been a case of anorexia nervosa, he wrote that "to all appearance it seemed as though she would soon waste away and die." In July, she was taken to Manteno to stay with him at the Doles', where she slowly "began to amend." After several months, Libby apparently recovered and in December she returned to her mother's home.[51]

During this time, George and Arthur remained with their mother. However, nine-year-old Arthur spent summers with his father and never seemed to adjust to living with his mother, from whom he had been separated at the age of eighteen months.[52]

Meanwhile, Packard scaled back her legislative work, but continued to promote woman's rights laws. Despite passage of the Married Women's Earnings Act, she believed she was "in all other respects . . . as much a slave as before."

Although Theophilus had relinquished the children to her, she did not have legal custody. Thus, she recorded that in the winter of 1871, she again sent to the Illinois legislature the "bill to equalize the rights and responsibilities of husband and wife" that had been rejected by the judiciary committee in 1869. Once again, the bill failed.[53]

However, Packard recorded that at the end of the 1871 legislative session, state senator John C. Dore wrote to tell her that the main features of her bill had passed "in one form or another."[54] In April 1871, the *Chicago Legal News* reported that the legislature had passed a child custody law, which stated: "Neither parent shall dispose of the custody of a minor child without the consent of the other, and in all cases the surviving parent, being a fit and competent person, shall be entitled to the guardianship of his or her minor child."[55] Thus, Packard told her readers, "I succeeded in getting an equal right with Mr. Packard to the children." "Little by little," she said, the common law in Illinois had been modified to grant her "protection as a married woman."[56]

Five months later, on 8 October 1871, tragedy struck the city of Chicago as a fire started on the southwest side of the city and burned northward to the lakefront, killing more than three hundred people and destroying $200 million in property.[57] The great Chicago fire spared Packard's house, but burned the printing shop of Clarke and Company, destroying her stock of books and bookplates. These materials were not insured and Packard was now left with no books to sell, no bookplates with which to print more, and no source of income. To create at least some income, she rented out part of her house; however, supporting a family would now be a struggle.[58]

A week after the fire, Theophilus came to Chicago and took Libby back to Manteno.[59] Meanwhile, George accepted an offer to work in the bookkeeping business of his uncle and namesake, George Hastings, in New York. Theophilus recorded that Samuel was "burnt out" in the fire, but his life, "though imperiled, was saved."[60] Samuel, with the help of an office boy, apparently managed to save much of his library, including his substantial personal library of law books. In November 1871 he left Chicago for Denver, Colorado, in search of a fresh start and healthier climate.[61]

Two months later, in January 1872, Theophilus returned to Chicago and removed twelve-year-old Arthur from his mother, claiming he did so "because of her mistreatment and abuse" of the boy. Arthur was to stay at the Doles' until Theophilus could "find a place for him."[62] Theophilus was relieved that Arthur and Libby were again under his care—away from the "error and false sentiments" of their mother and the "irreparable injury" they had, in his opinion, experienced while under her influence.[63]

Packard did not mention Libby, but wrote that her husband took Arthur from her "guardianship, care and custody, without my consent." However, she confessed that, although she regretted that event "so far as Arthur's welfare" was concerned, she was "greatly relieved of a heavy responsibility."[64] Furthermore, she saw the hand of Providence in her emancipation from family responsibilities. God, she decided, had "kindly gratified the great desire of my maternal heart" to have her children for a while. At this point, He seemed to be asking her to entrust her children to Him and "go work in [His] vineyard." Now, she could devote her "undivided energies to the great work, I seem peculiarly capacitated by my experiences, to perform."[65] To this calling—perhaps with more enthusiasm than regret—Packard responded, "I will."[66]

14   Working in Her Calling

IN 1872 WITH HER REFORMS in place in Illinois and her family scattered, Packard looked for other fields of service. Iowa was a logical choice. Not only did she still have good friends in Mount Pleasant, but also her son, Theo, and his wife had settled there.

Her focus in Iowa was patients' rights legislation, and she recorded that she began her efforts with letters to Representatives J. Vanderventer and J. M. Hovey. Hovey was chair of the House Committee on Insane Asylums. When both men discouraged her from pursuing this legislation, she again turned to the press, which provided its usual assistance.

The *Davenport Gazette,* for example, carried a 19 March 1872 editorial on "Rights of the Insane," which declared that, although "Lunatic Asylums were founded in the interest of humanity" to relieve past barbarity in treatment of the insane, recent evidence revealed that "great cruelties and outrages were practiced within their walls." The writer was appalled to report, "These palatial structures, built and supported at the public expense, have been converted into prison houses of persons not insane, especially married women." The editorial called for better regulation of modern asylums and restriction of the authority of asylum superintendents, who possessed "powers well nigh autocratic."[1]

The newspaper campaign worked. Packard's bill was referred to the Committee on Insane Asylums. She immediately traveled to Des Moines, where she boarded at the Pacific House and began to lobby legislators. To the great consternation of Dr. Mark Ranney, superintendent of the Mount Pleasant asylum, she secured passage of a comprehensive patients' rights package entitled, "Act to Protect the Insane." Passed on 23 April 1872, this legislation became known across the nation as "Packard's Law."[2]

Packard's Law provided for a visiting committee of three persons (one of whom must be a woman) to inspect Iowa asylums "at their discretion" and report annually to the governor. The visiting committee was authorized to examine witnesses under oath and to obtain papers and testimony necessary to investigate allegations of false commitment or abuse. The committee also had authority to fire any attendant or employee "found guilty of misdemeanor, meriting such discharge."[3]

Packard's Law required that the names and addresses of members of the visiting committee must be posted in every ward, and the asylum superintendent was required to inform patients of their right to correspond with whomever they chose. The superintendent could not read or censure patients' mail, but could forward their letters to the visiting committee for inspection before giving them to the addressee. Patients were also to be given material needed to write and mail letters, unless otherwise ordered by the visiting committee. The superintendent was charged with ensuring that the patients' letters were properly mailed.[4] Finally, the law required a coroner's inquest in the event of the sudden or "mysterious" death of a patient. Penalties attached to the law included imprisonment of not more than three years and a fine of up to $1,000 for failure to comply.[5]

This legislation passed in Iowa despite a belated assault by the superintendents' lobby. Packard "supposed [they] had lost track of my programme, having remained quiet so long with my children in Chicago." However, she said, in Iowa "as in Connecticut, the conspiracy followed me."[6]

Superintendent Ranney of the Mount Pleasant asylum protested Packard's legislation using much the same language McFarland had used to oppose her Illinois laws. He complained that the law took control away from asylum superintendents, disrupted the order of the institution, and "unjustly impugn[ed] the integrity of the officers of the hospital." Ranney argued that the visiting committee was far less qualified to evaluate hospital conditions than the board of trustees, "most of whom serve faithfully for such periods as to become intelligently acquainted with the managements and needs of the hospital."[7]

But when Ranney protested that the law would make the task of "subduing his patients" more difficult, Packard turned his own argument against him. She fumed, "Subduing his Patients! They were not placed under his care to be subdued, like criminals—but to be treated as unfortunates, with kindness and suitable medical treatment."[8]

Despite her apparent success in obtaining this law, Packard soon discovered that Ranney had persuaded members of the visiting committee that the new law was of dubious benefit and, insofar as possible, should be quietly ignored. Thus, she said, she learned "that the opposition from the Legislature was but a small part of the opposition to be overcome."[9]

After receiving a rude reception from Superintendent Ranney and a member of the visiting committee during an attempt to visit the Mount Pleasant asylum, Packard again turned to political allies and the press.[10] Going to the top, she reported her adverse experience to Governor Carpenter and asked his help in enforcing the law. Meanwhile, Iowa newspapers, including the *Mount Pleasant Journal,* published accounts of her unsuccessful attempt to visit the asylum as well as her letter-to-the-editor that declared "Self-Defense an Inalienable Right."[11]

Packard wrote that she also contacted Judge R. Lowe in Keokuk, a former governor of Iowa (and apparently a member of the visiting committee), enclosing a petition signed by "four thousand men of the first standing in Iowa" who had backed the new law. According to Packard, Lowe met with her on 2 July 1872 at Theo's home in Mount Pleasant. Evidently she persuaded Lowe that the new law was necessary, and he promised to support its enforcement.

Content that these efforts had moved Iowa toward compliance with the law, Packard traveled to New York in the fall of 1872 to promote legislation there as well as to "superintend" publication of her newest book. Soon after arriving in New York, she read an article in the *New York Tribune* describing the method used in Belgian asylums to evaluate patient complaints and secure their mail privileges. Asylum patients there placed their outgoing mail in locked boxes. The letters were then reviewed by an independent official and evaluated for evidence of legitimate complaints. Packard recorded that she immediately wrote Judge Lowe in Iowa urging him to encourage this practice there.[12]

Packard reported that while in New York City she attended the 21 October 1872 meeting of the commissioners appointed by Governor Hoffman to investigate New York's public and private institutions for the insane.[13] She also wrote several articles for the *New York Times* and *New York Tribune* calling for legislation similar to that passed in Iowa to protect the rights of the insane.[14] Packard did not mention specific legislation resulting from her activities in New York.

During this period, the AMSAII continued to denounce her legislative activities and minimize her successes. At the annual meeting in May 1873, John P. Gray, superintendent of the asylum in Utica, New York, reported on recent attempts to modify legislation in New York and advised colleagues, "We have had Dr. McFarland's former patient, Mrs. Packard, in consultation with the Legislature." Gray had evidently provided legislators with a copy of her old love-letter to McFarland. Suggesting that this intervention was effective he continued, "She had two or three bills there and she might have done some mischief, but the fact was too apparent that she had herself a record." Gray concluded his update on Packard, saying, "I suppose she will soon be up in Massachusetts . . . at least we commend her to some other State."[15]

While Packard's specific proposals in New York were apparently not adopted, the spirit of her efforts to protect asylum patients is evident in the legislation passed there the following year. This legislation assigned licensing power over institutions for the insane to the state Board of Charities and appointed a state commissioner in lunacy as an ex-officio member of the board. The commissioner's role was to prevent and investigate abuses in commitment and care of the insane.[16]

Not surprisingly, among the concerns discussed at the 1873 gathering of the AMSAII was how the Association should respond to calls in several states for oversight commissions. Pliny Earle cautioned that they should not overreact to criticism and suggested that "any action by this Association, at the present time, would do more harm than good."[17] Isaac Ray dismissed the public clamor about asylums as "a craving for sensation which must be gratified." It was the same feeling, he continued, that "sends crowds of people to hear Mr. Alger lecture against hospitals [and] induces other crowds to listen to George Francis Train, or Victoria Woodhull."[18] Ray reiterated his conclusion that asylums were not "materially affected" by such complaints, despite the negative publicity.[19]

Meanwhile, in the eighteen months since the fire in Chicago, Packard had found a new printer and prepared another book for publication. Early in 1873, she released *Modern Persecution*, "in an elegant type and style of binding," from the New York publishing house of Pelletraus & Raynor. She recorded that the cost to publish a thousand copies of the book, including new stereotype plates, was $2,500.[20]

Modern Persecution was indeed an impressive book in two richly embossed, gilt-edged volumes that included several illustrations. Volume I, *Modern Persecution; or Insane Asylums Unveiled,* was essentially the same as *The Prisoner's Hidden Life,* with chapters only slightly rearranged. Volume II, *Modern Persecution; or Married Woman's Liabilities, as Demonstrated by the Action of the Illinois Legislature,* carried Packard's story forward from her release from the asylum in 1863 through her activities in Illinois, Massachusetts, Connecticut, Iowa, and New York in 1872.

To further establish her credibility, *Modern Persecution* reprinted the statement from the *Journals* of the Illinois House and Senate (dated 20 February 1869) approving the *Report of the Investigating Committee* and accepting its recommendations. Packard was careful to note that this statement was signed by the twenty-two members of the House and Senate Committees on State Institutions, whose names she listed.[21]

Packard reported that she had sold only half of the first edition of *Modern Persecution* when a fire at her New York printer's shop again destroyed her stock of books and bookplates. This time, however, they were insured for $1,000, and she was able to reproduce the plates a third time.[22]

During the next year Packard traveled throughout the Northeast promoting legislation and provoking investigations of asylums in New York and Vermont. As word of Packard's "Herculean effort" became known across the country, verbal attacks against her in professional literature of the psychiatric profession increased almost in proportion to the support she was receiving in the popular press. The *Philadelphia Medical Times* for 14 March 1873, for example, lambasted "amateur philanthropists" and the state legislatures that seemed to be "endeavoring to outdo one another in absurd and mischievous" legislation regarding the insane. The article complained of demagogues clamoring "about tyranny and wrong, and people's rights" and lamented the "gross violations of common sense" that marked the efforts of such reformers and sympathizing legislators.[23]

Undoubtedly referring to Packard, the writer declared it would "become one of the curiosities of human credulity" that "a poor crazy woman, relying only on her nimble tongue," could convince several state legislatures to pass laws that ignored "every principal [*sic*] of moral management" established by educated men of science.[24] The article reported that harmful laws had recently passed in Iowa and Maine, but gratefully noted that the woman had not been as successful as she claimed, even though "with that sort of glamour which bewilders so many persons of deranged intellects, she imagines, and so represents that she has never failed."[25]

This was, of course, not true. Packard wrote with openness about her failures as well as her successes, even including an entire chapter entitled "Why My Bill Failed" in volume II of *Modern Persecution*. But hyperbole often prevailed over truth as the superintendents put the weight of their rising profession against the "talkative crazy lady."

In June 1873, Packard returned to Connecticut, the scene of her humiliation in 1866, to encourage passage of both woman's rights and patients' rights bills. This time she evidently succeeded, despite opposition from the superintendents' lobby. Legislation enacted 1 July 1873 established a Board of Charities to oversee inspection of asylums. Packard further noted, that although passage of her comprehensive "married woman's bill" was deferred, Connecticut did pass legislation entitling women to property rights.[26]

Maine was the next stop in her New England campaign. She wrote that she arrived in Augusta in the winter of 1873–74 and enlisted the aid of lawyer and former Augusta mayor Samuel Titcomb. Slightly adjusting her tactics, she sought support from the wives of legislators as well as the men themselves. And, to save expense, she blanketed legislators with handbills instead of her books, timing their distribution to coincide with introduction of her bill.[27]

According to Packard, she visited the Augusta asylum, accompanied by a commissioner from the Maine Board of Charities. She was gratified by the cordiality of the asylum superintendent, H. M. Harlow, who permitted her to inspect the facility freely, apparently hoping to disarm the by now well-known "evil hunter in insane asylums." She granted his good intentions and treated him kindly in her book, but, nevertheless reported that she believed more than fifty patients who were not insane were confined at his institution.[28]

She was apparently received cordially by Maine Governor and Mrs. Nelson Dingley, Jr.; Senate President John E. Butler; and Senator Webb of Kennebec, who introduced her bill in the Senate. Gratified by this warm reception, she was confident that her bill in Maine, which encompassed the same measures as Packard's Law in Iowa, would pass.[29]

However, she wrote that on the day the bill was to be brought to a third reading in the House, she detected "a noticeable and very painful coldness." One of the legislators took her aside and asked if she had read the morning papers. The newspapers, she learned, had published the now infamous love-letter. Packard wrote that she retreated to a sofa outside the House chambers. There, she said, "I sat in solitary loneliness . . . [and] wept to think of this sad reverse."[30] Action on her bill was deferred. Packard left Maine the next morning, assuming defeat. But she was astonished to learn that the Maine legislature had passed her bill on 4 March 1874 "without a dissenting vote!"[31]

In *Modern Persecution,* Packard used testimonials from Maine to counter accusations that her laws were regressive and harmful to the mentally ill. According to Packard, Governor Dingley assured her, "Thus far the law has worked well, and has been instrumental in bringing about improvements in the hospital, and in inspiring increased confidence in its management." Mrs. C. A. Quinby, a member of the visiting committee, reportedly told her, "Say to the opposers of your bill, it is *not true* that it had been a failure, in my judgment, and that of the best men and women of our city and State."[32]

From Maine, Packard traveled to Providence, Rhode Island, where the Judiciary Committee of the legislature had set aside her bill for the protection of the insane on the advice of Drs. Isaac Ray and J. N. Sawyer. In her address, Packard rebutted Ray's arguments against the bill with specific examples of cases in which present law had failed to protect patients at the Butler, Rhode Island, asylum. To substantiate her statements, she brought with her former patients and family members of patients in the Butler asylum. Like her other legislative addresses of this period, this speech was well organized and her points were argued in lawyerly fashion. In concluding her remarks, Packard assured legislators that her intent was not to lessen public confidence in the asylum, but "on the contrary, to secure and hold this confidence, by inducing you to furnish the public with a sure guarantee that henceforth" the rights of asylum patients would be protected by law.[33]

By April, Packard was in Boston advocating passage of a comprehensive law comparable to that passed in Iowa two years earlier. In her printed address to the Massachusetts legislature Packard noted that her bill had languished in the Committee on Public Charitable Institutions for nearly ten weeks. She urged legislators to act now to provide asylum patients the same protection under the law that other citizens enjoyed. She told Massachusetts legislators that, thus far, no state had "absolutely refused this appeal" and she hoped Massachusetts would not be the first exception.[34]

One key to Packard's success as a lobbyist is perhaps suggested in the reported comment of a Massachusetts legislator who, according to Packard remarked, "We passed the bill because we could not do otherwise, for Mrs. Packard was so very persistent, we could not bluff her off."[35] However, her success also had much to do with her political tactics and choice of allies.

In Massachusetts, for example, passage of postal rights legislation in June 1874 was due in large part to support from Commissioners of Lunacy Nathan Allen and Wendell Phillips. The new law stated that a patient must be given writing materials and allowed to write monthly to the superintendent, the state Board of Charities, and the commissioners of lunacy.[36]

John Gray had heralded the appointment of Allen and Phillips as Massachusetts commissioners of lunacy in the *American Journal of Insanity*, noting that Allen had been known to the profession for years not only for "his scientific investigation on medical and social questions" but also for his ten years' experience on the state Board of Charities. Meanwhile, Gray continued, "The name of Wendell Phillips carries to all minds a conviction that his action will be characterized by honesty of purpose in the interest of humanity, without fear or favor."[37]

Gray's tone changed, however, when Phillips expressed views similar to those of Packard in the commissioners' published report.[38] Like Packard, Phillips argued that persons accused of a crime had more protection under the law than did an individual alleged to be insane. Phillips repeated the now-familiar criticism of asylum attendants and management. He also objected to the use of opiates and complained that the patients' diet lacked healthy variety.[39]

Gray heatedly suggested that Phillips had expressed "the most decided views of the subject . . . without even visiting the hospital in question." He complained that Phillips seemed to view "an asylum as a place of 'imprisonment' [and] 'close confinement' . . . in which people are confined with the design of robbing them of their liberty and property."[40] Gray jabbed that Phillips, "who by the way is not a physician," seemed to believe "that asylums should be conducted on the 'European plan' of a first class hotel." He concluded with the AMSAII's usual defense that the report's criticisms reflected an "ignorance" of the "practical workings" of an asylum that most persons "would hesitate to display."[41]

Nathan Allen's argument in favor of postal rights was more difficult to dispute. He compared the right to send letters to the right of petition, which, he said, "In a republican government, should always be granted to the lowest and humblest individual." Restricting correspondence was a direct encroachment of the "principle of personal liberty," Allen insisted, and argued that "even in lunatic hospitals," there should be "serious objections to submitting always to the 'one-man power.'"[42] Allen's powerful appeal to republican values and his call to restrain the authority of the asylum superintendent matched Packard's rhetorical tactics precisely.

During her whirlwind campaign in New England, Packard apparently lost contact with her family. In 1874 Samuel Packard, who had returned to Chicago from Colorado, tried to reach his mother to tell her about his impending marriage to Clara A. Fish of Lombard, Illinois. In addition to inviting her to his wedding, Samuel advised his mother that he had "rerented" her house in Chicago for $30 per month, adding, "That is all the place is now worth for the furniture is pretty much all used up." He advised her to sell the property and invest the money elsewhere since the rent no longer covered the taxes. He also updated her on the whereabouts of the rest of the family, noting that he heard from Manteno that "Libby was about the same."[43]

Samuel's admiration for his mother was apparent as he laid out his future plans and asked her advice. He told her he hoped someday to devote himself "to carrying on some great and noble reformation—as you do." The lengthy letter was signed "with much love, your son, Samuel W."[44]

There is no indication that Packard received the letter or attended his wedding on 23 June 1874. She apparently remained on the East Coast throughout much of 1873, 1874, and 1875. Comments in the *American Journal of Insanity* suggest that, along with Maine, Rhode Island, and Massachusetts, she may have been in Pennsylvania and Ohio in 1874 and early 1875. For example, noting that Pennsylvania had passed legislation making it a penal offense to prevent asylum patients from writing their lawyers, *Journal* editor John Gray complained that public "contempt for all special knowledge" led them "to follow the lead of crazy women and amateur reformers" rather than heeding "the counsels of those who have made [mental medicine] the study of their lives." Soon, he feared, "we shall be following the example of Iowa and Maine."[45] Gray remarked that most of these "pseudo-philanthropists" knew little about care of the insane and did not have "the true interest of the insane at heart."[46]

Packard did, of course, have the best interest of asylum patients at heart and she happily accepted credit for the "multiplication of laws" protecting the civil rights of the mentally ill. She clearly influenced much of this legislation through her books and well-publicized campaigns in various states. However, it is not always clear which laws she lobbied for personally. The *American Journal of Insanity* noted, for example, that in 1873–74 an effort was underway in Ohio "to enact the law of trial by jury before committal to asylums" and that Illinois was considering placing "all State Asylums under the control of a State Board of three, to be elected by the people."[47] However, Packard does not mention those laws. She did record that New Hampshire passed legislation related to postal rights 10 July 1874, but did not claim any involvement in that effort.[48]

The next campaign for which Packard provided details took place in January 1875 in Washington, D.C., where she lobbied for a national law assuring asylum patients uncensored access to their mail. Apparently rebuffed by the postmaster general and unceremoniously excused from his office, Packard wrote that she "returned in sadness to [her] lonely room . . . to ruminate over my sore disappointment . . . and to consider what next must be done." She decided to take her cause directly to President Ulysses S. Grant at the White House.[49]

According to Packard she arrived at the White House alone the next day and asked the porter to tell Mrs. Grant "that a lady friend from Chicago would like to see her." Expecting to see a personal friend, a disappointed Julia Dent Grant nevertheless apparently greeted her graciously and listened to her story. Packard recorded that she held the president's wife "spell-bound" with her saga, after which Mrs. Grant purchased two of her books and arranged an appointment for her with the president.[50]

Packard wrote that she arrived at the White House the next day and waited in the reception-room outside the president's office until her name was called. She recalled, "I entered, and took a seat at the side of the table, close by the President, who sat at the end of the table, alone, in his private office." Then, she said, "with as few words as possible" she told him about her proposed postal rights bill and sought his advice.[51]

According to Packard, President Grant told her that he received letters almost daily from asylum patients and he agreed that their postal rights deserved protection. He apparently advised her to forgo a petition and to instead take her bill directly to Congressman J. B. Packer, chair of the House committee responsible for such legislation. Grant, she said, then signed his calling card and gave it to her "as your introduction to my cabinet" and told her to indicate to them his approval of her legislation. Packard wrote that she left the ten-minute interview elated by the "gentlemanly consideration" given her by the president. "Now," she wrote, "I felt myself fully equipped for my Washington work, for I well knew the power attached to this little piece of paper."[52]

Packard apparently also sought support from the ablest attorney and woman's rights advocate she could find in the nation's capital. Belva A. Lockwood, a pioneer woman lawyer and close friend of Myra Bradwell, was then battling for the right to practice before the federal courts in the District of Columbia and the U.S. Supreme Court.[53] Packard reported that it was Lockwood to whom she turned for direction in preparing a national law to ensure asylum patients' postal rights.[54]

Like Packard's Iowa law, the national postal rights bill guaranteed a patient's right to uncensored correspondence. It also called for placement of a post-office box in every asylum at an estimated cost of $4 each.[55] Packard's memorial to Congress in support of this bill was masterful and reflected the substantial knowledge about treatment of the mentally ill that Packard had gained since her own incarceration. It noted precedents for her bill in England, Belgium, and Germany and cited similar legislation she had fostered in Iowa, Maine, Massachusetts, Connecticut, and New Hampshire.[56]

Calling asylums "American bastilles," the memorial declared that postal rights legislation was the key by which asylums could be "unlocked and transmuted into republican institutions by holding this before-autocratic power" accountable under the law. Packard recounted her personal story to show that the writ of *habeas corpus* had proved useless both in preventing her commitment and in obtaining her release from the asylum. Friends, she explained, could not obtain a writ in her behalf without her husband's consent while she was incarcerated and she was not permitted to communicate her request for a writ directly to any authority. She described how it was actually correspondence in the form of a note slipped to a friend that led to her freedom.[57]

Packard's memorial stated that she had been working in this cause for ten years and had secured legislation of one kind or another in seven states. She added that it was her intention "to pursue this work until every State had been appealed to place the inmates of their insane asylums under the protection of their laws." She again distanced herself from potentially detracting political or organizational affiliations and identified herself as a "self-moved and self-appointed defender of the rights" of the insane, saying, "I work under no organization or party. I receive no remuneration, for services rendered, from any organization or individual. I work without money and without price, and bear my own expenses, which I defray by the sale of my own books."[58]

Despite the president's apparent support and favorable reports from the Committees on Post-Offices and Post-Roads in both the House and Senate, the postal rights bill was not called to a vote during the 1875 session of Congress. It was reintroduced the following year by Representative James Monroe as H.B. 452, and Packard returned to the capital for seven weeks to lobby for it. By then, however, the AMSAII had organized opposition to the bill. Packard reported that, at the request of Dr. Sawyer, superintendent of the asylum in the District of Columbia, Andrew McFarland was invited to Washington to meet with the Post-Office and Post-Roads committees.[59] In this battle, McFarland and the AMSAII prevailed and the postal rights bill died in committee.

Indeed, 1875 marked the beginning of an organized state-by-state effort by the AMSAII to block or repeal Packard's laws. At the superintendents' May 1875 gathering, Association president Charles H. Nichols introduced his report on the national postal rights bill by telling colleagues he believed it was important that they "be apprised of Mrs. Packard's movements in Washington last winter."[60]

Nichols described the content of the postal rights bill and reported that "immediately upon hearing what was going on, Dr. McDill and I called upon the Chairman of the House Committee, Hon. J. B. Packer of Pennsylvania, and had a full conversation with him, in relation to this measure." They learned that Packard had impressed members of the committee and that many favored her bill.[61]

However, Nichols said, the information he and McDill provided caused "some members of the Committee to doubt and hesitate, and others to change their minds and wholly oppose the measure" and the bill was killed in committee. Nichols urged AMSAII members to take similar pains to fully inform their state legislators of the dangers of such "unjust and mischievous" bills adding, "A word to the wise is sufficient."[62]

Much of the remainder of the meeting involved discussion of the Association's efforts to counteract Packard's crusade either directly or indirectly. Isaac Ray declared it was the duty of the AMSAII "to enquire into and pass judgement upon any scheme, project, or change" proposed for the welfare of the insane.[63]

Ray then presented resolutions from the ongoing "Project of the Law" representing the AMSAII's official position as of 1875. The resolutions restated the Association's opposition to oversight commissions, visiting committees, and postal rights for the insane. "Without arrogating to ourselves any extraordinary wisdom," Ray intoned, "we believe that the accomplished work of this Association, as well as the character and reputation of its present members, fairly entitles it to a respectful hearing in any matter of legislation, affecting the interests of the insane."[64]

The resolutions passed with only two dissenting votes. But discussion about Packard evidently continued. Clement Walker noted that much of the report submitted by Massachusetts Commissioners of Lunacy Nathan Allen and Wendell Phillips "fell dead before the Legislature of Massachusetts" without "producing a ripple." In an oblique reference to Packard, Walker remarked, "We do not fear Mr. Phillips, with his evolutions and withering imprecation, half as much as we fear these half-cured lunatics who go around button-holeing every Senator, and whose work is such that we can not get at them."[65]

At least one doctor, however, was perplexed by the Association's venom toward Packard. William M. Compton, from the Jackson, Mississippi, asylum, argued that the resolutions before the Association were unnecessary and gave "too much importance, too great a notoriety" to those proposing such "revolutionary reform." He continued, "I do not think that we should fear Mrs. Packard. If she is insane, as is alleged, she is to be pitied and not scourged. If she is an impostor she can be exposed."[66]

But the doctors did fear Mrs. Packard, and their opposition to her was as persistent and, at times, as vitriolic as her campaign against asylums and the men who managed them.

15 "Great and Noble Work"

IMPLEMENTATION OF THE AMSAII's "Project of The Law" clearly slowed, but did not stop, Packard's progress. From 1875 on in state after state, asylum superintendents promoted legislation to repeal or amend Packard's laws. Indeed, the degree of Packard's success is remarkable given the countermeasures of the AMSAII.

Because of these countermeasures, the effectiveness and longevity of the specific laws for which Packard was responsible varied from state to state. In Iowa, for example, comments by Superintendent Albert Reynolds of the Hospital for the Insane in Independence indicated that the visiting committee in that state remained relatively ineffective, despite Packard's efforts. Noting in May 1875 that Packard's Law was still in force, Reynolds remarked that he had "received only kindness and courtesy" at the hands of the Iowa visiting committee and that they had "never made a suggestion towards the control or management of the Hospital."[1]

In April 1876, *American Journal of Insanity* editor John Gray was delighted to report that Mark Ranney, who had resigned rather than work under Packard's Law, had returned to his position as superintendent at the Mount Pleasant, Iowa, asylum after the portion of Packard's Law affecting postal rights had been amended to return "control of correspondence where it formerly was, in the hands of the superintendent." Gray declared, "Thus has the folly of legislation, brought about by pseudo philanthropists, urged on by the specious pleas of an uncured lunatic . . . been fully manifested."[2]

However, by the latter decades of the nineteenth century, the AMSAII had become the object of substantial criticism, not only from former patients like Elizabeth Packard, but also from other professionals. British psychiatrists believed that American psychiatrists "relied too much on restraint." They also suggested that American asylums had become largely custodial in nature.[3] An Australian physician visiting American asylums in the early 1880s reported that "superintendents were so overburdened with the details of management and clinical duties that they had no time or inclination for scientific studies, or even for the proper care of their patients."[4]

The AMSAII had by then conceded the issue of external oversight of asylum superintendents and trustees. However, rather than resisting the establishment of Boards of Charity, commissioners of lunacy, and visiting committees, the Association now pressed for inclusion of asylum superintendents as members of such groups. They also opened AMSAII meetings to members of state Boards of Charities with the expressed aim of "educating" lay members of the boards and cultivating their support. The effectiveness of this effort is apparent in comments by Reverend Fred H. Wines, secretary of the Illinois state Board of Charities, who attended the AMSAII's conferences in 1876 and 1877. In his remarks to the superintendents, Wines professed "a sincere and profound respect" for the profession and sought their advice regarding the need for additional institutions for care of the insane in Illinois.[5]

In 1876, Dr. Thomas Kirkbride, presiding over the annual meeting of the AMSAII, touted the achievements of the AMSAII and assured colleagues that their Association had, since its founding, done more "to promote the best interest of the insane than all other causes combined." He was gratified that the Association's "carefully matured declarations" were "recognized as authority, by legislative bodies, building commissions, boards of management, and others" who were interested in the insane, "both at home and abroad."[6] He did not mention that these building commissions and boards of management would probably not have existed without the persistent efforts of Elizabeth Packard and those who shared her views.

Although the superintendents at times succeeded in regaining some of the authority and control denied them by Packard's laws, they were rarely able to escape investigation or to overturn her laws completely. This was especially true in states where others continued to monitor legislation when Packard's attention was diverted elsewhere.[7]

It is evident from the work of the Bradwells in Illinois and men such as Nathan Allen and Wendell Phillips in Massachusetts that Packard's reform efforts were neither solitary nor anomalous. Although she was unable to establish a national organization and considered herself an independent humanitarian, she clearly worked within a network of like-minded individuals.

In Illinois, for example, Myra Bradwell used the increasingly prestigious voice of her *Chicago Legal News* to sustain the legislation put in place in response to Packard's work. Bradwell spoke out against the "Private Mad-House" bill, which had been introduced in the legislature following passage of the 1865 jury trial law. This bill tacitly promoted equal treatment of men and women by rescinding the jury trial requirement for both. But Bradwell reminded readers that, while this would apparently remove the discriminatory aspect of the old law, everyone—especially women—needed the protection of a jury trial. Bradwell recalled that before passage of the jury trial law, "a great many people were sent to the insane asylums who were as sane as the person that sent them."[8]

Even when she was not directly involved or mentioned specifically, Packard's laws and the public notoriety of her story loomed like a specter over other cases, including the 1875 insanity trial of Mary Todd Lincoln. Lincoln's case is perhaps the most notable historical example of contested, involuntary commitment. Historians Mark Neely, Jr. and Gerald McMurtry have suggested that those involved with Lincoln's commitment were well aware of the similarities with Packard's case and adjusted their strategy accordingly. They note, for example, that Robert Lincoln's attorneys were careful not to link insanity with religion, and thus did not bring up Spiritualism in Mary Lincoln's trial.[9] They suggest, too, that Lincoln's doctor, Richard J. Patterson, possibly with Packard in mind, was also "careful to avoid any suspicion of false confinement."[10]

Andrew McFarland was one of two prominent psychiatrists invited to examine Mary Lincoln. Alexander McDill, superintendent of the Hospital for the Insane in Madison, Wisconsin, declined, probably due to ill health; he died a few months later.[11] However, McFarland did examine Lincoln and, expressing "grave apprehensions" as to the consequences, advised against her release.[12] Neely and McMurtry lamented the fact that McFarland was the only psychiatrist other than Patterson who actually examined Mary Lincoln that summer. Suggesting that McFarland's professional opinion was tainted by his involvement in Packard's case, they wrote that McFarland's "gloomy prognosis" regarding Lincoln "was, unfortunately for history, the work of Elizabeth Packard's oppressor, a man with a well-documented history of insensitivity to the problems of important female patients."[13] Despite McFarland's recommendation, Robert Lincoln ultimately bowed to pressure from his mother, her friends, and the press and consented to his mother's release.

Lincoln's case, however, demonstrated that the right to a jury trial did not necessarily ensure a fair trial. She was notified about her trial little more than an hour in advance and, thus, had little opportunity to prepare for it. Furthermore, her attorney was recommended by the prosecution and presented a scant, pro forma defense.[14] Like Packard's Spiritualist friend Tirzah Shedd, Lincoln could—and her defenders did—complain that hers was a "mock trial."[15]

Neely and McMurtry suggest that Packard's greatest impact on the Lincoln case, and perhaps her most lasting achievement, was her success in establishing postal rights for asylum patients. Because of that right, Mary Lincoln was able to write her friends, attorneys James and Myra Bradwell, for help.[16] In response to this correspondence, the Bradwells visited her at Belleview Place in the summer of 1875, bringing with them a reporter (incognito) from the *Chicago Tribune*. Convinced that Lincoln's condition did not require institutionalization, they pressured her doctor, son, and sister, Elizabeth Edwards, to release her.[17]

Packard apparently did not write about the Lincoln case although she must certainly have been aware of it from newspaper accounts. Following defeat of her national postal rights bill in the spring of 1875, she wrote that she "retired from my public duties" and returned to Illinois to care for Libby, whose condition had deteriorated. For three years she maintained a "temporary home" in Aurora, just outside Chicago, and devoted herself to caring for Libby. Packard attributed Libby's recurring bouts of mental illness to the fact that she had been deprived of a mother's "care and training" at the "very important age of budding womanhood."[18]

In 1876, Packard briefly returned to Washington, D.C., where she campaigned, again unsuccessfully, for a national postal rights bill for asylum patients. She then returned to Illinois to care for Libby and work in her book business. Two years later, she published her *magnum opus, The Great Drama; or, The Millennial Harbinger.* She explained that this extraordinary four-volume work, written during her last six months at the Jacksonville asylum, had "not been changed to adapt itself to the present time."[19] Only the introduction and the last chapter, entitled "The Mystic Key," were new.

The 1,600 pages of *The Great Drama* included recollections of happier times interspersed with earnest defense of Packard's beliefs and actions, testimonials to her sanity and success, and recriminations against those who deemed her insane. An interesting social history, the book contains detailed descriptions of home furnishings, children's clothing, homeopathic medicines, midwifery, and other minutiae of a nineteenth-century mother's daily life.

But the book is maddeningly fragmented with digressions that flit in and out of the narrative with no apparent regard for order. Often a sentence or short paragraph stands alone almost as if it were a proverb. Images of asylum horrors are interrupted by recollections of her children and events in their lives, followed by a lament of her lost family, then a return to her narratives of asylum evils. Emotion flies unrestrained from each page as tender memories resolve into fury and frustration at the injustice of her incarceration. A quick perusal suggests why McFarland considered the manuscript evidence of insanity—as well as why Packard may have withheld its publication for sixteen years.

Packard warned her readers that the style of this book was "wholly original" and explained that, since her mind was "constituted on the 'high-pressure' principle," her thoughts naturally came "by flashes through my instincts." Accordingly, she could truly say her "trains of thought [were] engineered by the "lightning Express."[20]

Thus, she cautioned, "Now, my dear reader, as the 'lightning Express' dashes on, allowing you only a 'glance and a glimpse' of the passing panorama of thoughts chasing after each other in seemingly promiscuous, wild confusion, be not alarmed!"[21] *The Great Drama,* she advised, was "a book of simple facts and opinions; not a logical one." Its "simple and artless style" was adapted "to the comprehension of the common people for whom it was written."[22]

In this book Packard was openly emotional and uninhibited. Here, for example, she reveals her "amativeness" and longing for a male companion. She recalls former beaux and speaks of herself as a "grass widow" in search of a husband. This is also the only publication in which she describes her romantic involvement with Abner Baker.

The Great Drama also clearly reveals how deeply Packard embraced Spiritualism. In one passage, for example, she recounts a nighttime encounter with the spirit of George Washington. The episode occurred as she drifted in and out of sleep, listening as the mournful singing of two patients echoed across the ward. The singing, she said, likewise echoed in her mind. "It was the same thing over and over, over and over, again and again, without the least variation of time, order, or expression." She wrote that as she listened, a famous statue of Washington flashed before her mind.[23] The image "was instantly caught up and associated with the music," reminding her of spirit mediums, who perfectly echoed or channeled another being. In her ephemeral state between wakefulness and sleep Packard imagined, "There is Washington, and I, his medium, transcribing his dictations for his beloved country's welfare."[24]

Historians have noted that Founding Fathers such as Benjamin Franklin, Thomas Jefferson, and, especially, Washington, held great symbolic meaning for Spiritualists, who frequently invoked them as guides. Historian Bret Carroll, for example, suggested that "Spiritualists hoped these patriotic spirit guides" would help them eliminate tyranny, "restore public virtue," and "usher in the millennium, that perfect social and moral order" hoped for by Christians.[25]

Whether Packard's visitation from Washington was allegorical and merely a literary device rather than either channeling or hallucination could be debated. However, such a visitation would have seemed perfectly familiar to her Spiritualist friends and readers. Furthermore, this "conversation" with Washington provided an ideal forum for exhorting the principles of liberty and citizens' rights that would become the hallmark of Packard's public rhetoric.

Her introductory caveats aside, *The Great Drama* revealed Packard at the edge of sanity writing freely about matters she would later suppress. Whether or not she was deranged at the time of her commitment, it is clear from these volumes that Packard had struggled to maintain mental equilibrium as months turned into years of confinement at the Jacksonville asylum where most of those around her were "lost to reason."[26]

Given its content, it is not surprising that Packard waited sixteen years before publishing this book. One wonders why, in fact, she chose to publish it at all. She explained that she withheld publication of this version of her story at first for lack of money and afterward "for want of courage," afraid that she was so far ahead of her time in her thinking that she would be returned to the asylum if her book were read. "Prudence," she said, "suggested that its publication be delayed until my sanity had become more fully recognized through the publication of books of a less radical nature."[27]

By 1878 Packard apparently felt sufficiently secure in her personal reputation to risk its publication. Times had also changed and, she wrote, "I now so often hear the radicalism of my book echoed, both from the American pulpit and press, that much longer delay may expose its author to the charge of being herself the echo, instead of the originator, of the thoughts of 'The Great Drama.'"[28]

Indeed, by then her readers were perhaps numbed by the escapades of such public figures as Victoria Woodhull and Packard's old acquaintance, Henry Ward Beecher. By comparison, Packard's radical feelings and opinions must have seemed unexceptional. Woodhull's published accusations of Beecher's scandalous affairs, particularly with the wife of his friend Theodore Tilton, had captivated the national press in the 1870s when Tilton sued Beecher for alienation of affection.

When Woodhull accused Beecher of hypocritically preaching chastity and fidelity, while practicing free love, Beecher defended himself in language much like that Packard had used, only slightly more convincingly, a decade earlier to explain her feelings for Abner Baker and Andrew McFarland. As Richard Whitman Fox noted, Beecher framed his story as one of victimization and persecution while claiming that "with a nature like his he could not stop loving." Beecher had intoned, "You may rebuke me for loving where I should not love" but only if you also "rebuke the twining morning-glory," which "holds on to that which is next to it." Thus, Fox explained, Beecher considered himself blameless for having loved Tilton's wife because he could not help it.[29] Historian Altina Waller suggested that, in Beecher's "private system" of morality, "moral affinity or spiritual love had replaced institutional obligations as the basis for human relationships—at least for those on the higher, nobler plane."[30]

Packard, like Beecher, considered herself on a higher plane of spirituality than most others. Thus, she explained, it was part of her nature to love a Christ-like man, such as Baker or McFarland. Believing her God-given nature was implicitly good, she trusted her conscience and her honest feelings even when those feelings embraced love for a man other than her husband. This confidence in her own essential goodness made it impossible for her to see any carnal or sinful motive in her affection for Baker or McFarland.

The substantial impact of Beecher's thought on Packard becomes especially apparent in the many references to him sprinkled throughout the text of *The Great Drama*. For example, in commenting that she and her husband "simply grew apart," Packard recalled a sermon in which Beecher had remarked, "Some people grow apart although living close together, while others grow together, although far separated . . . and those who are unlike, can no more be united by coming together than can a drop of oil and a drop of water unite by being brought together." Packard agreed "with Brother Beecher," and applied this analogy to the "impassable gulf" between her and her husband.[31]

In the last chapter of *The Great Drama*, entitled "The Mystic Key," Packard compared her case to the Beecher–Tilton scandal, and suggested that, if Beecher had "immediately challenged his accuser to substantiate those charges . . . [few] would ever have doubted his innocence afterwards."[32] She asked rhetorically, "If this great man was innocent, why did he not thus defend his good name, and the American's esteem of his character? He was guilty of a great breach of trust by not denying it, if he was innocent."[33]

The Mystic Key, published as a separate book later in 1878 and again in 1879, was Packard's most determined effort to defend her love-letter to McFarland and to diffuse intensified attacks by the AMSAII that, by then, were seriously undermining her crusade. She wrote that she sold this book "at a very low price to render its general circulation more hopeful," hoping it would "be an efficient aid" to her legislative work "by removing the greatest obstacle I have hitherto encountered in the passing my reform bills, viz., the false interpretation of my 'love letter!'—so Dr. McFarland has seen fit to christen it—which I wrote him while in the asylum."[34]

Suggesting that the letter was an attempt to manipulate the doctor's feelings in hopes of obtaining his aid, she wrote, that, unfortunately, "circumstances do exist that drive defenseless woman to use such means of self-defense, simply because she has no other resort."[35] That she was in her own mind a hostage subject to her doctor's control is evident as she recalled her feelings, saying, "The awe of the tyrant [had settled] into a reverence for a mighty power, adequate to this great emergency." She continued, "As he had had almost omnipotent power to crush, so he now had this same power to raise and defend me. The power of the Husband, the power of the Trustees, the power of the State, had all been delegated to him. As to the power of protection, he was all in all to me now."[36]

While *The Mystic Key* clearly had a purpose in supporting her reform work, *The Great Drama* seemed far less helpful in that regard. It is possible that sale of her earlier books had waned and that, in publication of this book (five years after *Modern Persecution*), financial exigency reigned over prudence. She would release another edition of *Modern Persecution* a year after publication of *The Great Drama*.

Packard, of course, hints at no such thing. In *The Mystic Key* she boasted that, "from the avails of this publishing business," she had supported herself, educated three children, and saved enough money to publish *The Great Drama*. She claimed to have sold "nearly forty thousand books and pamphlets . . . throughout twelve different States of this Union." She also noted that her legislative work had by then resulted in passage of twelve bills.[37]

She also reported proudly on the accomplishments of her children. Theo, then thirty-six years old, was a banker in Kellogg, Iowa, who "had the extra good fortune" of securing for his wife the woman "best calculated to make him a suitable companion." He was the father of "three smart children living" and, sadly, had "buried two little twin baby boys."[38]

Isaac (whom she called I.W.), then thirty-four, lived in Webster City, Iowa, with his wife, son, and daughter. After leaving the mercantile business in Chicago, he had established a grain business in Iowa. Packard reported that, by 1878, he had grown rich through profits of the several grain elevators he owned and employed his younger brothers, George and Arthur, as "clerks and partners" in "Packard Brothers" grain business.[39] Neither George nor Arthur, then twenty-five and twenty years old, was married at that time.

Packard told her readers that Samuel, age thirty-one, was "a very successful Christian lawyer" at the Chicago firm of Cooper, Packard and Gurley. He, too, had "a lovely wife" and a daughter, "dear little Stella." Packard again noted that Samuel had "repented of his disloyal act towards his mother," and now worked to further her reforms "by his legal knowledge" and as her "financial business agent."[40]

She was especially happy to note that her daughters-in-law, Mattie, Mary, and Clara, were "true and hearty sympathizer[s]" in her reform work. Each, she believed, held "a sincere and tender regard and respect for my character, personally, as their affectionate mother-in-law."[41]

Packard even managed a positive report on her daughter, Libby, who, she said, "like all my other children [has] good intellectual capacities" and a love for books. Libby wanted to be a teacher, but her health evidently precluded that. But, by 1878, Packard was able to write that, "by God's blessing" she now enjoyed "the inestimable blessing of a healthy, sound, naturally developed daughter for [her] solace and comfort in my future labors." She announced that Libby was going to become her "traveling companion and co-laborer" in her "book business and legislative work."[42]

Meanwhile, Packard reported that her husband was then living in Manteno, supported by their three oldest sons "as a boarder in Mr. M. Wright's family." She wrote that he was in poor health and suggested "his declining years" were spent in solitude "with but little of the solace of love and human sympathy to cheer his approach to his . . . lonely tomb." In a final dig, she recalled that his parents "were own cousins" and wondered "how much of the dark phases of his character" could be attributed to that fact of heredity.[43]

Despite Packard's best efforts, Andrew McFarland seemed by then to have moved beyond his humiliation at her hands and his professional reputation appeared unsullied. Several months before publication of Packard's *Great Drama,* McFarland, then sixty years old and recently widowed, presented his "Reminiscences and Reflections" on the history of the AMSAII to an appreciative audience at the Association's May 1877 meeting in St. Louis, Missouri.

In his address, he noted the achievements of the AMSAII, especially in perfecting the design and organization of hospitals for the insane and in reaching "substantial agreement" on the jurisprudence of insanity. He praised the Association for achieving unanimity in its aim and purpose as well as for the collegiality that fostered sharing of knowledge and experience within the profession. The objectives of their Association, he said, had been "abundantly reached."[44]

Colleagues recognized his address as a "labor of love towards those with whom he was so long connected."[45] It is clear that, for McFarland, the Association was like a closely knit family. Indeed, on the evening following his address, the Association was called to order to witness his marriage to Miss Abby King. His colleagues approved a congratulatory resolution that became part of the Association's proceedings for that year.[46] The couple returned to Oak Lawn Retreat, where McFarland continued to practice mental medicine and to monitor related legislation.

In March 1879, responding to reports from the recent legislative session, McFarland published an open letter to Illinois state representative Thomas P. Rogers of McLean County. Noting that Illinois now required physicians to be certified by the state Board of Health, he suggested that ample safeguards were in place to guarantee a doctor's integrity, making the Illinois jury trial law unnecessary. He reiterated his position that, public opinion to the contrary, false commitments were rare. Acknowledging that he was the "unwilling root" of the jury trial law, McFarland observed that countering charges of false commitment was "almost like fighting a phantom, which re-appears again, whole as ever, after the sword has gone through it."[47]

Meanwhile, with her book business booming and Libby's health improved, Packard resumed her legislative work. This time she took her crusade westward where, from 1879 to 1881, she campaigned for married women's rights in Washington Territory, Oregon, and Idaho Territory. She noted briefly that both Washington Territory (14 November 1879) and Oregon (20 October 1880) had passed legislation similar to the bill to equalize the rights of husbands and wives that she had introduced a decade earlier in Illinois.[48] Washington Territory also passed a postal rights law for asylum patients in 1879; however, Packard does not indicate her involvement, if any, in this legislation.[49]

In Oregon, she added to her cache of testimonials a note from a group of women expressing appreciation for her "great and noble work" in achieving passage of S.B. 42. The group gave her a gold watch and chain "as a slight token of esteem and regard."[50]

From Oregon, Packard traveled to Idaho Territory, where in December 1880 she presented her equal rights legislation to members of the Idaho legislature and the general public at the Methodist Episcopal church in Boise City. The *Boise Republican* reported that, for two hours, Packard "held the audience spell-bound, and every ear was intent on receiving her utterances, as she related her most remarkable experience, in a clear and forcible manner."[51]

But promoting equal rights proved difficult in Idaho Territory, and her bill failed when a group of legislators blocked its passage by invoking the "Bible argument for the subjection of the wife." She responded with a vitriolic thirty-five-page publication entitled *The Woman Hating Party in the Idaho Legislature Exposed!* This pamphlet, printed in Boise City in 1881, was vintage Packard, replete with testimonials from newspaper editors and politicians, arguments for her bill, castigation of her detractors, and the obligatory defense of her sanity. It included glowing reports from the *Idaho Democrat* and *Oregon Daily Bulletin* crediting her with passage of seventeen bills "in the same number of States and Territories." She pointed to her past successes and lauded the "manliness" of the legislators who had assisted her. She also named those in the Idaho legislature who did not support her or, worse yet, who had only pretended to support the bill.[52]

She related that her opponents had, on several occasions, canceled scheduled discussions of her bill without notice. This had apparently caused Packard much consternation as she tried to rally her cadre of supporters and "a company of ladies" that she had hired to keep transcripts of the floor debates.[53] She condemned her opponents as "unmanly" legislators who wanted their wives to remain subjugated to them. She assured the men that, "As your vote is cast on this question of the emancipation of woman, so will its record either consign your name to rot in oblivion, or it will be held in everlasting remembrance as your own well merited inheritance."[54] After twenty years of campaigning, Packard had lost none of her fire and enthusiasm.

Packard was in western legislatures at the same time as suffragists were there demanding the ballot and equal rights for women.[55] As usual she distanced herself from the suffragists and stressed the fact that, unlike the laws they proposed, her bill did not give women the right to vote, but would give them "equal rights in all else" with their husbands.[56]

However, in the *Woman Hating Party in the Idaho Legislature Exposed!* Packard suggested that the Idaho campaign led her to reconsider the question of woman's suffrage. She suggested that, if legislators there opposed fair laws protecting women, she would be forced to concede there was "but little hope for woman's cause, except through the ballot." Women, she warned them, would "be fairly driven by those who would be our protectors, to thus become our own protectors."[57] She told the legislators she hoped they would prefer her style of equal rights over such a prospect.[58]

In 1880, Libby Packard, then thirty years old and apparently in good health, married Henry Gordon of Portland, Oregon. Packard thus lost her "traveling companion and co-laborer." However, she named Libby as her West Coast book agent. An advertisement at the back of *The Women Hating Party in the Idaho Legislature Exposed!* directed buyers to send orders for Packard's publications to "Mrs. E. W. P. Gordon, 305 Market Street, Portland, Oregon," as well as to the Western News Company in Chicago and the Case, Lockwood, Brainard & Company in Hartford, Connecticut. The ad indicated that Packard paid her agents 15 percent commission on books and 20 percent on pamphlets. Four publications were listed: *The Great Drama* sold for $7, *Modern Persecu-*

tion for $5, *The Mystic Key* for $1, and *The Woman Hating Party in the Idaho Legislature Exposed!* was priced at 25 cents.

The AMSAII seems to have ignored Packard's work in the West. By the 1880s, her claims of despotism and abuse in American asylums were being echoed not only in the pamphlets and narratives of former patients, but in respected literary and medical journals. In addition, other professional groups, notably neurologists and social workers, now competed with the AMSAII for authority in matters related to the care of the mentally ill.

The New York Neurological Association (forerunner of the American Neurological Association), founded in 1872, viewed the AMSAII as a stodgy, narrow-minded autocracy that excluded non-institutional psychiatrists and neurologists from its membership, failed to encourage scientific research, and showed more interest in "plumbing and heating apparatus than in active therapeutic measures."[59] The National Conference of Charities (predecessor of the National Association of Social Workers) formed two years later and joined the chorus, urging increased regulation of institutions for the insane.[60] An alliance between these two groups led to founding of the National Association for the Protection of the Insane and the Prevention of Insanity. Founded in Boston in 1880, this group denounced the "supreme control and somewhat arrogant guardianship" exercised over the insane by asylum superintendents.[61]

Thus, Packard's menace to the AMSAII in her endeavors as an "independent humanitarian" faded somewhat as the superintendents shifted their defense to attacks from these reputable and increasingly vocal organizations. In a paper presented at the 1881 meeting of the AMSAII, Orpheus Everts (Cincinnati, Ohio, asylum) noted criticism that had recently appeared in publications such as the *Medical Record* and the *Journal of Mental and Nervous Disease* (organization of the American Neurological Association), which characterized the AMSAII as "unscientific and selfish in character and purpose." These critics also described the AMSAII as "a closed corporation" and "a power as autocratic and domineering in asylum medicine and asylum politics throughout the Union, as are the authorities of each institution behind their own walls and locks."[62] Everts launched the Association's standard defense against these new critics denigrating them, as the Association had once dismissed Packard, as "born agitators" and "professional reformers, who live and move upon the borderland of insanity . . . ever intent upon turning the world upside down."[63]

Evert's defense was largely aimed at an article entitled "Despotism in Lunatic Asylums" published in the respected *North American Review.*[64] The article, penned by social reformer Dorman Eaton, denounced American asylums as "a vicious and defective system . . . which excludes light and wisdom from without and breeds and screens abuses within the circle of administration."[65] Eaton applauded the recent founding of the National Association for the Protection of the Insane and Prevention of Insanity (of which he was a member) with the hope that it would help lift "the grave question of insanity . . . from the secrecy, the mystery, and the professional metaphysics of the asylums and the doctors" into the light of "public debate and criticism."[66]

Within the AMSAII, a few younger members showed a willingness to confront such criticism with corrective action. For example, Dr. J. Z. Gerhard of Harrisburg, Pennsylvania, while hesitating "as a very young member of this Association" to speak "in the presence of so many old members," suggested that the superintendents might perhaps be blinded to criticism by their own good intentions. Gerhard continued, "There is a feeling sometimes among men who are engaged in any special work that they are doing just right, that they have reached the highest point of excellence, and that there is no room for progress or advancement."[67] Citing "radical changes" implemented by the legislature of his home state, Gerhard noted that while some superintendents in the state were not sympathetic to the changes, others intended to give the reforms "a fair chance with the hope also that they may be a success."[68]

Despite such glimmers of openness to reform, most attending the AMSAII's 1881 meeting joined Orpheus Everts in roundly condemning the Association's critics. They concluded, perhaps with more hope than confidence, that Eaton's unfair criticism, like that of "the pamphleteers generally," would be recognized by "unprejudiced and intelligent readers" as "coarse," "crude," and "baseless."[69]

Packard had by then disappeared from the proceedings of the AMSAII, but her message resonated through the voices of the new organizations and individuals demanding change in America's system of care for the mentally ill. The AMSAII would continue in its defensive position almost to the turn of the century; but the impetus for reform had been sown, both within and without the profession.

16 Final Campaigns

THERE IS CONSIDERABLE EVIDENCE that Packard's legislative activities continued during the 1880s and 1890s. An article in the *Atchison Daily Champion* notes that she appeared before the Kansas legislature in 1881 "to secure additional legal protection for married women and for inmates of insane asylums."[1]

In 1883 she sent an "Open Letter to the Legislatures of Nebraska, Kansas, and Colorado," requesting passage of a postal rights bill and a bill to protect the personal identity of married women. The letter included statements of support from ministers, doctors, and lawyers along with signatures of 804 legal voters. One testimonial noted that the bills would "secure to American people some of their most sacred liberties," while another praised the married women's "Identity Act" as "a cure for the woman suffrage complaint."[2]

In the letter, Packard noted that she had presented these bills in four other states during the past winter. The Nebraska legislature evidently responded with passage of postal rights legislation.[3] Senator L. E. Finch introduced her bills in the Kansas legislature; however, neither bill was enacted that year.[4]

There is some evidence that she turned her attention to the South and successfully shepherded two bills through the South Carolina legislature in December 1884.[5] By February 1885, she was in Raleigh, North Carolina, where she addressed the state Senate Judiciary Committee in support of a bill to establish the "legal identity and personality of married women." The local newspaper reported Packard was "a fine talker" who was "calm, deliberate and self possessed." The writer added that it was the "most interesting committee meeting" that had occurred or would occur during that legislative session.[6]

In May 1886 Packard was back in Illinois, staying at the Leland Hotel in Springfield. A Springfield newspaper reported that she had traveled to nearby Jacksonville "with a lady friend and her lawyer, Judge S. R. Moore, of Kankakee," to confront Andrew McFarland. The article explained that Packard felt "hampered in her humane work" by McFarland, and was now trying to extract from him a written promise to stop libeling her by calling her insane.[7] McFarland refused to sign any such document and Moore instituted suit against him in Packard's behalf, claiming $25,000 damages for libel. The editor opined that this "was quite considerate, when this claim might easily have been $50,000."[8]

McFarland told a *Chicago Tribune* reporter that he had received Packard and her companions "courteously" at his Oak Lawn asylum and confirmed that he had been summoned to appear at the Kankakee County Circuit Court the coming September. He suggested that the whole thing was a publicity stunt to sell books.[9]

Kankakee County Circuit Court records confirm that Summons No. 7881 was delivered in the case of *Elizabeth P.W. Packard v. Andrew McFarland and others*. Abijah Dole, John Ure, and William Schrock were also named as defendants. The suit claimed the men had attempted "to impair and utterly destroy" Packard's book business and humanitarian work in a "false, scandalous, malicious and defamatory article" published in the *Newark Sunday Call* in December 1885.[10]

The fragmentary records of the case still extant at Kankakee County court house appear to have been written by Stephen Moore. The evidence presented appears to be a rehash of the testimony and depositions given during and immediately following Packard's 1864 trial. The available records do not indicate a verdict in the case.

After enduring twenty years of personal attacks, it is unclear why Packard chose this time to sue McFarland and other detractors. It may have been, as McFarland suggested, an effort to draw publicity to her cause or to generate material for a new book. There is no evidence that suggests she was in financial distress at the time.

Perhaps the most interesting information gleaned from records of the suit is the physical description of Packard offered by one witness for the defense. He described his encounter with Packard as she canvassed for her books in New Jersey in 1885: "She is at least sixty-five years of age . . . but in the dark hair she wears there is not one thread of silver. Intelligence and shrewdness gleam in her brown eyes . . . Her features are thin and sharp." This somewhat witch-like image of the diminutive Packard, who was actually seventy years old at the time, suggests the strength she still projected as well as the trepidation she inspired in her opponents.[11]

In his statement regarding the suit, Abijah Dole indicated that Theophilus Packard was near death at the Doles' Manteno home. Theophilus died three months later and was buried in a family plot in Manteno's Elmwood Cemetery where a small rectangular stone bears his name and dates of birth and death. An obituary in the *Congregational Year-Book* provides the dates of his schooling, marriage, and ministerial appointments and states that he died of consumption at the age of eighty-three.[12]

No will is on record for Theophilus Packard. Apparently, his diary and collection of theological books were the only legacy he hoped to leave his children. He noted in the diary that he had left marginal notes in volumes by theologian Jonathan Edwards "for my beloved children." He hoped that they would "remember [that] those books reflect in general what their father believed, loved and enjoyed."[13]

Packard's reaction to her husband's death is unknown. By April 1886 she was again on the East Coast campaigning for postal rights legislation. Writing from Annapolis, Maryland, she sent "An Open Letter to the Members of Maryland Legislature" urging passage of S.B. 181 and opposing H.B. 122. She argued that the latter bill, which had been proposed by the Maryland Board of Lunacy, was "a pretence—designed for the very purpose of supplanting, and thus defeating the just and humane object of the Postal Rights bill." She declared that asylum patients did not "want a Board of Lunacy to stand between them and the laws already enacted for the protection of personal liberty." Instead, she continued, they want "direct access to these laws, as a personal right."[14]

By 1888 Packard was back in the nation's capital, testifying before the Senate Judiciary Committee. In a memorial on the "Emancipation of Married Women by Congress" she urged passage of S.B. 2174, which would "change the common-law or marriage to the custom of modern civilization by the emancipation of married women."[15] The report that accompanied that House version of the bill indicates that the bill was tabled because similar laws were already in effect.[16]

The next evidence of Packard's whereabouts is a letter that she sent to Samuel's wife, Clara, in December 1888 from a Minneapolis hotel. The letter recalled an earlier visit with their "happy family." She also enclosed $50, saying, "It affords me pleasure to bestow this gift upon one so deserving of appreciation, as a Christian mother, and a philanthropist."[17]

By that time Samuel and Clara Packard were respected members of Oak Park's upper class, and both apparently possessed his mother's dedication to reform. In addition to various church activities, Clara was active in the temperance movement and also served as president of Oak Park's Nineteenth-Century Woman's Club. Packard told Clara, "You like me, seem to have had your field of labor assigned by the providence of God," and added: "It is ennobling to work for Christ, and if ever you have to suffer for him, as I have done, you will then, and only till then, know how to sympathize with me. But thank God! I have learned to live without human sympathy and without appreciation . . . To have God's approval is my sole ambition."[18]

Packard told Clara she planned to be in Chicago later that month to meet with an old friend from Shelburne. It would be a brief visit, she wrote with a hint of sadness, since she "had no home in Chicago to invite her into." (Apparently, her Prairie Avenue house was still rented out at the time.) She was planning to stay at the Windsor Hotel in Chicago and invited Clara to join her there.

Packard wrote that she was planning "to return to her field of labor at St. Paul" when the legislature resumed the first week of January 1889, but did not indicate the nature of the legislation she intended to pursue in Minnesota. She closed the letter saying she hoped her dear grandchildren would never forget their grandmother, "who feels quite proud of them."[19]

Packard evidently returned to her home on Prairie Avenue later that year. The *Chicago Daily Inter Ocean* reported in September 1889 that the house had been burglarized. Among the items stolen was the treasured watch given to her by the women of Oregon upon passage of her married woman's rights legislation there in 1880. Packard offered a reward for return of "this beloved testimonial of public appreciation and esteem," saying that she carried it with her and often used it in talking about her woman's rights efforts.[20]

There is evidence that Packard continued her legislative activities as late as 1891. In Indiana, she argued in support of a bill to protect patients' postal rights, prevent false incarceration of the sane, and impose penalties on those who violated provisions of this law.[21] Meanwhile, she continued to oppose efforts by the superintendents' lobby to overturn her jury trial law in Illinois. Although not mentioned by name, she was clearly a concern of physicians attending a joint meeting of the Chicago Medical Society and Medico-Legal Society of Chicago in February 1891.

Under discussion at this meeting was H.B. 5555, which sought to amend Packard's 1867 Personal Liberty Law to make the jury trial for commitment optional. Section five of the bill stated that lunacy inquests by jury or commission should be at the discretion of the court, except "when a jury shall be demanded by the person alleged to be insane or by any person acting in his interest."[22]

In support of this measure, Dr. Richard Dewey summarized the usual arguments against jury trials for commitment. Dr. Archibald Church related horror stories of abuse endured by patients as they traveled to court for trial, and Dr. D. R. Brower admitted that he circumvented the law by sending his patients to out-of-state institutions for treatment.[23]

However, the doctors were not optimistic about passage of H.B. 5555. Dr. James G. Kiernan reminded colleagues that there was "a female paranoiac in Springfield armed with a recommendation from every newspaper proprietor in this city, who will work tooth and nail against a modification of the jury trial law."[24]

Brower agreed with Kiernan that any amendment was unlikely to succeed at the moment. He added: "Dr. Kiernan has told you of a lady, who is now at Springfield, and just the moment the Medical Society starts this agitation [to change the law] she goes to Springfield and stays there and she has more power with the legislature there than the entire medical fraternity in the State of Illinois. I quite indorse Dr. Kiernan's classification of her."[25]

The doctors agreed that a committee should be appointed "to investigate the whole question" and hoped they could "formulate some law" that might "satisfy the opposition." Perhaps, Brower suggested, it would "be sufficient to simply ask the legislature to give the judge discretionary power, in cases that do not demand a jury trial, to order an investigation by a commission of physicians at some other place than the court-house," for example, at the patient's home.[26]

Kiernan suggested that they should adopt the method used successfully in New York, which was "to recommend appointment of a commission to investigate and report upon the whole subject to the next legislature."[27] He believed such a commission would give more weight to the doctors' recommendation and could also frame laws for later passage that could not be passed now. Anticipating Packard's argument against such a law, Kiernan conceded, "The arguments of that paranoiac would be stronger than those of a dozen physicians."[28]

In the end, the group agreed to send resolutions to the legislature asking that Illinois commitment law be modified "to conform somewhat" with laws in "successful and satisfactory operation in the states of New York and Wisconsin." They also appointed a committee to lobby for modifications to law.

At the end of February 1891, Packard sent a printed letter to the Illinois legislature in support of legislation to secure postal rights for asylum patients. The *Chicago Tribune* reported much of the contents of the letter, which detailed her "celebrated case." However, in April the *Tribune* reported that "the Packard bill" aimed at securing postal privileges for Illinois asylum patients was tabled by the Illinois Senate's Committee on State Charitable Institutions.

This action followed testimony by Dr. Richard Dewey, a nationally respected Illinois psychiatrist.[29]

The asylum superintendents' efforts were further rewarded in 1893 as the Illinois legislature amended Packard's Personal Liberty Law to make the jury trial optional.[30] Despite claims by the AMSAII, it is inaccurate to say that the Personal Liberty law was "overturned" since the amended law continued to require a jury trial upon the request of the person alleged insane or someone acting in that person's behalf.[31] The 1893 law also provided for the postal rights of asylum patients. In addition, it provided for two, court-appointed medical commissioners to examine the patient and report their findings. The court could order all those not directly involved in the case to leave the courtroom during the inquest. The law required hospitals for the insane to maintain a record of all restraint or seclusion of patients and specified that only the physician in charge could apply the restraint. And, for the first time in Illinois, the 1893 law provided for voluntary commitment.[32] Packard apparently did not contest the new law, which still implemented, in one form or another, many of her recommendations.

Andrew McFarland did not live to see the successful effort to amend the Illinois jury trial law. In November 1891 he hanged himself in an upstairs room of Oak Lawn Retreat. The coroner's jury ruled that the cause of death was "death by strangulation . . . while suffering from mental aberration."[33]

The *Jacksonville Journal* reported that he had suffered a head injury during a fire at the Retreat some years earlier, after which he was "much troubled with his head." His son, George, testified at the coroner's inquest that his father "had been much depressed in spirits for some time" and was troubled about the financial condition of the Retreat.[34] Indeed, McFarland's last years were difficult. His marriage to Abby King had ended in less than four years with an ugly divorce in which she claimed physical and emotional abuse. She demanded an "equal share" of their house and property as well as an equal share in profits from his business during their marriage and "a reasonable sum of money . . . for her support and maintenance."[35] However, McFarland's countersuit prevailed, and Abby King disappeared from his life with no share of his house or business.[36]

Following a funeral at Oak Lawn Retreat, McFarland was buried at Diamond Grove Cemetery in Jacksonville.[37] There his grave is marked by an impressive monument that replicates the roofline of the main building of Oak Lawn Retreat, which McFarland adapted from Melrose Abbey near Edinburgh, Scotland.[38] Today, McFarland is memorialized in the naming of the Andrew McFarland Mental Health Center in Springfield, Illinois.[39]

Packard's feelings about McFarland's death and the changes to her Personal Liberty Law in Illinois can only be surmised. Her son, Samuel, reported that, during the early 1890s, she "kept house" in her Prairie Avenue home, leaving on occasion to visit her children and grandchildren.[40]

In July 1893 she sent a note to the *Chicago Inter Ocean,* saying that she was resting at home from her legislative work and would be happy to provide friends visiting Chicago for the World's Fair "such accommodations as she [could] furnish." In return, she asked only that they purchase or help sell some of her books and pamphlets.[41]

In February 1895, her home was again burglarized. This time, Packard was badly beaten during the robbery. The *New York Times* reported that she was in Chicago's Hahnemann Hospital suffering from a broken arm and other injuries sufficiently severe that her recovery was in question.[42] The iron-willed reformer did recover, only to face other difficulties.

Within the year, Libby Packard Gordon again succumbed to derangement and was placed in a California asylum. About this time she was also divorced from Harry Gordon. Packard traveled to California and removed her daughter from the asylum with the intention of caring for her.[43] For several months they lived at the Pasadena home of Theo Packard, who was by then a widower with four teenage children. His daughter, Ina, recalled that her father constructed a five by ten enclosure with webbed wire, "just large enough for a cot and a table," for Libby in Packard's bedroom. Ina wrote that "Aunt Lizzie" usually did not talk much, but sometimes "would be quite noisy, and disturb Grandma while she was asleep." Ina was embarrassed that "all the neighbors were well aware" an insane person was living with them.[44]

However, Ina was proud of her grandmother's books and advocacy on behalf of the insane. "Grandma was not insane," she wrote, "but in those days husbands could do what they pleased with their wives." She related the saga as her grandmother had told it to her: "Grandpa Packard . . . believed that if a baby was born it should be immediately baptized or it would go to Hell, but Grandma did not believe that and in her Sunday School class did not teach that. Well, that made Grandpa angry, so he put her in the insane asylum . . . Grandma Packard has told me personally, she was no more insane than you or I."[45] Ina recalled that her Grandmother "could show a record of $50,000.00 from the sale of those books."[46]

In the summer of 1897, Packard evidently decided to return to Chicago with Libby. The train trip back was arduous as the frail Packard, now eighty-one years old, struggled to control her troubled daughter. Less than a week after their return, Elizabeth Packard's crusades for married women and the mentally ill ended. She died 26 July at Hahnemann Hospital in Chicago from complications following surgery for a strangulated hernia.[47]

Packard's obituary in the *Kankakee Times* recounted her life story, saying, "Mr. Packard and the deacons . . . believed her insane, but the neighbors in Manteno did not . . . The general impression is that Mr. Packard was mildly insane, himself and that his actions nearly drove his wife insane."[48]

The *Chicago Tribune* carried news of Packard's death on page two with the headline, "Wise Friend of the Insane Is Dead." The article reported that she had earned "thousands of dollars and spent much of it" in her work in behalf of the insane. It credited her with introducing thirty-four bills "in as many states."[49]

The next day the *Tribune* noted that Packard's funeral had been held at the First Presbyterian Church in Chicago with burial at Rosehill Cemetery. Noting her reputation as "a good business woman and a philanthropist," the *Tribune* lauded, "Although not a rich woman she spent during her life $25,000 in her work for the insane."[50]

Packard left no will, but probate records indicate she left an estate valued at $15,700 to her five living children. It included the house on Prairie Avenue, valued at $10,000, and the property in Springfield, valued at $3,000. Among other assets was $59.44 collected from Case, Lockwood & Brainard Co. for 2,320 pounds of plates and 144 books. Packard's total personal property, including furniture, was valued at $93.50.[51]

Samuel acted as executor of his mother's estate and it was undoubtedly he who selected her gravestone. The modest gray stone bears no scripture or reference to her career as a writer and reformer. It is marked instead with the simple epitaph, "Mother."

CONCLUSION

The great drama of Elizabeth Packard's life is indeed a tale of triumph and tragedy. In her books she framed herself as a heroine who by her own effort and ability overcame great odds to become a successful writer and reformer. She claimed agency in the choices and consequences of her life, saying, "I deliberately chose to obey God rather than man, and in that choice I made shipwreck of all my earthly good things."[52] But, although she relished her victories over her husband, her doctor, and "the asylum system," her personal life was never easy. Valuing home and family, she was able to enjoy little of either in the latter half of her life.

However, by the beginning of the twentieth century the spirit, if not the letter, of Packard's laws to protect the civil rights of the mentally ill was evident across the nation in more stringent commitment procedures, oversight commissions, visiting committees, and a greater degree of privacy with regard to patients' mail. Her success was in part a matter of timing as her voice was added to a crescendo of criticism that asylum superintendents found increasingly difficult to dismiss as the babbling of deranged minds. Packard was also more persistent than most, both in publishing and selling her books and in persuading important individuals to support her legislation. By its breadth, persistence, and general credibility, her crusade consolidated the public outcry, activated official inquiry, and led to corrective action.

Her increasingly vocal and wide-ranging criticism could not have begun at a less convenient moment for the psychiatric profession. Unfolding as questions about the efficacy of asylums were emerging, her compelling story quickly became a dramatic symbol that seemed to affirm the public's worst fears about asylums. Her intimations of fraud and abuse captured the attention of the taxpayers and legislators responsible for asylum funding.

She infuriated asylum superintendents by challenging their authority and competence just as they were trying to establish themselves as a profession. They could no longer, as they had done for decades, base a diagnosis of insanity only on opinion backed by upright professional and personal character as vouchsafed by an attained professional position. Packard's case also raised the professional debate over what some superintendents came to call the "bugbear" of moral insanity to a fevered pitch. Her critique of asylums and asylum superintendents clearly added impetus to efforts within the psychiatric profession to clarify definitions and diagnosis of insanity and to improve patient care.

Packard's political intuition was superb. Certainly, some of her political allies were as intent on their own political motives as they were convinced by the "intrinsic merits" of her arguments. Nevertheless, she was able to maneuver adeptly through the legislative process, learning from her successes and failures while pressing relentlessly for reform.

Packard's business acumen was equally impressive as she marketed her publications personally and through the press. Her writing, despite its occasional allegorical meanderings, skillfully captured the rhetoric of liberty and accommodated it to her compelling personal drama. The arguments of asylum superintendents seemed petulant and self-serving when heard alongside Packard's drumbeat on "the sacredness of personal liberty." In taking personal liberty as her motto and liberty of conscience as her creed, Packard drew on the most deeply held convictions of republican citizens. The rhetoric of liberty had worked in the Revolution, had worked in abolition of slavery, and it worked for Elizabeth Packard in her advocacy for the civil rights of the mentally ill and married women.

EPILOGUE—THE PACKARD CHILDREN

The Packard children received a mixed legacy from their ill-suited parents. Immediately following her mother's death, Libby Packard Gordon was placed in the Illinois Eastern Hospital for the Insane at Kankakee, a cottage-style asylum. Her brother Isaac served as her conservator. She died there in 1901 from chronic kidney disease.[53]

According to family members, Theo became a Spiritualist and "free lover" who "embarrassed the family by living with a woman not his wife." Isaac (Ira) also lived in Pasadena with his wife and children, Herbert and Mabel. Reportedly he committed suicide "at an advanced age, due to great suffering from cancer which he probably refused to treat . . . since he was a reader in the Christian Science church."[54]

George, who never married, contracted tuberculosis and preceded his mother in death in 1889.[55] Arthur, Packard's youngest son, settled with his wife, Emily, and two sons in Iowa, where he was a station agent for the Rock Island Railway. He later moved to Avoca, Illinois. Family members remembered him as "a mild, unimpressive sort of man" who eventually committed suicide.[56]

Of the Packard children, Samuel seems to have been most like his mother in temperament and reform spirit. He was remembered in the family as "a first rate story teller" with "a flashing blue eye, almost hypnotic and compelling" who fascinated his children with tales of buffalo hunting in Colorado.[57] Among the most notable achievements of his long legal career was the Yankton bond case in 1879, in which he represented investors who had purchased railroad bonds from Yankton County in Dakota Territory. Samuel took the investors' case to the U.S. Supreme Court and won.[58] However, refunds to the investors were obstructed by special legislation in the Dakota legislature. Using his mother's methods, Samuel petitioned the U.S. Congress and flooded the nation with letters and pamphlets opposing statehood for South Dakota. The state finally capitulated and, in 1883, passed legislation refunding the bondholders.[59]

In 1898 Samuel, as legal counsel for John Alexander Dowie (an Australian minister who preached a gospel of "Divine Healing"), was instrumental in establishing Dowie's utopian religious community, Zion City, north of Chicago. Later, Samuel interceded with authorities to permit a group of English lace makers to immigrate to Zion City. As a result of this case, the alien contract labor law was amended, despite opposition from Samuel Gompers and the American Federation of Labor.[60]

Two years later, after nearly a decade as Dowie's legal counsel, Samuel quietly dissociated himself from Dowie and rejoined the First Congregational Church Oak Park, Illinois.[61] He served as a deacon and Sunday school superintendent, and was remembered as "the single largest contributor" to the church.[62] He was an ardent advocate of temperance and a supporter of the Anti-Saloon League. Samuel was also a peace advocate and, in a 1915 booklet entitled *Plan for Permanent Peace by the Disarmament of Every Nation in the World,* proposed a plan for an international organization similar to the League of Nations, but with authority to enforce its edicts. In 1910, Samuel and Clara moved to Pasadena, California, where they continued to be active in the church and community. Samuel Packard died at his home in Pasadena in 1937 at the age of ninety.

Notes

Introduction

1. Neely and McMurtry, *Insanity File,* 21, 26. See also Baker, *Mary Todd Lincoln,* 221. For the best recent study of Mary Lincoln's mental illness, see Emerson, *Madness of Mary Lincoln.*

2. Slovenko, "Highlights in the History of Law and Psychiatry," 464.

3. See Hatch, *Democratization of American Christianity;* Wacker, *Religion in 19th Century America;* and Butler, *Awash in a Sea of Faith.*

4. For more on the development of institutional care and treatment of the insane, see works by Deutsch, Digby, Dwyer, Grob, Hurd, McGovern, and Tomes cited in the bibliography.

5. Jennifer Levison refers to Packard similarly as a "border woman." See Levison, "Elizabeth Parsons Ware Packard," 1075.

6. See Stanton et al., *History of Woman Suffrage* I, 465. See also Dixon, *Perfecting the Family,* 1997.

7. Packard, *Exposure,* 112.

8. Deutsch, *Mentally Ill in America,* 424n.

9. See Dunton, "Mrs. Packard and Her Influence," 419–23.

10. Ibid., 423.

11. Dunton, "Further Note on Mrs. Packard," 192–93.

12. Dewey, "Jury Law for Commitment," 575.

13. Ibid., 572–73.

14. Ibid., 581.

15. Deutsch, *Mentally Ill in America,* 306–7, 424n.

16. Szasz, *Manufacture of Madness,* 131.

17. Chesler, *Women and Madness,* 101.

18. Himelhoch and Shaffer, "Elizabeth Packard," 343–75.

19. Geller, "Women's Accounts of Psychiatric Illness," 1056, 1061.

20. Geller and Harris, *Women of the Asylum,* 7–8. For other anthologies that include excerpts from Packard's books, see Shannonhouse and Cullen-DuPont.

21. Huber, *Questions of Power,* 53.

22. Letter, J. C. Burnham to Barbara Sapinsley, 13 June 1971.

23. Ibid.

24. Wood, *Writing on the Wall,* 15, 30.

25. Levison, "Elizabeth Parsons Ware Packard," 1075.

26. Neely and McMurtry, *Insanity File,* 19–21, 26, 68, 108.

27. Friedman, *America's First Woman Lawyer*, 205–8.

28. Lightner, *Asylum, Prison, and Poorhouse*, 108, 114–17.

29. Hartog, *Man & Wife in America*, 123–24.

30. Basch, *Framing American Divorce*, 74–75.

31. Barton, *History and Influence*, 64.

32. Johnson, *Out of Bedlam*, 11–12.

33. Grob, *Mad Among Us*, 94, 133.

Chapter 1. "All the Love His Bachelor Heart Could Muster"

1. Packard, *Great Drama* III, 36.

2. *Catalogue of Amherst Female Seminary*, 7.

3. Packard, *Great Drama* III, 250.

4. Packard, *Exposure*, 36, 38.

5. Dunglison, *Dictionary of Medical Science*, 374, 667.

6. Ibid.

7. Commitment form for Elizabeth Parsons Ware, Worcester Insane Asylum Records. Used by permission of the Massachusetts Department of Mental Health. See also Deutsch, *Mentally Ill in America*, 149; Grob, *Mental Institutions in America*, 102; and Barton, *History and Influence*, 168.

8. Patient record No. 404, 1836, Worcester Insane Asylum Records.

9. Ibid.

10. Felter, *Eclectic Materia Medica*.

11. Dunglison, *Dictionary of Medical Science*, 565.

12. Patient record No. 404, 1836, Worcester Insane Asylum Records.

13. Ibid.

14. Dunglison, *Dictionary of Medical Science*, 60.

15. Packard, *Exposure*, 38–39.

16. Gosling and Ray, "The Right To Be Sick," 256–58. See also Smith-Rosenberg and Rosenberg, "The Female Animal," 332–56; and Smith-Rosenberg, "The Hysterical Woman," 652–78.

17. Packard, *Exposure*, 38.

18. Packard, *Modern Persecution* I, 77.

19. Packard, *Great Drama* II, 190.

20. Packard, *Great Drama* IV, 170.

21. Theophilus Packard, Diary, 2, 12–14.

22. Ibid., 11.

23. Tyler, *History of Amherst College*, 24–25, passim; and Theophilus Packard, Sr., letters to Mary Lyon, 26 March, 13 May and July 1834, Mary Lyon Collection.

24. Theophilus Packard, Diary, 14–15.

25. Ibid., 19, 29–30.

26. Ibid., 38, 40.

27. Ibid., 46–47, 55.

28. Dorrien, *Making of American Liberal Theology,* 346; Theophilus Packard, Diary, 61, 63.

29. Theophilus Packard, Diary, 63–66.

30. Dunglison, *Dictionary of Medical Science,* 308.

31. Theophilus Packard, Diary, 68.

32. Ibid., 69.

33. Ibid., 72–74.

34. Ibid., 74–75.

35. Ibid., 5.

36. Ibid., 182.

37. Ibid., 101–3.

38. Ibid., 106–7.

39. Ibid., 122.

40. Ibid., 77–78.

41. Ibid., 80; and Dorrien, *Making of American Liberal Theology,* 184.

42. Hatch, *Democratization of American Christianity,* 17.

43. Smith, *Revivalism & Social Reform,* 26–27; and Dorrien, *Making of American Liberal Theology,* 184.

44. Theophilus Packard, Diary, 81.

Chapter 2. "New Notions and Wild Vagaries"

1. Theophilus Packard, Diary, 147.

2. Packard, *Great Drama* IV, 68.

3. Theophilus Packard, Diary, 155. He traced his genealogy to Samuel Packard, who came "with his wife and child from Windham, England, in 1638, to Hingham in the Plymouth Colony," and proudly named his third son after this ancestor.

4. Ibid., 49.

5. Ibid., 51–52.

6. Butler, *Awash in a Sea of Faith,* 188.

7. Theophilus Packard, Diary, 159.

8. Ibid., 64.

9. Ibid., 175–76. Joseph Bellamy (1719–90), Samuel Hopkins (1721–1803), Ashahel Nettleton, Bennet Tyler (1783–58), and Timothy Dwight (1752–1817).

10. Packard, *Great Drama* III, 40.

11. Ibid., 40.

12. Ibid., 36.

13. Ibid., 39, 42.

14. Theophilus Packard, Diary, 147.

15. Packard, *Great Drama* III, 224.

16. Theophilus Packard, Diary, 151.

17. Packard, *Great Drama* II, 104.

18. Theophilus Packard, Diary, 152.

19. Ibid., 155.

20. Packard, *Great Drama* III, 375.

21. Theophilus Packard, Diary, 156.

22. Ibid., 157–58.

23. Packard, *Great Drama* II, 288.

24. Theophilus Packard, Diary, 161.

25. Packard, *Great Drama* II, 249.

26. Ibid., 250.

27. See Ryan, *Cradle of the Middle Class;* Welter, "Cult of True Womanhood," 151–74; and Kerber, "Separate Spheres," 9–39.

28. See Kelley, *Private Woman, Public Stage,* passim.

29. Packard, *Modern Persecution* II, 161.

30. See Tonkovich, *Domesticity with a Difference,* xi–xvi.

31. Beecher, *Treatise on Domestic Economy,* 2–3.

32. Tocqueville, *Democracy in America,* 566.

33. See Lerner, *Creation of Feminist Consciousness.*

34. Beecher, *Treatise on Domestic Economy,* 9.

35. Theophilus Packard, Diary, 161.

36. Ibid., 86.

37. Ibid.

38. Ibid.

39. Packard, *Great Drama* I, 363.

40. Ibid., 239.

41. Gaustad, *Documentary History of Religion,* 280, 283.

42. For more on Transcendentalism, see Capper and Wright, *Transient and Permanent.*

43. For more on American revivalism, see Smith, *Revivalism and Social Reform;* Hatch, *Democratization of American Christianity;* and Butler, *Awash in a Sea of Faith.*

44. For more on Spiritualism, see Brown, *Heyday of Spiritualism;* Moore, *In Search of White Crows;* Carroll, *Spiritualism in Antebellum America;* Braude, *Radical Spirits;* and McGarry, *Ghosts of Futures Past.*

45. Theophilus Packard, *History of the Churches and Ministers,* 322–56.

Chapter 3. Breaking the Mold

1. Packard, *Great Drama* II, 247.

2. Ibid., 297.

3. Ibid., 300–301.

4. Packard, *Great Drama* IV, 113, 145.

5. Theophilus Packard, Diary, 162.

6. Ibid.

7. At the time, Oberlin had Preparatory, Collegiate, and Seminary divisions. Given Theo's age, he probably was enrolled in preparatory classes.

8. For discussion of the Holiness Revival at Oberlin, see Smith, *Revivalism & Social Reform,* 103–13.

9. Theophilus Packard, Diary, 87.

10. Ibid., 162, 86.

11. Packard, *Great Drama* I, 238.

12. Ibid., 240.

13. Packard, *Great Drama* II, 247–48.

14. Packard, *Great Drama* I, 239.

15. Packard, *Great Drama* II, 207.

16. Ibid., 203.

17. Packard, *Mystic Key,* 46.

18. Packard, *Great Drama* I, 238, 240. She was alluding to the Old Testament figure Uzzah, the chief priest whose priestly power did not protect him from death when he dared to touch the Ark of the Covenant. See II Samuel 6:3–8.

19. Sage, *History of Iowa,* 55.

20. Ibid., 56.

21. Theophilus Packard, Diary, 88.

22. Sage, *History of Iowa,* 310 (Table 18.1).

23. Theophilus Packard, Diary, 164.

24. Packard, *Mystic Key,* 24–25.

25. Packard, *Exposure,* 100.

26. Packard, *Great Drama* II, 99; and Packard, *Great Drama* IV, 126.

27. Packard, *Modern Persecution* II, 166.

28. Packard, *Great Drama* IV, 126.

29. Ibid., 266.

30. Ibid., 124.

31. Ibid., 260–61.

32. Ibid., 261.

33. Ibid.

34. Ibid., 258.

35. Ibid., 118–19.

36. Ibid., 259.

37. Theophilus Packard, Diary, 163–64.

38. Sage, *History of Iowa,* 138.

39. Theophilus Packard, Diary, 164.

40. Ibid.

41. For more on Swedenborg, see Sigstedt, *Swedenborg Epic*; and Sig Synnestvedt, *Essential Swedenborg.*

42. Noyes, *History of American Socialisms,* 540.

43. Theophilus Packard, Diary, 164.

Chapter 4. Free Love and True Womanhood

1. "Brief Historical Sketch . . . First Presbyterian Church of Manteno," 2–3; and *Historical Sketches . . . First Presbyterian Church of Manteno,* passim.

2. Theophilus Packard, Diary, 165.

3. *Historical Sketches . . . First Presbyterian Church of Manteno,* 2.

4. Ibid., 2–3.

5. Ibid., 92.

6. Ibid., 167.

7. Ibid., 165.

8. Packard, *Great Drama* III, 20.

9. Ibid.

10. Ibid., 26–27.

11. Packard, *Great Drama* I, 332.

12. Packard, *Great Drama* III, 20.

13. Ibid., 26.

14. Ibid., 21.

15. Packard, *Modern Persecution* II, 167.

16. Packard, *Great Drama* III, 22.

17. Braude, *Radical Spirits,* 39–40.

18. Packard, *Great Drama* I, 46.

19. Packard, *Great Drama* IV, 210.

20. Packard, *Great Drama* I, 52.

21. Braude, "News from the Spirit World," 399–462. *Shekinah* was also the title of a Spiritualist periodical published in Connecticut and New York between 1851 and 1853.

22. Packard, *Great Drama* II, 331–32.

23. Lerner, *Creation of Feminist Consciousness,* 88–115, especially 90–93, 101–5.

24. James, *Varieties of Religious Experience,* 379–429, especially 380–82.

25. Packard, *Prisoner's Hidden Life,* 14.

26. Lerner, *Creation of Feminist Consciousness,* 142–66.

27. Packard, *Great Drama* II, 39–40.

28. Braude, *Radical Spirits,* 119.

29. Ibid., 117, 129, 140.

30. Packard, *Modern Persecution* II, 151.

31. Ibid., 151–52.

32. Ibid., 152.

33. Ibid., 152, 165.

34. Frances "Fanny" Wright, a Scotswoman who immigrated to the United States in 1818, became notorious as one of the first women to speak from a public stage. Her subjects were equally controversial since she opposed religion and favored abolition of slavery.

35. Letter, Angelina Grimke to Jane Smith, 17 December 1836, in Sklar, *Women's Rights Emerges,* 91.

36. See letter, Elizabeth Cady Stanton to Sarah Grimke and Angelina Grimke Weld, 25 June 1840, in Sklar, *Women's Rights Emerges,* 170.

37. Packard, *Modern Persecution* II, 165.

38. Ibid., 187.

39. Ibid., 152–53.

40. Ibid., 165.

41. Andreas, *History of the State of Nebraska,* 5.

42. Ibid.

43. Packard, *Great Drama* II, 13.

44. Packard, *Great Drama* I, 345.

45. Ibid., 343.

46. Ibid., 343–44.

47. Packard, *Great Drama* III, 89.

48. Packard, *Modern Persecution* II, 171.

49. Theophilus Packard, Diary, 165.

50. Ibid., 88.

51. Packard, *Great Drama* II, 283.

52. Packard, *Great Drama* I, 342.

53. Ibid., 367.

54. Packard, *Great Drama* II, 23.

55. Theophilus Packard, Diary, 165–66.

56. Ibid.

57. Packard, *Marital Power Exemplified,* 26.

58. Andreas, *History of the State of Nebraska,* Part 5: Biographical Sketches, accessed online at http://www.kancoll.org/books/andreas_ne/jefferson/jefferson-p5 .html#steelbio, 22 April 2007.

59. Packard, *Great Drama* II, 283.

60. Packard, *Modern Persecution* I, 34.

61. Ibid., 35.

62. Packard, *Prisoner's Hidden Life,* 26.

63. Packard, *Great Drama* I, 16–17.

64. Packard, *Great Drama* II, 328.

65. Packard, *Great Drama* III, 50.

66. Packard, *Marital Power Exemplified,* 33.

67. Ibid., 34.

68. Ibid.

69. Ibid., 35.

70. Packard, *Great Drama* II, 332.

71. Packard, *Modern Persecution* II, 155.

72. For discussion of popular religion, see Hatch, *Democratization of American Christianity,* passim, especially 3–14.

73. Packard, *Marital Power Exemplified,* 100.

74. Packard, *Modern Persecution* I, 149–50.

75. Packard, *Modern Persecution* II, 155.

76. Packard, *Modern Persecution* I, 35.

77. Ibid., 37–38.

Chapter 5. *"The Forms of Law"*

1. Samuel Ware, letter to Theophilus Packard, 1 May 1860, as printed in "The Question of Mrs. Packard's Sanity," *Northampton Free Press,* 13 April 1866, 1:3.

2. McDermott, "Dissolving the Bonds of Matrimony," 69, 71–75, 90. See also Cott, "Divorce and the Changing Status of Women," 568–614; and Farragher, *Sugar Creek,* 9–85.

3. Packard, *Modern Persecution* I, 77.

4. Ibid., 78.

5. Packard, *Exposure,* 112, 113.

6. Packard, *Modern Persecution* I, 78–79.

7. Packard, *Exposure, 7.*

8. Packard, *Modern Persecution* I, 79.

9. Packard, *Great Drama* IV, 121.

10. Packard, *Prisoner's Hidden Life,* 49.

11. Ibid., 37–38.

12. Sarah Rumsey as quoted in "The Question of Mrs. Packard's Sanity," *Northampton Free Press,* 20 April 1866, 1:3.

13. Petition dated 22 May 1860, as quoted in "The Question of Mrs. Packard's Sanity," *Northampton Free Press,* 1 May 1866, 1:3.

14. Fifteen members of Manteno Presbyterian Church, letter to Mrs. Elizabeth P. Packard, 24 May 1860, as quoted in "The Question of Mrs. Packard's Sanity," *Northampton Free Press,* 1 May 1866, 1:3.

15. Ibid.

16. Ibid., 1:4.

17. Commitment certificate for Elizabeth P. Ware, dated 29 January 1836, Worcester Asylum Records.

18. See "An Act to Amend the Act Establishing the Illinois State Hospital for the Insane," approved 15 February 1851, in *Public Laws of the State of Illinois* (1851), 97–99.

19. C. W. Knott, M.D., 5 June 1860, as quoted in "The Question of Mrs. Packard's Sanity," *Northampton Free Press,* 13 April 1866, 2:3.

20. A. B. Newkirk, M.D., 30 May 1860, as quoted in "The Question of Mrs. Packard's Sanity," *Northampton Free Press,* 1 May 1866, 1:3.

21. Ansel D. Eddy, D.D., and P. B. McKay, M.D., 8 June 1860, as quoted in "The Question of Mrs. Packard's Sanity," *Northampton Free Press,* 13 April 1866, 2:3.

22. Packard, *Great Drama* II, 321.

23. Theophilus Packard, as quoted in "The Question of Mrs. Packard's Sanity," *Northampton Free Press,* 16 May 1866, 1:5.

24. Ibid.

25. Theophilus Packard, Diary, 90–91.

26. Ibid.

27. Packard, *Great Drama* II, 321.

28. Packard, *Modern Persecution* I, 51.

29. Theophilus Packard, as quoted in "The Question of Mrs. Packard's Sanity," *Northampton Free Press,* 16 May 1866, 1:5.

30. Scull, *Social Order/Mental Disorder,* 55.

31. Elizabeth Packard, Jacksonville Record I, 232, dated 19 June 1863 [photocopy], Barbara Sapinsley Papers. Access to these records at the Illinois State Archives is now restricted by law.

32. Packard, *Exposure,* 39.

33. Stanton et al., *History of Woman Suffrage* I, 469.

34. Ibid., 469.

35. Tomes, *Generous Confidence,* 323–24.

36. "Fourth Biennial Report (1854)," in *Reports of the Illinois Hospital for the Insane, 1847–1863,* 155.

37. U.S. Census, 1860, 85.

38. See, for example, Chesler, *Women and Madness;* Masson, *Dark Science;* Gosling, *Before Freud;* Becker, *Through the Looking Glass;* Ussher, *Women's Madness;* Lunbeck, *The Psychiatric Persuasion;* Buhle, *Feminism and Its Discontents;* and Showalter, *Female Malady.*

39. Packard, *Great Drama* II, 139.

40. See, for example, Foucault, *Madness and Civilization;* Rothman, *Discovery of the Asylum;* and Scull, *Madhouses, Mad-Doctors, and Madmen.*

41. See McGovern, "Myths of Social Control," 3–23, especially 16–17; Dwyer, *Homes for the Mad,* 86–115; and Tomes, *Generous Confidence,* 113–23. McGovern also concluded that men were at a disadvantage in treatment of their mental illness both because doctors were more reluctant to label men with the stigma of insanity and because economic or legal obstacles sometimes forced families to endure "men's eccentric behavior longer." Furthermore, while women's insanity was typically ascribed to either emotional or gynecological causes, men's insanity was attributed to physical causes or lack of self-control (e.g., alcoholism, masturbation). Thus, men were viewed as more culpable in bringing on their insanity. See McGovern, "Myths of Social Control," 8.

42. Theophilus Packard, Diary, 168.

43. Ibid., 90.

44. Packard, *Modern Persecution* I, 95.

45. Ibid., 79.

Chapter 6. Andrew McFarland and Mental Medicine

1. Packard, *Modern Persecution* I, 80–81.

2. Dr. L. M. Glover, "Letter to Ministers of the Gospel in Illinois on Hospital for the Insane," *Jacksonville Journal,* 19 December 1867, 4A.

3. "Dr. Andrew McFarland Ends His Life," *Jacksonville Journal,* 24 November 1891.

4. *Portrait and Biographical Album of Morgan and Scott Counties,* 303.

5. McGovern, *Masters of Madness,* 46–52.

6. Ibid.

7. Ibid., 87.

8. Barton, *History and Influence,* 46.

9. Dain, *Concepts of Insanity,* xiv.

10. Ibid., 57–58.

11. *Reports of the Board of Visitors, Trustees and Superintendent of the New Hampshire Asylum for the Insane, June Session, 1852,* 20–21.

12. *Reports of the Illinois State Hospital for the Insane, 1847–1862,* 152.

13. *History of Morgan County,* 365.

14. For more about asylum architecture, see Yanni, *Architecture of Madness.*

15. Velek, *Jacksonville State Hospital,* 2. See also "Memorial of Miss Dix," 2–31; Lightner, *Asylum, Prison, and Poorhouse,* 4–30, 102–4; and Doyle, *Social Order of a Frontier Community,* 70–72.

16. Velek, *Jacksonville State Hospital,* 8.

17. *Reports of the Illinois State Hospital for the Insane, 1847–1862,* 112–13.

18. Ibid., 169–70.

19. Ibid., 175.

20. Ibid., 238–39.

21. Ibid., 254.

22. Ibid., 202–3.

23. Ibid., 202. Referring to American theologian Jonathan Edwards and English evangelist George Whitefield.

24. Ibid., 202. See Pollock, *Course of Time,* lines 578–79.

25. Rothman, *Discovery of the Asylum,* 122.

26. Ibid.

27. For example, McFarland was consulted by the defense regarding the trial of Charles Guiteau, assassin of President James Garfield. See "The United States, vs. Charles J. Guiteau," 303–448, especially 445 regarding Andrew McFarland.

28. Dain, *Concepts of Insanity,* 155–59.

29. Ibid., 192.

30. Ibid., 195.

31. Ibid., 183–93.

32. Ibid., 58.

33. Deutsch, *Mentally Ill in America,* 90, 92–94.

34. Grob, *Mental Institutions in America,* 168.

35. Samuel Woodward, Annual Report VII, Worcester State Lunatic Hospital (1839), 97, as quoted in Grob, *Mental Institutions in America,* 180–81.

36. McFarland, "Attendants in Institutions for the Insane," 52–61.

37. Ibid., 54–55.

38. Ibid., 52.

39. Ibid., 52–53.

40. Ibid., 66–67.

41. Ibid.

Chapter 7. "A World of Trouble"

1. Packard, *Prisoner's Hidden Life,* 69.

2. *Reports of the Illinois State Hospital for the Insane, 1847–1862,* 325, 374; Packard, *Great Drama* III, 291, 292, 294; and Packard, *Great Drama* IV, 41–42, 54–55.

3. Packard, *Mystic Key,* 58–59; and Packard, *Modern Persecution* I, 101.

4. "Charge Against Rev. Mr. Packard," *Boston Daily Advertiser,* 4 April 1865, 2:2–3.

5. Packard, *Great Drama* III, 136.

6. Packard, *Modern Persecution* I, 91.

7. Packard, *Exposure,* 61; and Packard, *Mystic Key,* 74.

8. Packard, *Modern Persecution* I, 102–3.

9. Ibid., 99.

10. Ibid., 99, 187.

11. Wood, *Writing on the Wall,* 42.

12. Packard, *Mystic Key,* 56, 72.

13. Packard, *Modern Persecution* I, 98.

14. Ibid.

15. Packard, *Mystic Key,* 57.

16. Packard, *Prisoner's Hidden Life,* 251.

17. Andrew McFarland, letter to Theophilus Packard, 11 August 1860, as quoted in "The Question of Mrs. Packard's Sanity," *Northampton Free Press,* 13 April 1866, 2:3.

18. Packard, *Great Drama* II, 219.

19. Packard, *Exposure,* cover.

20. Packard, *Modern Persecution* I, 94, 140.

21. Foucault, *Madness and Civilization,* 20.

22. Packard, *Great Drama* II, 218.

23. Ibid., 219.

24. Packard, *Modern Persecution* I, 78–79.

25. Packard, *Exposure,* 75.

26. Ibid.

27. Packard, *Great Drama* III, 173, 183. Her observation about wages held some merit. The trustees' *Third Biennial Report,* for example, showed that most female attendants were paid $10 per month; male attendants received $20 per month. The male cook/baker received $40 per month, and while the cook's male assistant received $15 per month, the female cook's assistant received $9. Even the washer man, making $20 per month, was paid more than the washerwoman, who made only $8. See *Reports of the Illinois State Hospital for the Insane, 1847–1862,* 130.

28. Ibid., 186, 213, 276.

29. Scull, *Social Order, Mental Disorder,* 68–70; Grob, *Mental Institutions in America,* 167–68; and Albanese, *Nature Religion in America,* 138–39. For positive aspects of hydrotherapy, see Wright, *Hydrotherapy in Psychiatric Hospitals.*

30. McFarland, "Attendants in Institutions for the Insane," 53–60.

31. Dwyer, *Homes for the Mad,* 163–85.

32. Ibid.

33. Grob, *Mental Institutions in America,* 215.

34. Packard, *Great Drama* II, 213.

35. Ibid.; and Packard, *Great Drama* IV, 58.

36. Packard, *Great Drama* III, 171–72.

37. Packard, *Modern Persecution* I, 120–37, especially 123–24.

38. Ibid., 126, 129–30, 136–37.

39. Packard, *Mystic Key,* 62.

40. Packard, *Modern Persecution* I, 143, 169–70.

41. Packard, *Great Drama* IV, 79–80.

42. *Reports of the Illinois State Hospital for the Insane, 1847–1862,* 324.

43. Packard, *Modern Persecution* I, 115. See also Packard, *Mrs. Packard's Reproof to Dr. McFarland for His Abuse of His Patients.*

44. Packard, *Modern Persecution* I, 116.

45. Packard, *Great Drama* IV, 51.

46. Packard, *Modern Persecution* I, 116. Packard was paraphrasing Acts 17:28: "For in Him we live, and move, and have our being."

47. U.S. Census, 1860, ciii.

48. Packard, *Modern Persecution* II, 176–77, 209–12.

49. Packard, *Modern Persecution* I, 162.

50. Ibid.

51. Report of the Investigating Committee, 1867, 41.

52. Packard, *Great Drama* II, 211.

53. Ibid., 212.

54. Packard, *Exposure,* 54–55.

55. Packard, *Modern Persecution* I, 143, 169–70.

56. Andrew McFarland, letter to Theophilus Packard, 2 February 1861, as quoted in "The Question of Mrs. Packard's Sanity," *Northampton Free Press,* 13 April 1866, 2:3.

57. Packard, *Mystic Key,* 72.

58. Sophia N. Olsen, "Mrs. Olsen's Narrative of Her One Year's Imprisonment, at Jacksonville Insane Asylum" in Packard, *Prisoner's Hidden Life,* 74.

59. Ibid.

60. Ibid., 75–76.

61. Ibid., 82.

62. Ibid., 87.

63. Andrew McFarland, letter to Theophilus Packard, 12 August 1861, as quoted in "The Question of Mrs. Packard's Sanity," *Northampton Free Press,* 13 April 1866, 2:3.

64. Packard, *Modern Persecution* I, 241.

65. Packard, *Prisoner's Hidden Life,* 212.

66. Andrew McFarland, letter to Theophilus Packard, 3 April 1862, as quoted in "The Question of Mrs. Packard's Sanity," *Northampton Free Press,* 13 April 1866, 2:3.

67. Ibid.

68. Packard, *Modern Persecution* I, 250. Packard's sons, Theo and Isaac, were at the time working as sutler's clerks following the Union army, but were able to visit her at the asylum "on their return from service in the Nebraska Regiment."

69. Packard, *Great Drama* IV, 200–201.

70. Ibid., 201.

71. *Reports of the Illinois State Hospital for the Insane, 1847–1862,* 364–65.

72. Packard, *Great Drama* IV, 115.

73. Packard, *Prisoner's Hidden Life,* 214–19.

74. Packard, *Modern Persecution* II, 122.

Chapter 8. "An Unendurable Annoyance"

1. *Special Report of the Trustees of the Illinois State Hospital for the Insane,* 31.

2. Theophilus Packard, Diary, 170.

3. Dr. A. B. Newkirk, 21 August 1862, as quoted in "The Question of Mrs. Packard's Sanity," *Northampton Free Press,* 1 May 1866, 1:4.

4. Charles A. Spring, 21 August 1862, as quoted in "The Question of Mrs. Packard's Sanity," *Northampton Free Press,* 1 May 1866, 1:4.

5. Packard, *Exposure,* 19.

6. Ibid., 19–21.

7. Ibid., 19–21, 23.

8. Ibid., 23.

9. Ibid., 24–25.

10. Ibid., 25–26.

11. Ibid., 26–27.

12. Packard, *Marital Power Exemplified,* 7.

13. *Special Report of the Trustees,* 31.

14. Theophilus Packard, Diary, 170.

15. Packard, *Modern Persecution* I, 355.

16. Packard, *Marital Power Exemplified,* 111–12.

17. Packard, *Modern Persecution* I, 355.

18. *Reports of the Illinois State Hospital for the Insane, 1847–1862,* 357.

19. Ibid., 360.

20. Ibid., 351.

21. See "An Act to Amend an Act Entitled 'An Act to Establish the Illinois State Hospital for the Insane,'" approved 12 February 1853, in *Reports of the Illinois State Hospital for the Insane, 1847–1862,* 394.

22. *Special Report of the Trustees,* 31.

23. *Reports of the Illinois State Hospital for the Insane, 1847–1862,* 364.

24. Packard, *Modern Persecution* I, 355.

25. Elizabeth Packard, letter to Andrew McFarland, 19 January 1863, as printed in *Report of the Investigating Committee,* 34.

26. *Report of the Investigating Committee,* 34.

27. Ibid., 35.

28. Packard, *Mystic Key,* 76.

29. Packard, *Great Drama* II, 345.

30. Trustees Records (unpublished) as cited in *Special Report of the Trustees,* 31.

31. Andrew McFarland, letter to Theophilus Packard, 14 April 1863, as quoted in "The Question of Mrs. Packard's Sanity," *Northampton Free Press,* 13 April 1866, 2:4.

32. Theophilus Packard, Diary, 170.

33. Andrew McFarland, letter to Theophilus Packard, 14 April 1863, as quoted in "The Question of Mrs. Packard's Sanity," *Northampton Free Press,* 13 April 1866, 2:4.

34. McFarland, "Minor Mental Maladies," 10–26.

35. Ibid., 17.

36. Ibid., 17–18.

37. Ibid., 18–19.

38. Ibid., 21.

39. Ibid.

40. Ibid., 23–24.

41. "Annual Meeting . . . AMSAII," *AJI* 20 (July 1863): 70.

42. Ibid., 72.

43. Ibid., 79–83.

44. Ibid.

45. Ibid., 84–86.

46. Ibid., 90.

47. Ibid., 90–91.

48. Ibid., 91.

49. Ibid.

50. Ibid., 92.

51. Ibid.

52. Ibid., 91.

53. Ibid., 94.

54. Ibid., 97.

55. Ibid., 98.

56. Ibid.

57. Ibid., 107.

58. Ibid., 135.

59. Packard, *Marital Power Exemplified,* 8.

60. Packard, *Great Drama* IV, 251, 253; and *Bailey's Chicago Directory.*

61. Packard, *Great Drama* IV, 251.

62. Ibid., 253.

63. Theophilus Packard III, letter to Theophilus Packard, 21 October 1863, as quoted in "The Question of Mrs. Packard's Sanity," *Northampton Free Press*, 8 May 1866, 1:6.

64. Packard, *Exposure,* 120.

65. Theophilus Packard, Diary, 172.

66. Packard, *Marital Power Exemplified,* 76–77; and *Historical Sketches,* 2–3.

67. Packard, *Modern Persecution* II, 107.

68. Theophilus Packard, Diary, 171.

69. Packard, *Great Drama* IV, 253.

70. Palmer, *Bench and Bar of Illinois,* 1024.

71. Isaac W. Packard, letter to Theophilus Packard, 15 November 1863, as quoted in "The Question of Mrs. Packard's Sanity," *Northampton Free Press*, 8 May 1866, 1:6.

72. Certificate of Samuel Packard, Elizabeth W. Packard, George H. Packard, 10 November 1863, as quoted in "The Question of Mrs. Packard's Sanity," *Northampton Free Press*, 8 May 1866, 1:6.

73. Packard, *Marital Power Exemplified,* 8–9.

74. Ibid., 10.

75. Theophilus Packard, Diary, 172.

76. State of Illinois, Kankakee County, "The People of the State of Illinois, to Theophilus Packard," dated January 11, 1864, signed by Charles R. Starr, Judge of the Twentieth Judicial Circuit of the State of Illinois, endorsed by the Habeas Corpus Act, as reproduced in Packard, *Modern Persecution* II, 25–28 and *Marital Power Exemplified,* 14–15.

77. Theophilus Packard, Diary, 92.

Chapter 9. From Courtroom to Activism

1. *Portrait and Biographical Record of Kankakee County,* 211–14, 240–42; and "Reply to Mr. Sewall's Rejoinder," *Boston Daily Advertiser,* 3 May 1865, 2:4–5.

2. Ibid.

3. Robson, *Biographical Encyclopaedia of Illinois,* 139–40.

4. Stephen R. Moore, letter-to-the-editor of the *Boston Daily Advertiser,* ca. May 1865 [transcript], Barbara Sapinsley Papers.

5. Palmer, *Bench and Bar of Illinois,* 980.

6. Packard, *Marital Power Exemplified,* 13.

7. Packard, *Great Drama* I, 372.

8. Packard, *Marital Power Exemplified,* 17–18.

9. Packard, *Prisoner's Hidden Life,* 107.

10. Packard, *Marital Power Exemplified,* 21.

11. Ibid., 22.

12. Ibid., 23–24.

13. Ibid., 25.

14. Ibid.

15. Ibid., 26–27.

16. Ibid., 31.

17. Ibid., 28–29, 32.

18. Ibid., 32–33.

19. Ibid., 33–34.

20. Ibid., 35–36.

21. Ibid., 36.

22. Ibid., 37.

23. Ibid.

24. Ibid., 38.

25. Ibid., 39.

26. Theophilus Packard, Diary, 93, 172.

27. Packard, *Marital Power Exemplified,* 42.

28. Ibid., 130.

29. Packard, *Modern Persecution* II, 75.

30. Ibid., 73, 76.

31. Packard, *Modern Persecution* II, 164.

32. Bill of complaint for divorce, Kankakee County Circuit Court, 1864.

33. Chancery Summons No. 1808, Kankakee County Circuit Court, 1864.

34. Theophilus Packard, Diary, 172.

35. "The Question of Mrs. Packard's Sanity," *Northampton Free Press,* 16 May 1866, 1:7.

36. Packard, *Marital Power Exemplified,* 61–62.

37. Hartog, *Mrs. Packard on Dependency,* 22–23.

38. Packard, *Modern Persecution* II, 366.

39. Packard, *Mystic Key,* 10.

40. Theophilus Packard III, letter to Samuel Ware, 29 March 1864, as quoted in "The Question of Mrs. Packard's Sanity," *Northampton Free Press,* 15 May 1866, 1:7.

41. Packard, *Modern Persecution* II, 86.

42. Packard, *Marital Power Exemplified,* 49.

43. Packard, *Modern Persecution* II, 86.

44. Packard, *Mrs. Packard's Reproof,* 17–20.

45. Ibid., 21.

46. Packard, *Modern Persecution* II, 88.

47. Packard, *Exposure,* 6.

48. Ibid., 10–13.

49. Ibid., 41–42.

50. Ibid., 50.

51. Ibid., 51.

52. Ibid., 45.

53. Packard, *Modern Persecution* II, 161.

54. *Proceedings of the Woman's Rights Conventions,* 5–6.

55. Ibid.

56. Lerner, *Creation of Feminist Consciousness,* 14.

57. Packard, *Exposure,* 109.

58. Ibid., 15.

59. Ibid.

60. Ibid., 11–12.

61. Ibid., 11.

62. Packard, *Modern Persecution* II, 391.

63. Ibid., 71.

64. Ibid., 69.

65. Sklar, *Women's Rights Emerges,* 59.

66. Ibid., 13.

67. Packard, *Exposure,* 113.

68. Packard, *Modern Persecution* II, 391.

69. Packard, *Marital Power Exemplified,* 64.

70. Packard, *Modern Persecution* II, 391–92; and Packard, *Marital Power Exemplified,* 63–64.

71. Hartog, *Mrs. Packard on Dependency,* 28–29, 33.

Chapter 10. *"My Pen Shall Rage"*

1. Packard, *Great Drama* IV, 137.

2. See, for example, Fuller, *Account of Imprisonment;* Stone, *Exposing the Modern Secret Way;* and Hunt, *Astounding Disclosure.* See also Grob, *Mental Institutions in America,* 254n, 265.

3. Torrey and Miller, *Invisible Plague,* 256.

4. U.S. Census, 1860, iii-cvii.

5. Ibid.

6. Ibid., lxxx.

7. Ray, "American Legislation on Insanity," 21–62.

8. Ibid., 25.

9. Ibid.

10. Ibid., 26.

11. Ibid., 27.

12. Ibid.

13. Ibid., 27, 29.

14. Ibid., 29–31.

15. Ibid., 33–34.

16. "Proceedings . . . AMSAII," *AJI* 21 (July 1854): 153.

17. Ibid., 153–55.

18. Parigot, "Legislation on Lunacy," 222.

19. Ibid., 200–223.

20. Ibid., 213.

21. Ibid., 209–10.

22. Ibid., 213.

23. Ibid., 214–16.

24. Chipley, "Summary," 299–300.

25. Packard, *Modern Persecution* II, 96.

26. Grob, *Mental Institutions in America,* 86–87; and Grob, "Transformation of the Mental Hospital," 639–54.

27. Packard, *Marital Power Exemplified*, 118–20.

28. "The Question of Mrs. Packard's Sanity," *Northampton Free Press,* 15 May 1866, 1:5.

29. Ibid.

30. Packard, *Modern Persecution* II, 96.

31. "Defects in the Laws Respecting Insanity," *Boston Daily Advertiser,* 10 January 1865, 2:2–3.

32. Ibid.

33. Tiffany, *Samuel E. Sewall,* 128–29.

34. Packard, *Modern Persecution* II, 98.

35. Ibid.

36. Ibid., 99.

37. Ibid.

38. Ibid., 97.

39. Ibid., 100.

40. Ibid., 104–5; "Last Will and Testament of Samuel Ware," Wills, vol. 49, 365; and Death Index, vol. 192, 238, Vital Statistics Records, Massachusetts State Archives.

41. Packard, *Modern Persecution* II, 92–93, 104–5.

42. "Charge Against Rev. Mr. Packard," *Boston Daily Advertiser,* 4 April 1865, 2:2–3.

43. Ibid.

44. Ibid.

45. "Rejoinder to Rev. Mr. Packard," *Boston Daily Advertiser,* 7 April 1865, 2:2.

46. "Reply to Mr. Sewall's Rejoinder," *Boston Daily Advertiser,* 7 April 1865, 2:2–3.

47. Stephen R. Moore, letter-to-the-editor of the *Boston Daily Advertiser,* ca. May 1865 [transcript], Barbara Sapinsley Papers.

48. Ibid.

49. Ibid.

50. "Proceedings . . . AMSAII," *AJI* 23 (July 1866): 115.

51. Ibid., 121.

52. Ibid., 90.

53. Packard, *Modern Persecution* II, 176.

54. Packard, *Mystic Key,* 54.

55. Packard, *Marital Power Exemplified,* 69.

56. Ibid., 109.

57. Ibid., 106–7; and Packard, *Modern Persecution* II, 174–77.

58. Packard, *Marital Power Exemplified,* 122.

59. Ibid.; and Packard, *Modern Persecution* II, 185.

60. Packard, *Marital Power Exemplified,* 77.

61. Theophilus Packard, Diary, 175.

62. Theophilus Packard, as quoted in "The Question of Mrs. Packard's Sanity," *Northampton Free Press,* 13 April 1866, 2:5 and 20 April 1866, 1:3.

63. Ibid., 1:4.

64. Packard, *Modern Persecution* II, 211; and "Petition," *New Haven Daily Morning Journal and Courier,* 18 May 1866, 2:4.

65. "The Rights of Married Women," *New Haven Daily Morning Journal and Courier,* 21 May 1866, 2:1; and Packard, *Modern Persecution* II, 291–92.

66. Packard, *Modern Persecution* II, 400.

67. Ibid., 291–93.

68. "Mrs. Packard's Plea in Defence of Married Woman's Emancipation," *New Haven Daily Morning Journal and Courier,* 14 June 1866, 2:4–7; and Packard, *Modern Persecution* II, 394.

69. Packard, *Modern Persecution* II, 395–96.

70. "Mrs. Packard's Plea in Defence of Married Woman's Emancipation," *New Haven Daily Morning Journal and Courier,* 14 June 1866, 2:4–7; and Packard, *Modern Persecution* II, 396.

71. Ibid.

72. Ibid.; and Packard, *Modern Persecution* II, 397.

73. Ibid.; and Packard, *Modern Persecution* II, 406.

74. Packard, *Modern Persecution* II, 295; and Packard, *Mystic Key,* 103.

75. Theophilus Packard, letter-to-the-editor of the *New Haven Daily Morning Journal and Courier,* 22 May 1866, 2:4–5.

76. Andrew McFarland, letter to Alma E. Eaton, as quoted in the *New Haven Daily Morning Journal and Courier,* 22 May 1866, 2:4–5.

77. Ibid.

78. Ibid. Referring to Tom Paine's book, *The Age of Reason* (1795), which called Christianity a mythology.

79. "Mrs. Packard's Plea in Defence of Married Woman's Emancipation," *New Haven Daily Morning Journal and Courier,* 14 June 1866, 2:4–7.

80. Packard, *Modern Persecution* II, 300–301.

Chapter 11. Shooting the Rattlesnakes

1. Packard, *Modern Persecution* II, 105.

2. "Last Will and Testament of Samuel Ware," 365.

3. See Probate Docket #5009, Registry of Probate, Franklin County Probation and Family Court, Greenfield, Mass. By a prenuptial agreement, Olive Ware was to receive only the clothing and furniture she had brought to the marriage plus a keepsake Bible and $200 to cover her husband's debts and burial expenses. She asked instead that the estate be divided as if her husband had died without a will,

thereby significantly increasing her share. The estate was not settled until June 1870, when she released her claim.

4. Packard, *Mystic Key,* 37–38.

5. Ibid., 38.

6. Theophilus Packard, Diary, 175.

7. *Ninth Biennial Report of the Trustees, Illinois State Hospital for the Insane,* 34–35.

8. *Public Laws of the State of Illinois* (1865), 85–86.

9. *Tenth Biennial Report of the Trustees, Illinois State Hospital for the Insane,* 39.

10. Bradwell was admitted to the Illinois bar (1890) and licensed to practice before the U.S. Supreme Court in 1892, becoming the first woman to achieve those objectives. See *Bradwell v. The State, Supreme Court of the United States,* 83 U.S. 130; 21 L.Ed. 442; 1872 LEXIS 1140.

11. *Report of the Investigating Committee* (1867), 29.

12. Packard, *Modern Persecution* II, 213.

13. Ibid., 190.

14. Packard, *Mystic Key,* 11–12.

15. Packard, *Great Drama* IV, 261.

16. Letter, "A Lover of Justice," to the editor of the *Illinois State Journal,* 26 January 1867.

17. Packard, *Prisoner's Hidden Life,* 339–40.

18. Packard, *Modern Persecution* II, 220.

19. *Illinois State Register,* 3 January 1867.

20. *Illinois State Journal,* 15 January 1867.

21. *Eddy v. the People,* 15 Ill. 386; 1854 Ill. LEXIS 18.

22. "Our Laws Relative to Insane Persons," *Jacksonville Journal,* 31 January 1867.

23. Packard, "Mrs. Packard's Address to the Illinois Legislature," 3, 11.

24. *Journal of the Illinois House* (1867), vol. I, 253 and vol. II, 42, 268; and *Journal of the Illinois Senate* (1867), vol. I, 799, 897, 947, 1247.

25. Packard, *Modern Persecution* II, 203–4.

26. "Protection of Personal Liberty," *Public Laws of the State of Illinois* (1867), 139–40.

27. Packard, *Modern Persecution* II, 212.

28. "Summary," *AJI* 27 (October 1870): 261.

29. Ibid., 261–62.

30. See *Journal of the Illinois Senate* (1867), 46, 278, 289, 382, 591, 1053, 1184; and *Journal of the Illinois House* (1867), 119, 580, 587, 594, 658, 884, 894, 913.

31. *Illinois State Journal,* 11 January 1867.

32. Ibid.

33. *Illinois State Journal,* 29 January 1867.

34. "From Jacksonville," *Illinois State Journal,* 14 February 1867. See also *Jacksonville Journal,* 13 February 1867.

35. Packard, *Modern Persecution* II, 220.

36. "Letter from an Attendant in the Jacksonville Insane Asylum, Jacksonville, to his Excellency, the Governor of Illinois," January 1866, *Illinois State Register,* 22 February 1867.

37. *Jacksonville Journal,* 25 February 1867.

38. *Illinois State Register,* 25 January 1867.

39. *Illinois State Journal,* 25 February 1867.

40. Fuller was a Republican from Boone County. See *Bench and Bar of Illinois, Historical and Reminiscent,* vol. II, 787.

41. "Concurrent Resolutions," *Public Laws of the State of Illinois* (1867), 189.

42. *Journal of the Illinois Senate* (1867), 1184; and *Journal of the Illinois House* (1867), 981.

43. Sangamon County Deed Records, 1822–1902, Deed Record No. 5005.

44. See, for example, "Horrible Revelations," *Jacksonville Journal,* 19 April 1867.

45. *Jacksonville Journal,* 6 May 1867.

46. *Report of the Investigating Committee,* 15.

47. *Jacksonville Journal,* 17 May 1867; and "Mrs. Packard's Personal Liberty Law Again," *Jacksonville Sentinel,* 16 May 1867.

48. *Report of the Investigating Committee,* 5; and "Journal of the Joint Committee."

49. *Report of the Investigating Committee,* 4–5.

50. "Proceedings . . . AMSAII," *AJI* 24 (January 1868): 290–91.

51. Ibid., 295.

52. *Report of the Investigating Committee,* 2–3, 6.

53. *Report of the Investigating Committee,* 29. Bradwell also believed that patients from Cook County were refused admittance because other counties had been permitted to exceed their proper quota of patients; however, the committee found no evidence of this.

54. Ibid., 32.

55. Ibid., 31.

56. Ibid., 32.

57. Ibid., 38–39.

58. Ibid., 69.

59. Ibid., 43–45.

60. Ibid., 46, 70–71.

61. Ibid., 47–48.

62. Packard, *Mystic Key,* 78.

63. Ibid., 77–78.

64. Ibid., 76–77.

65. *Report of the Investigating Committee,* 52.

66. Ibid.

67. Ibid., 53.

68. Ibid., 55.

69. Ibid.

70. Ibid., 48.

71. Ibid., 37.

72. Ibid., 57–58.

73. Ibid., 58–59.

74. "The Mrs. Packard Agitation Against the Insane Hospital," *Jacksonville Sentinel*, 8 August 1867.

75. *Report of the Investigating Committee*, 64–65, 67.

76. Ibid.

77. Ibid., 66.

78. Ibid.

79. Ibid., 68–69.

80. Ibid., 77–78.

Chapter 12. Vindication and "Virtuous Action"

1. *Illinois State Register*, 6 December 1867.

2. *Jacksonville Journal*, 10 December 1867.

3. Palmer, *Bench and Bar of Illinois*, 337. Dummer was a former Cass County judge and a respected member of the Illinois bar. Sturtevant was president of Illinois College. Turner, a professor at Illinois College, was a noted educational reformer who had influenced passage of the Morrill Act (1862) and was instrumental in founding the University of Illinois as one of the first land-grant agricultural schools. See Carriel, *Life of Jonathan Baldwin Turner*.

4. "The Meeting Last Night—A Large Attendance—Vindication of Dr. McFarland," *Jacksonville Journal*, 13 December 1867.

5. *Chicago Tribune*, 14 December 1867.

6. *Illinois State Register*, 21 December 1867.

7. *Illinois State Register*, 14 December 1867.

8. Ibid.

9. "A Note From Judge Dummer," *Jacksonville Journal*, 14 December 1867; and J. B. Turner, letter-to-the-editor of the *Jacksonville Journal*, "The Insane Hospital," *Jacksonville Journal*, 16 December 1867. For other examples, see *Illinois State Register*, 27 January 1868; and "Editorial," *Jacksonville Journal*, 17 December 1867.

10. "Letter to the Ministers of the Gospel in Illinois on Hospital for the Insane, from Dr. Glover," *Jacksonville Journal*, 19 December 1867.

11. Ibid.

12. *Jacksonville Journal*, 21 December 1867.

13. Ibid.

14. Packard, *Modern Persecution* II, 258–59.

15. Andrew McFarland, letter to Edward Jarvis, 2 January 1868, Edward Jarvis Papers.

16. Ibid.

17. Andrew McFarland, letter to Edward Jarvis, 12 August 1868, Edward Jarvis Papers.

18. *Special Report of the Trustees* (1868), 97–98.

19. Ibid.

20. Ibid., 96–97.

21. Ibid., 96–98.

22. Ibid., 99.

23. Ibid., 100.

24. Ibid., 104.

25. Ibid.

26. Ibid., 100.

27. Ibid., 101.

28. Ibid., 100.

29. Ibid., 106.

30. Gray, "Illinois Legislation Regarding Hospitals for the Insane," *AJI* 26 (October 1869): 204.

31. Ibid., 207, 216.

32. *Eleventh Biennial Report of the Trustees* (1868), 33–34.

33. Gray, "Summary," *AJI* 27 (October 1870): 260–62.

34. "History of Oak Lawn Sanatorium," 1–3; and *Portrait and Biographical Album of Morgan and Scott Counties,* 303–4. In addition to McFarland, managers of the Oak Lawn asylum included former Jacksonville state asylum trustees Ludwig M. Glover, Lloyd W. Brown, Felix G. Farrell, M. P. Ayers, John Cassell, and Isaac Morrison.

35. For introduction of the term "female Gothic," see Moers, *Literary Women.*

36. Winter, *Subjects of Slavery,* 21.

37. DeLamotte, *Perils of the Night,* 179.

38. Ibid., chapter 5, passim.

39. Winter, *Subjects of Slavery,* 2.

40. Packard, *Prisoner's Hidden Life,* 14.

41. Ibid., 202.

42. Ibid., 89.

43. Ibid., 140.

44. Ibid., 14.

45. Ibid., 140.

46. Ibid., iii.

47. Ibid., 338.

48. Ibid., 140.

49. Ibid.

50. Ibid.

51. Dain, "Critics and Dissenters," 9. Beers acknowledged that he had been insane and later worked with the psychiatric profession for reform. Following his recovery, Beers wrote *A Mind That Found Itself* (Longmans, 1908) and founded

the influential National Committee on Mental Hygiene, later the National Association for Mental Health.

52. Packard, *Prisoner's Hidden Life,* 364.

Chapter 13. Triumph and Disaster

1. Packard, *Modern Persecution* II, 366.

2. Packard, *Mystic Key,* 38.

3. Samuel Packard, Diary, 74.

4. Packard, *Modern Persecution* II, 373.

5. Ibid., 374.

6. Ibid.

7. Stanton, *History of Woman Suffrage* III, 562. See also Beldon, "A History of the Woman Suffrage Movement in Illinois," 5.

8. "An Act to Protect Married Women in their Separate Property," *Public Laws of the State of Illinois* (1861), 143.

9. "Law Relating to Women," *Chicago Legal News,* 17 October 1868, 22:1.

10. Stanton, *History of Woman Suffrage* III, 562.

11. Packard, *Modern Persecution* II, 367.

12. See *Journal of the Illinois House* (1869) I, 358.

13. Packard, *Modern Persecution* II, 369–71.

14. Ibid.

15. Ibid., 366–67.

16. *Chicago Tribune,* 5 February 1869; and *History of Woman Suffrage* III, 565–70. See also Buechler, *Transformation of the Woman Suffrage Movement,* 67–76.

17. Stanton, *History of Woman Suffrage* III, 569–70.

18. Ibid.

19. Packard, *Modern Persecution* II, 372–73.

20. *Journal of the Illinois House* (1869) II, 671; and Packard, *Modern Persecution* II, 372–73 (1869).

21. Packard, *Modern Persecution* II, 372.

22. See "An Act in Relation to the Earnings of Married Women," approved 24 March 1869, *Public Laws of the State of Illinois,* 255. See also Packard, *Modern Persecution* II, 372.

23. *Journal of the Illinois House* (1869) II, 546, 591.

24. Stanton, *History of Woman Suffrage* III, 569–70.

25. Friedman, *America's First Woman Lawyer,* 196, 200–201.

26. Packard, *Modern Persecution* II, 373.

27. Friedman, *America's First Woman Lawyer,* 196, 200–201.

28. Gray, "Illinois Legislation Regarding Hospitals for the Insane," *AJI* 26 (October 1869): 204, 207.

29. Ibid., 206.

30. Packard, *Mystic Key,* 104.

31. Grob, *Mental Institutions in America,* 278.

32. Although the name and agency responsible has changed over the years, state oversight of state care for the mentally ill continues today under the Illinois State Department of Mental Health and Developmental Disabilities.

33. See Jaffary, *Mentally Ill,* 8.

34. McFarland, *What Shall Be Done with the Insane of the West?* 13–15.

35. Packard, *Modern Persecution* II, 374.

36. Ibid., 376–77.

37. Ibid., 378.

38. Ibid.

39. Theophilus Packard, Diary, 93.

40. Packard, *Modern Persecution* II, 379.

41. Theophilus Packard, Diary, 177.

42. Ibid.

43. Packard, *Modern Persecution* II, 381.

44. Samuel Packard, Diary, 77.

45. Packard, *Modern Persecution* II, 382–83.

46. Ibid.

47. Theophilus Packard, Diary, 177.

48. Packard, *Mystic Key,* 39.

49. Packard, *Modern Persecution* II, 383.

50. Samuel Packard, Diary, passim.

51. Theophilus Packard, Diary, 94–95.

52. Ibid., 178.

53. Packard, *Modern Persecution* II, 373.

54. Ibid.

55. *Chicago Legal News,* 29 April 1871, 243:4.

56. Packard, *Mystic Key,* 16.

57. For more on the fire, see Miller, *Great Chicago Fire;* and Sawislak, *Smoldering City.*

58. Packard, *Modern Persecution* II, 384; and Packard, *Mystic Key,* 52–53.

59. Theophilus Packard, Diary, 180.

60. Ibid., 180–81.

61. John C. Packard, Jr., letter to Barbara Sapinsley, 28 June 1981.

62. Theophilus Packard, Diary, 180–81.

63. Ibid., 179–80, 182.

64. Packard, *Modern Persecution* II, 384.

65. Ibid.

66. Ibid.

Chapter 14. Working in Her Calling

1. "Rights of the Insane," *Davenport Gazette*, 19 March 1872; and Packard, *Modern Persecution* II, 305–6.

2. *Laws of Iowa*, Chapter 91, 1872; and Packard, *Modern Persecution* II, 326–28.

3. Packard, *Modern Persecution* II, 326–28.

4. Ibid., 327.

5. Ibid., 326–27.

6. Ibid., 315.

7. "Reports from American Asylums," 482.

8. Packard, *Modern Persecution* II, 309.

9. Ibid., 318.

10. Ibid., 318, 333–39.

11. Ibid., 330–32.

12. Ibid., 341.

13. Ibid., 345.

14. See, for example, *New York Times*, 1 April 1872, 4; 7 August 1872, 2; and 24 August 1872, 5.

15. "Proceedings . . . AMSAII," *AJI* 30 (October 1873): 176.

16. Grob, *Mental Institutions in America*, 280.

17. "Proceedings . . . AMSAII," *AJI* 30 (October 1873): 239.

18. Ibid., 239–40.

19. Ibid.

20. Packard, *Mystic Key*, 53.

21. Packard, *Modern Persecution* II, 264–65. See also *Journal of the Illinois Senate* (1869) I, 153; and *Journal of the Illinois House* (1869), 128.

22. Packard, *Mystic Key*, 52–53.

23. *Philadelphia Medical Times*, 14 March 1873, as quoted in *AJI* 30 (April 1874): 486.

24. Ibid., 484–85.

25. Ibid., 486.

26. Packard, *Mystic Key*, 14, 103.

27. Ibid., 109.

28. Ibid., 120.

29. Ibid., 117–20.

30. Ibid., 116–17.

31. Ibid., 118; and *Laws of Maine*, Chapter 256, 1874.

32. Packard, *Mystic Key*, 123–24.

33. Packard, "Mrs. Packard's Exposure of Doctor Ray's Fallacies," 4.

34. See Packard, "A Bill to Remedy the Evils of Insane Asylums," 6, 8, 11.

35. Packard, *Mystic Key*, 132.

36. *Laws of Massachusetts*, Chapter 363, 1874.

37. "Commissioners in Lunacy," 273.

38. See Report of the Commissioners of Lunacy, House Document No. 60, Docu-

ments of the House of Representatives of Massachusetts, 1875; and "Report of the Commissioners of Lunacy," 476–77.

39. Ibid.

40. Ibid.

41. Ibid., 482–83.

42. Ibid., 474.

43. Samuel W. Packard, letter to Mother, Chicago, 1874.

44. Ibid.

45. "Bibliographical, Iowa," 486–87.

46. Ibid., 489.

47. Ibid.

48. U.S. House, Miscellaneous Documents No. 59, 43rd Congress, 2nd Session, 1874–75, "Postal Rights of Inmates of Insane Asylums," 1.

49. Packard, *Mystic Key,* 127.

50. Ibid., 128.

51. Ibid., 130.

52. Ibid., 131–33. Packard credited several in the Grant administration who assisted her, including J. R. Hawley, who introduced her bill in the House; A. A. Sargent, who introduced it in the Senate; John B. Packer, chairman of the House Post-Offices and Post-Roads Committee; Alexander Ramsey, chairman of the comparable Senate committee; Representative Thomas C. Platt; and Senator T. W. Ferry. She reported that Hannibal Hamlin initially opposed the bill, but was won over by her personal appeal and ultimately reported favorably on the bill.

53. Friedman, *America's First Woman Lawyer,* 135–46.

54. Packard, *Mystic Key,* 133.

55. U.S. House, Miscellaneous Documents No. 59, 43rd Congress, 2nd Session, 1874–75, "Postal Rights of Inmates of Insane Asylums," 1.

56. Ibid.

57. Ibid.

58. Ibid., 3.

59. Packard, *Mystic Key,* 139.

60. "Proceedings . . . AMSAII," *AJI* 32 (January 1876): 322.

61. Ibid.

62. Ibid.

63. Ibid., 346.

64. Ibid.

65. Ibid., 352.

66. Ibid., 354.

Chapter 15. "Great and Noble Work"

1. "Proceedings . . . AMSAII," *AJI* 32 (January 1876): 306.

2. "Bibliographical, Iowa," *AJI* 32 (April 1876): 561.

3. Barton, *History & Influence,* 64–65. For the AMSAII's rebuttal of accusations against it published in the British medical journal, *The Lancet,* see the AMSAII Proceedings in *AJI* 34 (October 1877): 218–24.

4. Barton, *History & Influence,* 64–65.

5. "Proceedings . . . AMSAII," *AJI* 33 (October 1876): 211–12; and "Proceedings . . . AMSAII," *AJI* 34 (October 1877): 166, 188–90.

6. "Proceedings . . . AMSAII," *AJI* 33 (October 1976): 164.

7. Friedman, *America's First Woman Lawyer,* 205.

8. *Chicago Legal News,* 3 March 1879, 267:3–4.

9. Neely and McMurtry, *Insanity File,* 21, 26.

10. Ibid., 80–81. See also, Baker, *Mary Todd Lincoln,* 327, 338–39.

11. "Proceedings . . . AMSAII," *AJI* 34 (October 1877): 214.

12. Andrew W. McFarland, letter to Robert Todd Lincoln, 8 September 1875, as quoted in Neely and McMurtry, *Insanity File,* 72.

13. Neely and McMurtry, *Insanity File,* 141.

14. Ibid., 21–26.

15. Packard, *Prisoner's Hidden Life,* 128, 130.

16. Neely and McMurtry, *Insanity File,* 68.

17. James Bradwell, letter to R. J. Patterson, 15 August 1875, as quoted in Neely and McMurtry, *Insanity File,* 65. See also Neely and McMurtry, *Insanity File,* 68–69; and Randall, *Mary Lincoln,* 430–35.

18. Packard, *Mystic Key,* 45, 49.

19. Packard, *Great Drama* I, 9.

20. Ibid., 8.

21. Ibid., 11.

22. Ibid., 8.

23. Ibid., 87.

24. Ibid., 88.

25. Carroll, *Spiritualism in Antebellum America,* 38–39.

26. Packard, *Great Drama* II, 364.

27. Ibid., 11.

28. Ibid.

29. Fox, *Trials of Intimacy,* 38.

30. Waller, *Reverend Beecher,* 116.

31. Henry Ward Beecher, [Sermon], *The Independent,* 5 March 1863, as cited in Packard, *Great Drama* II, 277.

32. Packard, *Mystic Key,* 13–14.

33. Ibid., 14.

34. Ibid., 7, 86.

35. Ibid., 88–89.

36. Packard, *Modern Persecution* I, 371. Packard's explanation suggests the phenomenon psychologists have identified in hostages who exhibit emotional attachment to the captors on whom they are dependent for their relative security and comfort.

37. Packard, *Mystic Key,* 11.

38. Ibid., 42–43.

39. Ibid., 44–45.

40. Ibid., 47–48.

41. Ibid.

42. Ibid., 45, 49.

43. Ibid., 41–52.

44. McFarland, "Association Reminiscences and Reflections," 359.

45. Proceedings . . . AMSAII," *AJI* 34 (October 1877): 213.

46. Ibid., 216, 280–81.

47. McFarland, "Commitments to Institutions for the Insane," 15, 17.

48. Packard, *Woman Hating Party,* unpaged introduction.

49. *Laws of Washington Territory,* 1877–88, 913, as cited in Himmelhoch and Schaffer, "Elizabeth Packard," 372.

50. Packard, *Woman Hating Party,* 23–24.

51. *Boise Republican,* 1 January 1881, as cited in Packard, *Woman Hating Party,* 23.

52. Packard, *Woman Hating Party*, unpaged introduction.

53. Ibid., 16.

54. Ibid., 13.

55. Stanton, *History of Woman Suffrage* III, 767–88.

56. Packard, *Woman Hating Party,* 4.

57. Ibid., 31.

58. Ibid.

59. Deutsch, "History of Mental Hygiene," 336.

60. Johnson, *Out of Bedlam,* 11–12.

61. Grob, *Mental Institutions in America,* 282, 293–94. See also Brown, "Neurology's Influence on American Psychiatry," 519–31.

62. Everts, "American System," 118, 119, 124.

63. Ibid., 117.

64. Eaton, "Despotism in Lunatic Asylums," 263–75.

65. Ibid., 267.

66. Ibid., 264.

67. "Proceedings . . . AMSAII," *AJI* 38 (October 1881): 187.

68. Ibid.

69. Ibid., 228.

Chapter 16. Final Campaigns

1. *Atchison (Kansas) Daily Champion,* 14 March 1886, Issue 46, col. C, accessed online via InfoTrac Web: Nineteenth-Century Newspapers database, 13 April 2007.

2. Packard, "Open Letter to the Legislatures of Nebraska, Kansas, and Colorado."

3. *Laws of Nebraska,* Chapter 69, 1883, as cited in Himmelhoch and Shaffer, "Elizabeth Packard," 372.

4. See S.B. 157, "An Act to Protect the Inmates of Insane Asylums," and S.B. 158, "An Act to Declare and Protect the Identity of Married Women," Kansas Senate Journal (1883).

5. *Elizabeth P.W. Packard v. Andrew McFarland et al.,* suit filed 10 May 1886, Kankakee Circuit Court, Kankakee, Illinois.

6. "Mrs. Packard and the Committee," *The News and Observer* (Raleigh, North Carolina), 7 February 1885, issue 80, col. E, accessed via InfoTrac Web: Nineteenth-Century Newspapers database, 13 April 2007.

7. Clipping, "A Remarkable Woman: Mrs. Elizabeth P.W. Packard in Springfield," [photocopy], Barbara Sapinsley Papers.

8. Ibid.

9. "The Other Side of the Story: What Dr. McFarland Has to Say Concerning Mrs. Packard's $25,000 Damage Suit," *Chicago Tribune,* 14 May 1886, 5.

10. *Elizabeth P.W. Packard v. Andrew McFarland et al.,* suit filed 10 May 1886, Kankakee Circuit Court, Kankakee, Illinois.

11. Ibid.

12. *Congregational Year-Book, 1887,* 37.

13. Theophilus Packard, Diary, 153, 176, 182.

14. Packard, "Open Letter to the Members of Maryland Legislature," Annapolis, 3 April 1886.

15. Packard, "Emancipation of Married Women by Congress: Memorial in Support of United States Senate Bill 2174," 1888.

16. U.S. House, "Common Law of Marriage, Etc.," 17 March 1888.

17. E. P. W. Packard, letter to Clara Packard, 21 December 1888.

18. Ibid.

19. Ibid.

20. E. P. W. Packard, "The Emancipation Watch," letter-to-the-editor of the *Daily Inter Ocean* (Chicago), 15 September 1889, 23:1.

21. Packard, "Mrs. Packard's Argument in Support of the Bill for the Protection of the Postal Rights of the Inmates of Insane Asylums." Held by the Indiana State Library.

22. Illinois H.B. 5555, "A Bill for an Act to Revise the Law Relating to the Commitment and Detention of Lunatics" introduced 13 January 1891 by Representative Charles A. Partridge (Republican, Lake County). See Hoag, "Joint Meeting," 82.

23. Hoag, "Joint Meeting," 77.

24. Ibid., 84.

25. Ibid., 77.

26. Ibid., 76.

27. Ibid., 84.

28. Ibid.

29. "Life Behind the Bars of a Madhouse," *Chicago Daily Tribune,* 1 March 1891, 6; and "Work of the Senate Committees," *Chicago Daily Tribune,* 1 April 1891, 6.

30. Ibid.

31. Dewey, "Presidential Address," 208.

32. Dewey, "Jury Law for Commitment," 582–83.

33. "Suicide, Dr. Andrew McFarland Ends His Life by His Own Hand," *Jacksonville Journal,* 24 November 1891, 4:1–3.

34. Ibid.

35. *Abby K. McFarland v. Andrew McFarland,* Chancery Court, Morgan County, Jacksonville, Illinois, May 1881.

36. Ibid.

37. "Suicide, Dr. Andrew McFarland Ends His Life by His Own Hand," *Jacksonville Journal,* 24 November 1891, 4:3.

38. "History of Oak Lawn Sanatorium," compiled by T. O. Hardesty, [typescript], Special Collections, Jacksonville (Illinois) Public Library.

39. Founded in 1966 and built, appropriately, according to the cottage plan, the McFarland Zone Center originally served as an outpatient facility for children. Today the McFarland Mental Health Center is a state-operated in-patient facility for adults with acute or chronic mental disorders.

40. Estate of Elizabeth P. W. Packard, Will, Bond & Letter General No. 17–6535, Docket 46, Page 100, B-6-&-15, Office of the Clerk of the Circuit Court of Cook County, Chicago, Illinois.

41. "Mrs. Packard, A Card from the Humanitarian Worker to Her Friends," *Chicago Inter Ocean,* 21 July 1893, issue 119, col. A, accessed via InfoTrac Web: Nineteenth-Century Newspapers database, 13 April 2007.

42. "Aged Woman Beaten by a Burglar," *New York Times,* 17 February 1895, 6; and "Old Woman is Beaten and Robbed," *Chicago Daily Tribune,* 27 February 1895, 1.

43. Ibid.

44. Mrs. Ina (J. Hensley) Akins, Bloomsdale, Missouri, letter to Emma Packard, 22 January 1961, [photocopy], Barbara Sapinsley Papers.

45. Ibid.

46. Ibid.

47. Report of Death for Mrs. E. P. W. Packard, 25 July 1897, Bureau of Vital Statistics, Department of Health, City of Chicago.

48. "Mrs. Packard Dead: Celebrated Woman Dies Suddenly at Hahnemann Hospital," *Kankakee Times,* 28 July 1897, 2:7.

49. "Wise Friend of the Insane is Dead," *Chicago Tribune,* 27 July 1897, 2:6.

50. "Funeral of Mrs. E. P. W. Packard," *Chicago Tribune,* 28 July 1897, 10:4.

51. Estate of Elizabeth P. W. Packard, Will, Bond & Letter General No. 17–6535, Docket 46, Page 100, B-6-&-15, Office of the Clerk of the Circuit Court of Cook County, Chicago, Illinois.

52. Packard, *Modern Persecution* II, 388.

53. Kankakee County Death Records, 1877–1915, 135–36, Illinois Regional Archives Depository.

54. Emma L. Packard, letter to Barbara Sapinsley, 6 October 1965, Barbara Sapinsley Papers.

55. Estate of Elizabeth P. W. Packard, Will, Bond & Letter General No. 17–6535, Docket 46, Page 100, B-6-&-15, Office of the Clerk of the Circuit Court of Cook County, Chicago, Illinois.

56. Emma L. Packard, letter to Barbara Sapinsley, 6 October 1965, Barbara Sapinsley Papers.

57. Ibid.

58. *National Bank v. County of Yankton,* 101 U.S. 129, 25 L. Ed. 129, 1879 US LEXIS 1892.

59. Samuel W. Packard, *Dakota: Statement of Facts.* See also "Samuel Ware Packard," in *National Cyclopaedia of American Biography* (1939), vol. 27, 37–38; and "Samuel W. Packard" in Palmer, *Bench and Bar of Illinois,* 1024–26.

60. Cook, *Zion City, Illinois,* 38–39. See also, "Attorney Packard's Address," 148–49. *The Coming City* advertised itself as "a fortnightly paper published in the interests of Zion City, near Chicago, edited by the Rev. John Alexander Dowie."

61. Cook, *Zion City, Illinois,* 111–12.

62. "Memorial Service for Mrs. Samuel Ware Packard, First Congregational Church, Oak Park, IL, October 18, 1926," booklet, Walter E. Packard Papers, Bancroft Library, University of California at Berkeley.

Bibliography

Collections

American Antiquarian Society. Worcester, Mass.

Amherst College Archives. Amherst, Mass.

Barbara Sapinsley Papers. Oskar Diethelm Library, New York Hospital—Cornell Medical Center, New York.

Bills, Resolutions and Related General Assembly Records, 25th Illinois General Assembly, first session. 1867. Record Group 600.001. Illinois State Archives. Springfield, Ill.

Clements C. Fry Collection. Harvey Cushing/John Hay Whitney Medical Library, Yale University, New Haven, Conn.

Cole-Throop Family Collection, 1850–1933. Special Collections, State Historical Society of Iowa, Iowa City, Iowa.

Congregational Library Small Collections. Congregational Library of the American Congregational Association, Boston, Mass.

Edward Jarvis Papers. Rare Books & Special Collections, Francis Countway Library, Harvard Medical School, Boston, Mass. Church Records.

First Presbyterian Church of Manteno, Ill. Special Collections. Jacksonville Illinois Public Library. Jacksonville, Ill.

James and Myra Bradwell Papers, 1864–1884. Abraham Lincoln Presidential Library, Springfield, Ill.

Kankakee County Records. Illinois Regional Archives Depository. Williams Hall. Illinois State University. Bloomington, Ill.

Kankakee County Records. Kankakee County Court House. Kankakee, Ill.

Mary Lyon Collection. Five College Archives Digital Access Project. Five College Archives Digital Access Project, http://clio.fivecolleges.edu/mhc/lyon/a/2/. Accessed 29 April 2002.

Massachusetts State Archives. Boston, Mass.

Milne Special Collections and Archives, University of New Hampshire. Concord, N.H.

Miscellaneous Collections. Chicago Historical Society. Chicago, Ill.

Records of the New Hampshire Asylum for the Insane. New Hampshire Historical Society. Concord, N.H.

Sangamon County Records. Illinois Regional Archives Depository, Brookens Library. University of Illinois at Springfield. Springfield, Ill.

Special Collections. Idaho State Historical Society Library and Archives. Boise, Idaho.

Special Collections. The Jones Library, Amherst, Mass.

Walter E. Packard Papers. The Bancroft Library, University of California at Berkeley, Berkeley, Calif.

Worcester Insane Asylum Records. Francis A. Countway Library, Rare Books & Special Collections, Harvard Medical School, Cambridge, Mass. Used by permission of the Massachusetts Department of Mental Health.

Newspapers

Atchison Daily Champion (Atchison, Kan.)
Boston Daily Advertiser
Chicago Legal News
Chicago Tribune
Daily Illinois State Journal (Springfield, Ill.)
Davenport Gazette (Davenport, Ia.)
Greenfield Gazette and Courier (Greenfield, Mass.)
Illinois Journal (Springfield, Ill.)
Illinois State Journal (Springfield, Ill.)
Illinois State Register (Springfield, Ill.)
Jacksonville Journal (Jacksonville, Ill.)
Jacksonville Journal-Courier (Jacksonville, Ill.)
Jacksonville Sentinel (Jacksonville, Ill.)
Kankakee Gazette (Kankakee, Ill.)
Kankakee Times (Kankakee, Ill.)
New Haven Daily Morning Courier and Journal (New Haven, Conn.)
Northampton Free Press (Northampton, Mass.)
Philadelphia Medical News (Philadelphia, Pa.)
Springfield Register (Springfield, Ill.)

Public and Legal Documents

Bradwell v. The State. 83U.S.130; 21 L.Ed.442; 1872LEXIS1140.
Eddy v. the People. 15 Ill.386; 1854 Ill.LEXIS18.
Illinois. City of Chicago. Department of Health. Bureau of Vital Statistics. Report of Death for Mrs. E.P.W. Packard, 25 July 1897.
———. Cook County Circuit Court Archives. Office of the Clerk of the Circuit Court of Cook County. Estate of Elizabeth P.W. Packard, deceased. Will, Bond & Letter General, No. 17–6535, Docket 46, p. 100.
———. General Assembly. Joint Committee Appointed to Visit the Hospital for the Insane. Springfield: n.p., 1853.
———. General Assembly. *Journal of the House of Representatives of the Twenty-*

fifth General Assembly of the State of Illinois. Springfield: Baker, Bailhache & Co., 1867.

———. General Assembly. Journal of the Joint Committee. . . Appointed to Visit the Hospital for the Insane, 25th General Assembly, First Session, May 14, 1867–December 4, 1867, in "Bills, Resolutions and Related General Assembly Records, 25th General Assembly, 1st session." Record Group 600.001. Illinois State Archives. Springfield: Ill.

———. General Assembly. *Journal of the Senate of the Twenty-fifth General Assembly of the State of Illinois.* Springfield: Baker, Bailhache & Co., 1867.

———. General Assembly. *Laws of the State of Illinois, Passed by the Fifteenth General Assembly, Begun and Held in the City of Springfield, December 7, 1846.*

———. General Assembly. *Laws of the State of Illinois, Passed at the First Session of the Sixteenth General Assembly, 1849.*

———. General Assembly. *Laws of the State of Illinois, Passed by the Seventeenth General Assembly, at the Session Commencing January 6, 1851.*

———. General Assembly. *Laws of the State of Illinois, Passed by the Thirty-eighth General Assembly, 1893.*

———. General Assembly. *Laws of the State of Illinois, Passed by the Thirty-seventh General Assembly, 1891.*

———. General Assembly. *Public Laws of the State of Illinois, Passed by the Twenty-fourth General Assembly, Convened January 2, 1865.*

———. General Assembly. *Public Laws of the State of Illinois, Passed by the Twenty-fifth General Assembly, Convened January 8, 1867.*

Illinois. Illinois State Hospital for the Insane. *Biennial Report of the Trustees, Superintendent and Treasurer of the Illinois Central Hospital for the Insane at Jacksonville.* Springfield: D. W. Lusk, 1877.

———. Illinois State Hospital for the Insane. *Eighth Biennial Report of the Trustees, Superintendent, and Treasurer of the Illinois State Hospital for the Insane, at Jacksonville, December, 1862.* Springfield: Baker & Phillips Printers, 1862.

———. Illinois State Hospital for the Insane. *Eleventh Biennial Report of the Trustees, Superintendent and Treasurer of the Illinois State Hospital for the Insane, at Jacksonville, December, 1868.* Springfield: Illinois Journal Printing Office, 1868.

———. Illinois State Hospital for the Insane. *Ninth Biennial Report of the Trustees, Superintendent and Treasurer of the Illinois State Hospital for the Insane, at Jacksonville, December, 1864.* Springfield: Baker & Phillips, 1864.

———. Illinois State Hospital for the Insane. *Reports of the Illinois State Hospital for the Insane, 1847–1862.* Chicago: F. Fulton, 1863.

———. Illinois State Hospital for the Insane. *Special Report of the Trustees of the Illinois State Hospital for the Insane, in Review of a Report of a Legislative Committee Appointed by the Twenty-fifth General Assembly.* Springfield: Baker, Bailhache & Co., 1868.

———. Illinois State Hospital for the Insane. *Tenth Biennial Report of the Trustees, Superintendent and Treasurer of the Illinois State Hospital for the Insane, at Jacksonville, December 1866.* Springfield: Baker, Bailhache & Co., 1866.

————. Kankakee County. Circuit Court. Bill of Complaint for Divorce, Elizabeth P. W. Packard, 8 February 1864.

————. Kankakee County. Circuit Court. Chancery Summons No. 1808, E.P.W. Packard v. Theophilus Packard, 8 February 1864.

————. Morgan County. Circuit Court. Chancery Records. McFarland v. McFarland. May term, 1881.

————. Morgan County. Office of the County Clerk. Estate of Andrew McFarland, Record M, p. 17, 12 December 1891.

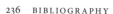

————. Office of the Governor. Report of the Investigating Committee on the Hospital for the Insane, and Other State Institutions, Made to the Governor of Illinois, December 1, 1867. Springfield: Illinois Journal Printing Office, 1869.

————. Sangamon County. Deed Records, 1822–1902. Deed Record No. 505, Thomas W. See to Elizabeth P.W. Packard, 5 April 1867.

Iowa. General Assembly. Laws of Iowa, Chapter 91, 1872.

Kansas. Senate Journal. Proceedings of the Senate of the State of Kansas, Third Biennial Session . . . at Topeka, January 9, 1883. Senate Bill 157, "An Act to Protect the Inmates of Insane Asylums," and Senate Bill 158, "An Act to Declare and Protect the Identity of Married Women." Topeka, Kans.: Kansas Publishing House. 1883.

Maine. General Assembly. Laws of Maine, Chapter 256, 1874.

Massachusetts. Franklin County. Franklin Probation and Family Court, Greenfield, Mass. Registry of Probate. Probate Docket #5009, Samuel Ware, 4 December 1866.

————. General Assembly. Laws of Massachusetts, Chapter 363, 1874.

————. Report of the Commissioners of Lunacy. House Document No. 60. Documents of the House of Representatives of Massachusetts, 1875.

————. Supreme Judicial Court Archives and Records Preservation. Last Will and Testament of Samuel Ware, 13 September 1865, Wills Vol. 49, p. 365.

————. Worcester Insane Asylum records. Commitment form for Elizabeth Parsons Ware. Francis A. Countway Library, Rare Books & Special Collections, Harvard Medical School, Cambridge, Mass. Used by permission of the Massachusetts Department of Mental Health.

————. Worcester Insane Asylum records. Patient record No. 404, 1836. Francis A. Countway Library of Medicine, Rare Books and Special Collections, Harvard Medical School, Cambridge, Mass. Used by permission of the Massachusetts Department of Mental Health.

National Bank v. County of Yankton. 101U.S.129, 25L.Ed.129, 1879US LEXIS1892.

Nebraska. General Assembly. Laws of Nebraska, Chapter 69, 1883.

New Hampshire. State Hospital for the Insane. Reports of the Board of Visitors, Trustees, Building Committee, and of the Superintendent of the New Hampshire Asylum for the Insane, June Session, 1851. Concord: Butterfield & Hill, State Printers, 1851.

————. Reports of the Board of Visitors, Trustees and Superintendent of the New Hampshire Asylum for the Insane, June Session, 1852. Concord: Butterfield & Hill, 1852.

U.S. Congress. Senate. Committee on the Judiciary. "Emancipation of Married Women by Congress: Memorial in Support of Senate Bill 2174, to change the common-law of marriage to the customs of modern civilization by the emancipation of married women . . ." by E.P.W. Packard. Washington, D.C.: [s.n.], 1888.

———. House. Committee on the Judiciary. "Common Law of Marriage, etc." Report to accompany bill H.R. 7594. Report 1189. 50th Congress, 1st Session, March 17, 1888.

———. Department of the Interior. *Population of the United States in 1860, Compiled From the Original Returns of the Eighth Census.* Washington, D.C.: GPO, 1864.

U.S. Congressional Serial Set. Serial Set No. 1654. House Miscellaneous Documents, 43rd Congress, 2nd session, No. 59 (1874–75). "Memorial in Support of the Bill for the Protection of the Postal Rights of the Inmates of Insane Asylums by Mrs. E. P. W. Packard, January 8, 1875." Referred to the Committee on the Post Office and Post Roads and ordered to be printed, February 1, 1875.

Books, Articles, and Other Documents

Albanese, Catherine. "On the Matter of Spirit: Andrew Jackson Davis and the Marriage of God and Nature." *Journal of the American Academy of Religion* 60 (1990): 1–17.

American Psychiatric Association. *One Hundred Years of American Psychiatry.* New York: Columbia University Press, 1944.

Andreas, A. T. "Biographical Sketches," in *History of the State of Nebraska, Part Five.* Chicago: Western Historical Company, 1882. Accessed online at http://www.kancoll .org/books/andreas_ne/jefferson/jefferson-p5.html#steelbio, 22 April 2007.

Appignanesi, Lisa. *Sad, Mad and Bad: Women and the Mind-Doctors from 1800.* Toronto: McArthur & Company, 2007.

Bailey's Chicago Directory. Chicago: John C. W. Bailey, 1864–65.

Baker, Jean. *Mary Todd Lincoln: A Biography.* New York: Norton, 1987.

Barton, Walter E. *The History and Influence of the American Psychiatric Association.* Washington, D.C.: American Psychiatric Press, Inc., 1987.

Basch, Norma. *Framing American Divorce: From the Revolutionary Generation to the Victorian.* Berkeley: University of California Press, 1999.

———. *In the Eyes of the Law: Women, Marriage, and Property in Nineteenth-Century New York.* Ithaca and London: Cornell University Press, 1982.

Becker, Dana. *Through the Looking Glass: Women and Borderline Personality Disorder.* Boulder, Colo.: Westview Press, 1991.

Beecher, Catharine. *A Treatise on Domestic Economy for the Use of Young Ladies at Home and at School.* Boston: Marsh, Capen, Lyon, and Webb, 1841.

Beers, Clifford. *A Mind That Found Itself.* New York: Longmans, Green & Co., 1908.

Behnke, Donna A. "Created in God's Image: Religious Issues in the Woman's Rights Movement in the 19th Century." M.A. thesis, Northwestern University, 1975.

Beldon, Gertrude May. "A History of the Woman Suffrage Movement in Illinois." M.A. thesis. University of Chicago, 1913.

Berry, Dawn Bradley. *The 50 Most Influential Women in American Law.* Los Angeles and Chicago: Lowell House and Contemporary Books, 1996.

"Bibliographical, Iowa, Seventh Biennial Report of the Iowa Hospital for Insane: 1872–73." *American Journal of Insanity* 30 (April 1874): 486–87.

Braude, Ann. *Radical Spirits: Spiritualism and Women's Rights in Nineteenth-Century America.* Boston: Beacon Press, 1989.

Brigham, Amariah. "Definition of Insanity—Nature of the Disease, October 1844." *American Journal of Psychiatry* 151 (June 1994): 97–102.

Brown, Edward M. "Neurology's Influence on American Psychiatry: 1865–1915." In *History of Psychiatry and Medical Psychology.* Ed. Edwin R. Wallace and John Gach, 519–31. New York: Springer, 2008.

Brown, Slater. *The Heyday of Spiritualism.* New York: Hawthorne Books, Inc., 1970.

Buechler, Steven M. *The Transformation of the Woman Suffrage Movement: The Case of Illinois, 1850–1920.* New Brunswick, N.J.: Rutgers University Press, 1986.

Buhle, Mari Jo. *Feminism and Its Discontents: A Century of Struggle with Psycho-analysis.* Cambridge, Mass: Harvard University Press, 1998.

Burbick, Joan. "'Intervals of Tranquility': The Language of Health in Antebellum America." *Prospects* 12 (1987): 175–99.

Burnham, John C., ed. "Elizabeth Parsons Ware Packard." In *Notable American Women, 1607–1950.* Ed. Edward T. James, Janet Wilson James, and Paul S. Boyer, vol. III, 1–2. Cambridge, Mass., and London: Belknap Press of Harvard University Press, 1971.

Butler, Jon. *Awash in a Sea of Faith: Christianizing the American People.* Cambridge, Mass. Harvard University Press, 1990.

Capper, Charles, and Conrad Edick Wright, eds. *Transient and Permanent: The Transcendentalist Movement and Its Contexts.* Boston: Massachusetts Historical Society, 1999.

Carroll, Bret E. *Spiritualism in Antebellum America.* Bloomington and Indianapolis: Indiana University Press, 1997.

Chesler, Phyllis. *Women and Madness.* Garden City, N.J.: Doubleday and Co., Inc.,1972.

Chicagoans As We See 'Em: Cartoons-Caricatures. Compiled by Frank Folwell Porter. Chicago: [Newspaper Cartoonists' Association], 1904.

Chipley, W. S. "Summary [of the Annual Report for the Eastern Lunatic Asylum, Lexington, Kentucky]." *American Journal of Insanity* 17 (January 1861): 299–300.

Chused, Richard H. "Married Women's Property Law: 1800–1850." *Georgetown Law Review* 71 (June 1983): 1359–1425.

———. *Private Acts in Public Places: A Social History of Divorce in the Formative Era of American Family Law.* Philadelphia: University of Pennsylvania Press, 1994.

Clark, Elizabeth B. "Matrimonial Bonds: Slavery and Divorce in Nineteenth-Century America." *Law and History Review* 8 (Spring 1990): 25–54.

"Commissioners in Lunacy, State of Massachusetts." *American Journal of Insanity* 31 (October 1874): 273.

Cook, Philip L. *Zion City, Illinois: Twentieth-Century Utopia*. Syracuse, N.Y.: Syracuse University Press, 1996.

Cott, Nancy F. "Divorce and the Changing Status of Women in Eighteenth-Century Massachusetts." *William and Mary Quarterly* 33 (October 1976): 568–614.

Cross, Whitney R. *The Burned-over District: The Social and Intellectual History of Enthusiastic Religion in Western New York, 1800–1850*. Ithaca: Cornell University Press, 1950; reprint, New York: Harper & Row, 1965.

Cullen-DuPont, Kathryn, ed. *American Women Activists' Writings: An Anthology, 1637–2002*. New York: Cooper Square Press, 2002.

Dain, Norman. *Concepts of Insanity in the United States, 1789–1865*. New Brunswick, N.J.: Rutgers University Press, 1964.

———. "Critics and Dissenters: Reflections on 'Anti-Psychiatry' in the United States." *Journal of the History of the Behavioral Sciences* 25 (January 1989): 3–25.

Dann, Norman. *Practical Dreamer: Gerrit Smith and the Crusade for Social Reform*. Hamilton, N.Y.: Log Cabin Press, 2009.

Davis, Andrew Jackson. *Principles of Nature, Her Divine Revelations, and a Voice to Mankind*. 1847, 8th ed. New York: S. S. Lyon & Wm. Fishbough, 1851.

Degler, Carl. *At Odds: Women and the Family in America from the Revolution to the Present*. New York: Oxford University Press, 1980.

DeLamotte, Eugenia C. *Perils of the Night: A Feminist Study of Nineteenth-Century Gothic*. New York: Oxford University Press, 1990.

Deutsch, Albert. "History of Mental Hygiene." In *One Hundred Years of American Psychiatry: 1844–1944*. Ed. J. K. Hall et al. New York: Columbia University Press, 1944.

———. *The Mentally Ill in America: A History of Their Care and Treatment From Colonial Times*. 2nd ed. New York and London: Columbia University Press, 1949.

Dewey, Richard. "The Jury Law for Commitment of the Insane in Illinois (1867–1893), and Mrs. E. P. W. Packard, Its Author, Also Later Developments in Lunacy Legislation in Illinois." *American Journal of Insanity* 64 (January 1913): 571–84.

———. "Presidential Address to the Association of Medical Superintendents of American Institutions for the Insane." *American Journal of Insanity* 53 (1897): 208.

Digby, Anne. *Madness, Morality and Medicine: A Study of the York Retreat, 1796–1914*. New York: Cambridge University Press, 1985.

Dixon, Chris. *Perfecting the Family: Antislavery Marriages in Nineteenth-Century America*. Amherst: University of Massachusetts Press, 1997.

Dorrien, Gary. *The Making of American Liberal Theology: Imagining Progressive Religion, 1805–1900*. Louisville, Ky.: Westminster John Knox Press, 2001.

Dowdall, George W. *The Eclipse of the State Mental Hospital: Policy, Stigma and Organization*. Albany: State University of New York Press, 1996.

Doyle, Don. *The Social Order of a Frontier Community: Jacksonville, Illinois 1825–70.* Urbana: University of Illinois Press, 1978, 70–72.

DuBois, Ellen Carol. "Outgrowing the Compact of the Fathers: Equal Rights, Woman Suffrage, and the United States Constitution, 1820–1878." *Journal of American History* 74 (December 1987): 836–62.

Dunton, W. R., Jr. "Further Note on Mrs. Packard." *Johns Hopkins Hospital Bulletin* 19 (July 1908): 192–93.

———. "Mrs. Packard and her Influence Upon Laws for the Commitment of the Insane." *Johns Hopkins Hospital Bulletin* 18 (October 1907): 419–23.

Dwyer, Ellen. *Homes for the Mad: Life Inside Two Nineteenth-Century Asylums.* New Brunswick and London: Rutgers University Press, 1987.

Eaton, Dorman B. "Despotism in Lunatic Asylums." *North American Review* 132 (March 1881): 263–75.

Edwards Annual Directory to the Inhabitants, Institutions, Incorporated Companies, Manufacturing Establishments, Business Firms, etc. in the City of Chicago for 1860–70, vol. 12. Chicago: Richard Edwards, Publisher, 1869–70.

Emerson, Jason. *The Madness of Mary Lincoln.* Carbondale: Southern Illinois University Press, 2007.

Everts, Orpheus. "The American System of Public Provision for the Insane." *American Journal of Insanity* 38 (October 1881): 113–39.

Failer, Judith Lynn. *Who Qualifies for Rights? Homelessness, Mental Illness, and Civil Commitment.* Ithaca and London: Cornell University Press, 2002.

Farragher, John Mack. *Sugar Creek: Life on the Illinois Prairie.* New Haven, Conn.: Yale University Press, 1985.

Finzsch, Norbert, and Robert Jutte. *Institutions of Confinement: Hospitals, Asylums, and Prisons in Western Europe and North America, 1500–1950.* New York: Cambridge University Press, 1996.

First Presbyterian Church of Manteno, Ill. "Brief Historical Sketch of the Development and Activities of the first Presbyterian Church of Manteno, Ill. From the Time of Its Organization, April 8th, 1853, until the Day of Re-dedication, January 19, 1905," AMs [photocopy].

———. Historical Sketches of the Development and Activities of the First Presbyterian Church of Manteno, Illinois, from the Time of its Organization April, 1853 until October 25, 1953 [photocopy].

Foucault, Michel. *Madness and Civilization: A History of Insanity in the Age of Reason.* Trans. Richard Howard. New York: Pantheon Books, 1965.

Fox, Richard Wightman. *Trials of Intimacy: Love and Loss in the Beecher-Tilton Scandal.* Chicago: University of Chicago Press, 1999.

Friedman, Jane M. *America's First Woman Lawyer: The Biography of Myra Bradwell.* Buffalo, N.Y.: Prometheus Books, 1992.

Fuller, Robert B. *An Account of the Imprisonment and Sufferings of Robert Fuller* . . . Boston: the author, 1833.

Gamwell, Lynn, and Nancy Tomes. *Madness in America: Cultural and Medical Perceptions Before 1914.* Ithaca, N.Y.: Cornell University Press, 1995.

Gaustad, Edwin S., ed. *A Documentary History of Religion in America to the Civil War.* 2nd ed. Grand Rapids, Mich.: William B. Eerdmans Publishing Company, 1993, 280.

Geller, Jeffrey L. "Women's Accounts of Psychiatric Illness and Institutionalization." *Hospital and Community Psychiatry* 36 (October 1985): 1056–62.

Geller, Jeffrey L., et al. "The Rights of State Hospital Patients: From State Hospitals to Their Alternatives." *Administration and Policy in Mental Health* 25 (March 1998): 387–401.

Geller, Jeffrey L., and Maxine Harris. *Women of the Asylum: Voices From Behind the Walls, 1840–1945.* New York: Anchor Books, 1994.

Goldsmith, Barbara. *Other Powers: The Age of Suffrage, Spiritualism, and the Scandalous Victoria Woodhull.* New York: Alfred Knopf, 1998.

Gosling, F. G. *Before Freud: Neurasthenia and the American Medical Community, 1870–1910.* Urbana: University of Illinois Press, 1987.

———, and Joyce M. Ray. "'The Right to Be Sick,' American Physicians and Nervous Patients, 1885–1910." *Journal of Social History* 20 (Winter 1986): 251–67.

Gray, John P. "Illinois Legislation Regarding Hospitals for the Insane." *American Journal of Insanity* 26 (October 1869): 204–29.

———. "Summary." *American Journal of Insanity* 27 (October 1870): 260–62.

Grob, Gerald N. "Abuse in American Mental Hospitals in Historical Perspective: Myth and Reality." *International Journal of Law and Psychiatry* 3 (1980): 295–310.

———. *The Mad Among Us: A History of the Care of America's Mentally Ill.* New York: Free Press, 1994.

———. *Mental Illness and American Society, 1875–1940.* Princeton, N.J.: Princeton University Press, 1983.

———. *Mental Institutions in America: Social Policy to 1875.* New York: Free Press, 1973.

———. "The Transformation of the Mental Hospital in the United States." *American Behavioral Scientist* 28 (5) (1985): 639–54.

Grossberg, Michael. *Governing the Hearth: Law and the Family in Nineteenth-Century America.* Chapel Hill and London: University of North Carolina Press, 1985.

Halttunen, Karen. "Gothic Mystery and the Birth of the Asylum: The Cultural Construction of Deviance in Early-Nineteenth-Century America." In *Moral Problems in American Life.* Ed. Karen Halttunen and Lewis Perry, New Perspectives on Cultural History, 40–57. Ithaca, N.Y.: Cornell University Press, 1998.

Hammerton, A. James. *Cruelty and Companionship: Conflict in Nineteenth-Century Married Life.* London and New York: Routledge, 1992.

Hartog, Hendrick. *Man & Wife in America.* Cambridge, Mass.: Harvard University Press, 2000.

————. *Mrs. Packard On Dependency.* Legal History Program Working Papers. Madison: University of Wisconsin Law School, 1988.

Hatch, Nathan O. *The Democratization of American Christianity.* New Haven: Yale University Press, 1989.

Himmelhoch, Myra Samuels, with Arthur H. Shaffer. "Elizabeth Packard: Nineteenth-Century Crusader for the Rights of Mental Patients." *Journal of American Studies* 13 (December 1979): 343–75.

"History of Oak Lawn Sanatorium," compiled by T. O. Hardesty, M.D., 1–3. Typescript. Bound with unpublished History of Oak Lawn T.B. Sanatorium. Special Collections. Jacksonville (Illinois) Public Library.

History of Morgan County, Illinois: Its Past and Present. Chicago: Donnelley, Lloyd & Co., 1878.

Hoag, Junius C. "Joint Meeting February 16, 1891, of the Chicago Medical Society and the Medico-Legal Society of Chicago." *Chicago Medical Record* 1 (1891): 75–86.

Hubert, Susan J. *Questions of Power: The Politics of Women's Madness Narratives.* Newark: University of Delaware Press and London: Associated University Presses, 2002.

Hunt, Isaac H. *Astounding Disclosure! Three Years in a Mad-House . . .* Shohegan, Me.: A.A. Mann, 1851.

Hurd, Henry M. *The Institutional Care of the Insane in the United States and Canada.* Baltimore: Johns Hopkins, 1916–17.

Jaffary, Stuart King. *The Mentally Ill and Public Provision for Their Care in Illinois.* Chicago: University of Chicago Press, 1942.

James, Henry. *The Secret of Swedenborg: Being an Elucidation of His Doctrine of the Divine Natural Humanity.* Boston: Fields, 1869.

James, William. *The Varieties of Religious Experience: A Study in Human Nature.* Ed. Martin E. Marty. New York: Longmans, Green and Co., 1902; reprint, New York: Viking Penguin, 1982.

Johnson, Ann Braden. *Out of Bedlam: The Truth About Deinstitutionalization.* New York: Basic Books, 1990.

Kelley, Mary. *Private Woman, Public Stage: Literary Domesticity in Nineteenth-Century America.* New York: Oxford University Press, 1984.

Kerber, Linda K. "Separate Spheres, Female Worlds, Woman's Place: The Rhetoric of Women's History." *Journal of American History* 75 (June 1988): 9–39.

————. *Women of the Republic: Intellect and Ideology in Revolutionary America.* Chapel Hill: University of North Carolina Press, 1980.

Lerner, Gerda. *The Creation of Feminist Consciousness: From the Middle Ages to Eighteen-Seventy.* New York and Oxford: Oxford University Press, 1993.

Levison, Jennifer Rebecca. "Elizabeth Parsons Ware Packard: An Advocate for Cultural, Religious, and Legal Change." *Alabama Law Review* 54 (Spring 2003): 985–1075.

Lightner, David L. *Asylum, Prison, and Poorhouse: The Writings and Reform Work of Dorothea Dix in Illinois.* Carbondale: Southern Illinois University Press, 1999.

Luchins, Abraham S. "The Rise and Decline of the American Asylum Movement in the 19th Century." *Journal of Psychology* 122 (September 1988): 471–86.

Lunbeck, Elizabeth. *The Psychiatric Persuasion: Knowledge, Gender, and Power in Modern America.* Princeton: Princeton University Press, 1994.

Marsden, George M. *The Evangelical Mind and the New School Presbyterian Experience: A Case Study of Thought and Theology in Nineteenth-Century America.* New Haven and London: Yale University Press, 1970.

McDermott, Stacy Pratt. "Dissolving the Bonds of Matrimony." In *In Tender Consideration: Women, Families, and the Law in Abraham Lincoln's Illinois.* Ed. Daniel W. Stowell, 71–103. Urbana: University of Illinois Press, 2002.

McGarry, Molly. *Ghosts of Futures Past: Spiritualism and the Cultural Politics of Nineteenth-Century America.* Berkeley: University of California Press, 2008.

McGovern, Constance M. *Masters of Madness: Social Origins of the American Psychiatric Profession.* Hanover and London: University Press of New England, 1985.

Mehr, Joseph J. *An Illustrated History of Illinois Public Mental Health Services: 1847–2000.* Victoria, B.C.: Trafford, 2002.

Miller, Ross. *The Great Chicago Fire.* Urbana: University of Illinois Press, 1990.

Moers, Ellen. *Literary Women.* New York: Anchor Press, 1977.

Mohr, James C. *Doctors and the Law: Medical Jurisprudence in Nineteenth-Century America.* New York: Oxford University Press, 1993.

Moore, R. Laurence. *In Search of White Crows: Spiritualism, Parapsychology, and American Culture.* New York: Oxford University Press, 1977.

Neely, Mark E., Jr., and R. Gerald McMurtry. *The Insanity File: The Case of Mary Todd Lincoln.* Carbondale and Edwardsville: Southern Illinois University Press, 1986.

Norgren, Jill. *Belva Lockwood: The Woman Who Would be President.* New York: New York University Press, 2007.

Noyes, John H. *History of American Socialisms.* Reprint ed. New York: Hillary House Publishers, 1961.

Ochberg, Frank M. *Post Traumatic Therapy and Victims of Violence.* New York: Brunner/Mazel, 1988.

McFarland, Andrew. Andrew McFarland to the Hon. Thos. P. Rogers of the Twenty-Eighth Representative District, of the Twenty-First General Assembly of the State of Illinois. Carrolton, Ill.: Patriot Printing, 1879. Abraham Lincoln Presidential Library, Springfield, Ill.

———. "Association Reminiscences and Reflections." *American Journal of Insanity* 34 (January 1878): 342–59.

———. "Attendants in Institutions for the Insane." *American Journal of Insanity* 17 (July 1860): 53–60.

———. *Draining and Sub-soil Plowing.* Concord: Butterfield and Hill Printers, 1853.

———. *The Escape, or, Loiterings Amid The Scenes of Story and Song.* Boston: B. B. Mussey & Company, 1851.

————. "Minor Mental Maladies." *American Journal of Insanity* 20 (July 1863): 10–26.

————. *What Shall Be Done with the Insane of the West?* Chicago: Western Association for the Promotion of Social Science, 1868.

McGovern, Constance M. "The Myths of Social Control and Custodial Oppression: Patterns of Psychiatric Medicine in Late Nineteenth-Century Institutions." *Journal of Social History* 20 (1) (1986): 3–23.

————. "Psychiatry, Psychoanalysis, and Women in America: An Historical Note." *Psychoanalytic Review* 71 (4) (1984): 541–52.

McHugh, Christine. "Phrenology: Getting Your Head Together in Ante-Bellum America." *Midwest Quarterly* 23 (1981): 65–77.

Minow, Martha. "'Forming Underneath Everything That Grows': Toward a History of Family Law." *Wisconsin Law Review* 819 (July–August 1985). Journal online. Avaiable from LexisNexis Academic Universe; accessed 5 May 2003. http://www.lexisnexis .com/us/lnacademic/results/docview/docview.do?docLinkInd=true&risb=21_ T891689229&format=GNBFI&sort=BOOLEAN&startDocNo=&resultsUrlKey= 29_T8916884287&cisb=22_T8916895900&treeMax=true&treeWidth=0&csi= 7368&docNo=3

Norbury, Frank. "Dorothea Dix and the Founding of Illinois' First Mental Hospital." *Journal of the Illinois State Historical Society* 92 (Spring 1999): 13–29.

Packard, Elizabeth Parsons Ware. "A Bill to Remedy the Evils of Insane Asylums and Mrs. E.P.W. Packard's Argument, in Support of the Same, Presented to the Massachusetts Legislature, April 28, 1874. [Boston: s.n.,] 1874. Courtesy of the American Antiquarian Society.

————. "Emancipation of Married Women by Congress, a Memorial in support of Senate Bill 2174, to Change the Common-Law or Marriage to the Customs of Modern Civilization by The Emancipation of Married Women in the District of Columbia, the Forts and Arsenals, and the Territories of the United States." Ordered to be printed by the Senate Judiciary Committee, March 5, 1888. Held by the Rutherford B. Hayes Presidential Center, Fremont, Ohio.

————. *The Exposure on Board the Atlantic & Pacific Car of Emancipation for the Slaves of Old Columbia, Engineered by the Lightning Express; or, Christianity and Calvinism Compared. With an Appeal to the Government to Emancipate the Slaves of the Marriage Union.* Cover title, *Exposure of Calvinism, and Defense of Christianity.* Chicago: the Authoress, 1864. Held by the Abraham Lincoln Presidential Library, Springfield, Ill.

————. *Great Disclosure of Spiritual Wickedness!! In High Places. With an Appeal to the Government to Protect the Inalienable Rights of Married Women.* Boston: the Author, 1864; reprint, New York: Arno Press, 1974.

————. *The Great Drama, or, The Millennial Harbinger.* 4 vols. Hartford: the Author, 1878.

————. *Marital Power Exemplified in Mrs. Packard's Trial, and Self-Defence From the Charge of Insanity; or, Three Years' Imprisonment for Religious Belief, by the*

Arbitrary Will of a Husband, With an Appeal to the Government to So Change the Laws as to Afford Legal Protection to Married Women. Hartford: Case, Lockwood & Co., 1867.

———. *Modern Persecution, or Insane Asylums Unveiled.* Hartford: Case, Lockwood and Brainard, 1875; reprint, New York: Arno Press, 1973.

———. "Mrs. Packard's Address to the Illinois Legislature" and "Action of Illinois Legislature on this Subject. February 12, 1867." Photocopy. Held by the American Antiquarian Society.

———. "Mrs. Packard's Argument in Support of the Bill for the Protection of the Postal Rights of the Inmates of Insane Asylums. [Indianapolis, Ind.], 1891." Held by the Indiana State Library, Indianapolis, Ind.

———. "Mrs. Packard's Exposure of Doctor Ray's Fallacies, Before the judiciary Committee of Rhode Island Legislature. March 10th, 1874." [Providence, Rhode Island: s.n.], 1874. Held by the American Antiquarian Society.

———. *Mrs. Packard's Reproof to Dr. McFarland for His Abuse of His Patients, and for which He Called Her Hopelessly Insane.* Chicago: Times Steam Job Printing House, 1864. Held by Rare Books & Special Collections, Francis Countway Library, Harvard Medical School, Boston, Mass.

———. *The Mystic Key; or, The Asylum Secret Unlocked.* Hartford: the Authoress, 1878.

———. "Open Letter to the Legislatures of Nebraska, Kansas, and Colorado." [January 1883]. Digital image. Accessed online at http://www.kansasmemory .org/item/206221, 21 October 2009.

———. "Open Letter to the Members of Maryland Legislature," Annapolis, 3 April 1886. Photocopy. Barbara Sapinsley Papers.

———. *The Prisoner's Hidden Life, or Insane Asylums Unveiled: As Demonstrated by the Report of the Investigating Committee of the Legislature of Illinois. Together with Mrs. Packard's Coadjutor's Testimony.* Chicago: the Authoress, 1868.

———. *The Woman Hating Party in the Idaho Legislature Exposed!* Boise City: Republican Print, Idaho Territory, 1881.

Packard, Samuel Ware. "Attorney Packard's Address." *The Coming City* 1 (December 12, 1900): 148–50. Walter E. Packard Papers, Bancroft Library, University of California at Berkeley.

———. *Dakota: Statement of Facts in Support of the Protest Made by the Yankton County Bondholders Against the Admission of Dakota.* N.p., 1882. Held by the Newberry Library, Chicago, Ill.

———. *Plan for Permanent Peace by the Disarmament of Every Nation in the World.* Pasadena, California: n.p., 1915. Walter E. Packard Papers, Bancroft Library, University of California at Berkeley.

Packard, Theophilus. Diary and Account Book. Walter E. Packard Papers. The Bancroft Library. The University of California at Berkeley.

———. *History of the Churches and Ministers of Franklin Association, in Franklin*

County, Mass. and an Appendix Respecting the County. Boston: S. K. Whipple and Co., Dutton & Wentworth, 1854.

Palmer, John M., ed. *The Bench and Bar of Illinois, Historical and Reminiscent.* Vol. II. Chicago: Lewis Publishing Company, 1899.

Parigot, J. "Legislation on Lunacy." *American Journal of Insanity* 21 (October 1864): 200–223.

Pollock, Robert. *The Course of Time: A Poem in Ten Books.* Edinburgh: William Blackwood and London: T. Cadell, 1827.

Portrait and Biographical Album of Morgan and Scott Counties, Illinois. Chicago: Chapman Brothers, 1889.

Portrait and Biographical Record of Kankakee County, Illinois. Chicago: Lake City Publishing Company, 1893.

Proceedings, Association of Medical Superintendent of American Institutions for the Insane and Proceedings, American Medico-Legal Association. As reported in the *American Journal of Insanity,* 1847–96.

Proceedings of the Woman's Rights Conventions, Held at Seneca Falls & Rochester, N. Y., July & August, 1848. New York: Robert J. Johnston, Printer, 1870; reprint, New York: Arno Press, 1969.

Randall, Ruth Painter. *Mary Lincoln: Biography of a Marriage.* Boston: Little, Brown, 1953.

Ray, Isaac. "American Legislation on Insanity." *American Journal of Insanity* 21 (July 1864): 21–62.

———. "An Examination of the Objections to the Doctrine of Moral Insanity." *American Journal of Insanity* 18 (October 1861): 112–38.

Reade, Charles. *Hard Cash: A Matter-of-Fact Romance.* London: Sampson Low, Son, & Marston, 1863 and Philadelphia: The Nottingham Society, 1863.

Reiss, Benjamin. *Theaters of Madness: Insane Asylums and Nineteenth-Century American Culture.* Chicago: University of Chicago Press, 2008.

"Report of the Commissioners of Lunacy, to the Commonwealth of Massachusetts, January 1875." *American Journal of Insanity* 31 (April 1875): 476–77.

"Reports from American Asylums." *American Journal of Insanity* 30 (April 1874): 482.

Robson, Charles, ed. *Biographical Encyclopaedia of Illinois of the Nineteenth Century.* Philadelphia: Galaxy Publishing Company, 1875.

Rosenberg, Charles E. *The Trial of the Assassin Guiteau: Psychiatry and Law in the Gilded Age.* Chicago and London: University of Chicago Press, 1968.

Rothman, David J. *The Discovery of the Asylum: Social Order and Disorder in the New Republic.* Boston and Toronto: Little, Brown & Co., 1971.

Russell, Denise. *Women, Madness and Medicine.* Cambridge: Polity Press, 1995.

Ryan, Mary P. *Cradle of the Middle Class: The Family in Oneida County New York, 1790–1865.* New York: Cambridge University Press, 1981.

Sage, Leland L. *A History of Iowa.* Ames: Iowa State University Press, 1974.

Sapinsley, Barbara. *The Private War of Mrs. Packard: The Dramatic Story of a Nine-teenth-Century Feminist.* New York: Paragon House, 1991.

Sawislak, Karen. *Smoldering City: Chicagoans and the Great Fire, 1871–1874.* Chicago: University of Chicago Press, 1995.

Scull, Andrew. *The Insanity of Place/The Place of Insanity.* New York: Routledge, 2006.

———. *Madhouses, Mad-Doctors, and Madmen: The Social History of Psychiatry in the Victorian Era.* Philadelphia: University of Pennsylvania Press, 1981.

———. *Social Order/Mental Disorder: Anglo-American Psychiatry in Historical Perspective.* Berkeley and Los Angeles: University of California Press, 1989.

Shannonhouse, Rebecca, ed. *Out of Her Mind: Women Writing on Madness.* New York: Random House, 2000.

Shepherd, Tonya. "The Spectacular Madwoman: Nineteenth-Century Women Writers Who Exposed the Ideological Bias of Psychiatric Objectivity and the Immorality of Moral Asylum Management." Ph.D. dissertation, Indiana University of Pennsylvania, 2003.

Shershow, John C., ed. *Delicate Branch: The Vision of Moral Psychiatry.* Oceanside, N.Y.: Dabor Science Publications, 1977.

Showalter, Elaine. *The Female Malady: Women, Madness, and English Culture, 1830–1980.* New York: Pantheon Books, 1985.

Sigstedt, Cyriel Odhner. *The Swedenborg Epic: The Life and Works of Emanuel Swedenborg.* New York: Bookman Associates, 1952.

Sklar, Kathryn Kish. *Catharine Beecher: A Study in American Domesticity.* New York: W. W. Norton, 1976.

———. *Women's Rights Emerges Within the Antislavery Movement, 1830–1870: A Brief History with Documents.* Boston and New York: Bedford/St. Martin's, 2000.

Slovenko, Ralph. "Commentary: Reviewing Civil Commitment Laws." *Psychiatric Times* 27 (October 2000). Journal online. Available from http://www.mhsource.com. Accessed 2 February 2001.

———. "Highlights in the History of Law and Psychiatry with Focus on the United States," *Journal of Psychiatry & Law* 25 (4) (1997): 445–579.

Smith, Stephen. "Unification of the Laws of the States Relating to the Commitment of the Insane." *American Journal of Insanity* 49 (October 1892): 157–83.

Smith, Timothy L. *Revivalism and Social Reform: American Protestantism on the Eve of the Civil War.* Nashville: Abingdon Press, 1957; reprint, New York: Harper & Row, 1965.

Smith-Rosenberg, Carroll. "The Female Animal: Medical and Biological Views of Woman and Her Role in Nineteenth-Century America." *Journal of American History* 60 (September 1973): 332–56.

———. "The Hysterical Woman: Sex Roles and Role Conflict in 19th-Century America." *Social Research* 39 (1972): 652–78.

———. "Puberty to Menopause: The Cycle of Femininity in Nineteenth-Century America." In *Clio's Consciousness Raised: New Perspectives on the History of Women.* Ed. Mary S. Hartman and Lois Banner. New York: Harper & Row, 1974.

Stanton, Elizabeth Cady, Susan B. Anthony, and Frances Gage, eds. 2nd ed. *History of Woman Suffrage*. Vols. I-III. Rochester, N.Y.: Charles Mann, 1889.

Staples, William G. *Castles of Conscience: Social Control and the American State, 1800–1985*. New Brunswick, N.J.: Rutgers University Press, 1990.

Stauffer, John. *The Black Hearts of Men: Radical Abolitionists and the Transformation of Race*. Cambridge, Mass.: Harvard University Press, 2002.

Stone, Elizabeth T. *Exposing the Modern Secret Way of Persecuting Christians in Order to Hush the Voice of Truth: Insane Hospitals are Inquisition Houses*. Boston: the Author, 1859.

Swedenborg, Emanuel. *The Delights of Wisdom Pertaining to Conjugial Love*. New York: American Swedenborg Printing and Publishing Society, 1903; reprint, translated by Samuel M. Warren. New York: Swedenborg Foundation, 1938.

Synnestvedt, Sig. *The Essential Swedenborg*. New York: Twayne Publishers, 1970.

Szasz, Thomas S. *The Age of Madness: The History of Involuntary Mental Hospitalization Presented in Selected Texts*. Garden City, N.Y.: Anchor Press/Doubleday, 1973.

———. *Coercion as Cure: A Critical History of Psychiatry*. New Brunswick: Transaction Publishers, 2007.

———. *Law, Liberty and Psychiatry*. New York: Macmillan, 1963.

———. *The Manufacture of Madness: A Comparative Study of the Inquisition and the Mental Health Movement*. New York: Harper & Row, 1970.

———. *The Myth of Mental Illness: Foundations of a Theory of Personal Conduct*. New York: Harper & Row, 1961.

Tiffany, Nina Moore. *Samuel E. Sewall: A Memoir*. Boston and New York: Houghton, Mifflin and Co., 1898.

Tocqueville, Alexis de. *Democracy in America*. London: Saunders and Otley, 1835–40; reprint, translated by Harvey C. Mansfield and Delba Winthrop. Chicago and London: University of Chicago Press, 2000.

Tomes, Nancy. *A Generous Confidence: Thomas Story Kirkbride and the Art of Asylum-Keeping, 1840–1883*. New York and London: Cambridge University Press, 1984.

Tonkovich, Nicole. *Domesticity with a Difference: The Nonfiction of Catharine Beecher, Sarah J. Hale, Fanny Fern, and Margaret Fuller*. Jackson: University Press of Mississippi, 1997.

Torrey, E. Fuller, and Judy Miller. *The Invisible Plague: The Rise of Mental Illness from 1750 to the Present*. New Brunswick: Rutgers University Press, 2001.

Tuke, Hack. "Psychological Retrospect: American Retrospect, The Insane in the United States, General Management and Treatment." *Journal of Mental Science* 31 (1885): 89–116.

Tyler, W. S. *History of Amherst College during its First Half Century, 1821–1871*. Springfield, Mass.: Clark W. Bryan and Company, 1873.

"The United States, vs. Charles J. Guiteau." *American Journal of Insanity* 38 (January 1882): 303–448.

Ussher, Jane M. *Women's Madness: Misogyny or Mental Illness?* Amherst: University of Massachusetts Press, 1991.

Valeri, Mark R. *Law and Providence in Joseph Bellamy's New England: The Origins of the New Divinity in Revolutionary America.* New York: Oxford University Press, 1994.

Velek, Miroslav. *Jacksonville State Hospital: The First Psychiatric Institution in Illinois.* Springfield: Department of Medical Humanities, School of Medicine, Southern Illinois University, 1982.

Wacker, Grant. *Religion in 19th Century America.* New York: Oxford University Press, 2000.

Wallace, Edwin R., and John Gach. *History of Psychiatry and Medical Psychology: with an Epilogue on Psychiatry and the Mind-Body Relation.* New York: Springer, 2008.

Waller, Altina L. *Reverend Beecher and Mrs. Tilton: Sex and Class in Victorian America.* Amherst: University of Massachusetts Press, 1982.

Welter, Barbara. "The Cult of True Womanhood: 1820–1860." *American Quarterly* 18 (Summer 1966): 151–74.

Wheeler, Adade Mitchell, with Marlene Stein Wortman. *The Roads They Made: Women in Illinois History.* Chicago: Charles H. Kerr Publishing Company, 1977.

Whitaker, Robert. *Mad in America: Bad Science, Bad Medicine, and the Enduring Mistreatment of the Mentally Ill.* Cambridge, Mass.: Perseus, 2002.

Winter, Kari. *Subjects of Slavery, Agents of Change: Women and Power in Gothic Novels and Slave Narratives, 1790–1865.* Athens: University of Georgia Press, 1992.

Wood, Mary Elene. *Writing on the Wall: Women's Autobiography and the Asylum.* Urbana: University of Illinois Press, 1994.

Wright, Rebekah. *Hydrotherapy in Psychiatric Hospitals.* Boston: Tudor Press, 1940.

Yanni, Carla. *The Architecture of Madness: Insane Asylums in the United States.* Minneapolis: University of Minnesota Press, 2007.

Yellin, Jean Fagan, and John C. Van Horne, eds. *The Abolitionist Sisterhood: Women's Political Culture in Antebellum America.* Ithaca: Cornell University Press, 1994.

Zwelling, Shomer. "Spiritualist Perspectives on Antebellum Experience." *Journal of Psychohistory* 10 (1982): 3–25.

Index

Page numbers in italics refer to illustrations.

abolitionism, 6, 38, 41, 116
Alabama Law Review, 13
Allen, Nathan, 171–72, 176, 178
American Journal of Insanity: on internal reform of organization, 121; on McFarland leadership position resignation, 77; on McFarland situation, 140; on Packard legislative efforts, 10–11, 119–21; on patient postal rights, 171, 172–73, 177; on professional expertise of members, 70
American Psychiatric Association, 3. *See also* AMSAII (Association of Medical Superintendents of Institutions for the Insane)
America's First Woman Lawyer: The Biography of Myra Bradwell (Friedman), 13
AMSAII (Association of Medical Superintendents of Institutions for the Insane): campaign to block or repeal Packard's Law, 175–76, 178–79; criticism from overseas, 177–78; defensive positions, 168, 188–89; formation, 68–69, 118; on investigation of Illinois Hospital for the Insane, 140; opposition to Massachusetts legislative change efforts, 124, 127; related groups, 188; sanity/insanity definition debates, 96–100, 120–21
"An Act in Relation to the Earnings of Married Women," 158

"An Act to Establish and Protect the Maternal Rights of Married Women," 156–58
"An Appeal in Behalf of the Insane" (Coe), 111
Andrew McFarland Mental Health Center, 195, 231n39
Anthony, Susan B., 64
Anti-Insane Asylum Society, 153–54
Association of Medical Superintendents of Institutions for the Insane (AMSAII). *See* AMSAII (Association of Medical Superintendents of Institutions for the Insane)
Asylum, Prison, and Poorhouse: The Writings and Reform Work of Dorothea Dix in Illinois (Lightner), 13
asylum administration, 70–71, 72. *See also* AMSAII (Association of Medical Superintendents of Institutions for the Insane); institutionalization of 1860–1863; McFarland, Andrew

Baker, Abner, 50–53, 107, 181
Baldwin, Elmer, 135, 139
Barton, Walter, 14
Basch, Norma, 14
Beecher, Catharine, 6, 30–31, 86
Beecher, Edward, 71
Beecher, Henry Ward, 16, 39, 143, 182–83
Beedy, Daniel, 102
Beers, Clifford, 154, 224–25n51
"Bible argument for the subjection of the wife," 186

Bible Class episode, 53–56, 59
Blessing, Mr. and Mrs. William, 78–79, 108
Boardman, William A., 122
Board of Public Charities, 159–60
Boise Republican, 186
Bond, Lester L., 157, 158
Bonfield, Thomas P., 104–5
Boston Daily Advertiser, 123, 125
Bradwell, James B., *133*; asylum abuse allegations, 140; Packard-Lincoln connection, 1; as Packard network participant, 178, 180; testimonials for Elizabeth Packard, 160, 180; women's suffrage reform efforts, 157
Bradwell, Myra, *134*; law career, influence and accomplishments, 133–34, 220n10; Packard-Lincoln connection, 1; as Packard network participant, 178–79, 180; as women's suffragist, 157
Braude, Ann, 46–50
Brie, Joseph E., 107
Brower, D. R., 194
Brown, J. W., 105–6
Brown, Tilden, 126–27
Burnham, John C., 12
Butler, John E., 170

Calvinism: conversion formula, 24–25; opposing views of Elizabeth Packard, 53–56; opposition sects, 33–34, 38–39; Packard (Elizabeth) treatise attacking, 91–92; Packard (Theophilus) interpretation of doctrine, 32–33; spiritualism v., 46–47. *See also* Congregationalism; Packard, Theophilus
"Calvinism and Christianity Compared," 91–92
Campbell, Alexander, 33
Carroll, Bret, 181
Channing, William Ellery, 33
Chauncy, Charles, 33
Chesler, Phyllis, 11

Chicago Daily Inter Ocean, 193, 196
Chicago fire, 163
Chicago Legal News, 13, 134, 163, 178–79
Chicago Medical Society, 193–94
Chicago Times, 135
Chicago Tribune: "anonymous" Packard articles published, 157; Jacksonville asylum investigation report, 145, 146–47; McFarland rebuttal to Packard, 112; Packard bill reporting, 194; praise for Packard, 8, 197; support for Packard, 135
child custody rights, 111, 125, 156, 160, 163
Chipley, W. S., 98
Christian Freeman, 78
Church, Archibald, 193–94
Coe, Mr. and Mrs. James, 111
Colorado legislative reform efforts, 190
commitment, 60, 63, 64–67. *See also* institutionalization for insanity; institutionalization of 1860–1863
Compton, William, 176
Congregationalism, 16, 24–25, 38–39, 59–60
Congregational Year-Book, 191–92
Connecticut legislative reform efforts, 128–31, 169
Cornett, Charles C., 143
Currier, T., 160–61
custody rights, 111
Cutler, Hannah Tracy, 156

Dain, Norman, 70, 75
Davenport Gazette, 165
Davis, Andrew Jackson, 42
Declaration of Sentiments, 115, 116
DeLamotte, Eugenia, 151
demographics, 3–5
desertion, 57
"Despotism in Lunatic Asylums" (Eaton), 188–89
Deutsch, Alfred, 11
Dewey, Richard, 10–11, 193, 195

Dictionary of Medical Science (Dunglison), 16–17
Dingley, Nelson, Jr., 170
divorce, 57, 95, 110–11
Dix, Dorothea, 2, 4, 63, 70, 86–87
Doggett, Kate N., 157
Dole, Abijah, 53, 56, 106, 109, 162–63, 191
Dole, Sybil, 106–7, 162–63
domestic feminism, 29–31, 117
Dummer, Henry E., 140, 145, 222n3
Duncanson, Dr., 109
Dunglison, Robley, 16–17
Dunton, William R., 10
Dwyer, Ellen, 83, 209n41

Earle, Pliny, 86, 118–19, 127, 168
earnings rights, 156
Eaton, Dorman, 188–89
Eclectic Materia Medica, Pharmacology and Therapeutics (Felter), 17
Eddy, Ansel D., 60, 79
Eddy v. the People (1854), 136
Edwards, Jonathan, 26
Elizabeth P.W. Packard v. Andrew McFarland and others, 190–91
"Emancipation of Married Women By Congress" (Packard), 192
Emerson, Ralph Waldo, 33, 86
Everts, Orpheus, 188, 189
ex-patients movement, 154
Exposure on Board the Atlantic & Pacific Car of Emancipation for the Slaves of Old Columbia, Engineered by the Lightning Express, Or Christianity and Calvinism Compared, With an Appeal to the Government to Emancipate the Slaves of the Marriage Union (Packard), 112–16

Failer, Judith Lynn, 14
Fellowes, Francis, 130
Felter, Harvey, 17
"female Gothic" literary style, 151–52. *See also* romance novels

feminism. *See* domestic feminism; feminist consciousness
feminist consciousness, 115–16
Field, Angeline, 46, 95, 100
Field, David, 46, 100
Finch, L. E., 190
First Awakening, 26. *See also* Calvinism; Second Great Awakening
Fish, Clara A. *See* Packard, Clara Fish
Fonerden, John, 143
Foucault, Michel, 11
Fowler, O. S., 39–40
Fox, Richard Whitman, 182–83
Framing American Divorce (Basch), 14
free love, 51–53
Friedman, Jane, 13, 158–59
Fuller, Allen C., 139, 145
Fuller, Buckminster, 8

Gage, Frances, 156
Garrison, William Lloyd, 116
Geller, Jeffrey, 11–12
Gerhard, J. Z., 189
Glover, Ludwig M., 146–47
Goodspeed, E., 157
Gordon, Henry, 187, 196
Graf, Mrs. P. L. Hosmer, 138–39
Grant, Julia Boggs Dent, 173
Grant, Ulysses S., 173–74
Gray, John P., 97, 148, 167–68, 171–72, 173, 177
Great Disclosure of Spiritual Wickedness!!! In High Places (Packard), 122–23
The Great Drama; or, The Millennial Harbinger (Packard), 10, 78, 180–81, 187, 205n18
Grob, Gerald, 14, 76, 83, 122

habeas corpus writ, 121, 122
Hanford, Zalmon, 102, 111
Hard Cash (Reade), 118
Harlow, H. M., 170
Harris, Maxine, 12

Hartog, Hendrik, 13–14, 117
Haslett, Mrs. William, 102, 109
Hastings, George (brother-in-law), 59
Hatch, Nathan, 3
Hawley, Joseph R., 129
Henry, John, 141
The History and Influence of the American Psychiatric Association (American Psychiatric Press), 14
A History of the Congregational Churches and Ministers of Franklin County (Packard), 32
The History of Woman Suffrage (Stanton, Anthony and Gage), 158
Hovey, J. M., 165
Howe, Elbridge G., 122
"How Godliness is Profitable" (Packard), 108
Hubert, Susan J., 12
Hunter, Andrew J., 139

Idaho Democrat, 187
Idaho Territory legislative reform efforts, 186–87
Illinois Hospital for the Insane (Jacksonville, Illinois), 72; challenges to administrators, 71–73; confinement hearings of 1867, 139; investigation by Illinois joint legislative committee, 139, 140–44; McFarland family, 84; operational statistics, 73; patient abuse allegations and testimony, 141, 143–44; patient classification methodology, 141, 143–44; patient demographics, 63, 64–65; politics and management, 72–73; women' rights and wages, 211n27. *See also* institutionalization of 1860–1863
Illinois legislative reform efforts, 132–44, 136, 145, 146, 193–95, 225n32
Illinois State Journal, 135–36, 138, 139
Illinois State Register, 135, 138, 145
Illinois Women's Suffrage Association, 157

incurable mental illness, 93–94
The Independent, 16, 39, 78
Indiana legislative reform efforts, 193
insanity: Calvinism influence, 74–75; as culture-bound concept, 8; definition problems, 5, 96–99, 118–22, 123–24. *See also* moral insanity
insanity as legal issue. *See* jurisprudence of insanity
The Insanity File: The Case of Mary Todd Lincoln (Neely and McMurtry), 13
institutionalization for insanity, 60, 63, 64–67
institutionalization of 1860–1863, 62; confinement with seriously ill patients, 84–88; Dix contact and relationship, 86–87; documentation of experience, 87–88; early period, 78–80; failure to "cure," 89–90; isolation and mail restriction, 86, 89; issues related to release, 91–99; McFarland family, 84; McFarland relationship, 80–81, 84–85, 91, 94–95, 99; Olsen narrative regarding, 87–88; Packard routine, 85–86; relationship with other patients, 87–88; release, 100; resistance tactics, 81–83, 88; stigma, 79; viewpoint, 79–81. *See also* Illinois Hospital for the Insane (Jacksonville, Illinois)
Iowa legislative reform efforts, 165–67, 177

Jacksonville asylum. *See* Illinois Hospital for the Insane (Jacksonville, Illinois); institutionalization of 1860–1863
Jacksonville Journal, 136, 138, 145, 146–47, 195
Jacksonville Sentinel, 135
Jarvis, Edward, 124, 147
Johns Hopkins Hospital Bulletin, 10
Johnson, Ann Braden, 14

Johnson, H. A., 143
Jones, Henry K., 143
Jones, S. S., 122
Jones, W. P., 143
Journal of American Studies, 11
Journal of Mental and Nervous Disease, 188
jurisprudence of insanity, 1–2, 5–7. *See also* insanity

Kain, Mrs. S. A., 138
Kain, S. A., 141
Kankakee Times, 197
Kansas legislative reform efforts, 190
Kiernan, James G., 194
King, Abby, 185–86, 195
Kirkbride, Thomas, 4, 77, 178
Knott, Christopher W., 60, 105

Lake, C. A., 104
Leavitt, Moses, 135, 136
legislative reform efforts: Colorado, 190; Connecticut, 128–31, 169; federal, 173–74, 192, 227n52; Idaho Territory, 186–87; Illinois, 132–34, 136, 145, 146, 193–95, 225n32; Indiana, 193; Iowa, 165–66, 177; Kansas, 190; Maryland, 192; Massachusetts, 122–28, 153; Nebraska, 190; New Hampshire, 174, 175; New York, 167–68; North Carolina, 190; Northeast region, 169, 172–73; Oregon, 186; Rhode Island, 170–71; South Carolina, 190; Southern region, 190; Washington, D.C. (federal), 173–74, 192, 227n52; Washington Territory, 186
Lerner, Gerda, 115
Levison, Jennifer Rebecca, 13
Lightner, David, 13
Lincoln, Mary Todd, 1, 179–80
Lincoln, Robert, 1, 179
Livermore, Mary, 157
Lockwood, Belva A., 173

Loomis, Mason B., 104
Loring, Harrison, 105
Lowe, R., 167
Lunbeck, Elizabeth, 14

The Mad Among Us (Grob), 14
Madness and Civilization (Foucault), 11
Maine legislative reform efforts, 170
Man and Wife in America (Hartog), 13–14
Mann, J. D., 107
Marital Power Exemplified (Packard), 127–28, 153
Married Women's Earnings Act, 158
married women's rights, 156–57, 163, 192. *See also* women's rights
Maryland legislative reform efforts, 192
Massachusetts legislative reform efforts, 122–28, 171
McConnell, Murray, 145
McDill, Alexander, 179
McFarland, Abby King, 185–86, 195
McFarland, Andrew, 68; on AMSAII, 185–86; biographical information, 68–69; death, 195; defense against Packard allegations, 130–31, 144, 150–51; discharge of incurables from institutions, 93–94; dismissal from Jacksonville Asylum leadership, 144, 147–48; education and training, 69; federal postal rights reform, 175; Illinois Personal Liberty Law of 1867, 137–38; Jacksonville asylum appointment, 71; libel suit, 190–91; Lincoln-Packard connection, 1; literature defending, 12; on moral insanity, 96, 132–33; Packard condition report, 87; Packard relationship, 141–43; on Packard's derangement, 8; personal liberty deprivation for mentally ill individuals, 93; philosophy about treatment of mental patients, 76–77; professional concerns, 70–71; religious views, 78; report on challenges

of institution administration, 83; reputation and expertise, 71, 73, 185, 210n27

McFarland, Harriet, 84

McFarland, Mary, 84

McGovern, Constance, 66, 69, 209n41

McKay, P. B., 60

McMurtry, R. Gerald, 13, 179

Medical Record, 188

Medico-Legal Society of Chicago, 193–94

mental medicine. *See* AMSAII (Association of Medical Superintendents of Institutions for the Insane); psychiatry

Miller, William, 33

"Minor Mental Maladies" (McFarland), 96–99

Missionary Herald, 78

Modern Persecution; or Insane Asylums Unveiled (Packard). *See also The Prisoner's Hidden Life* (Packard)

Modern Persecution; or Insane Asylums Unveiled (Packard), 10, 168–69, 187, 228n36

Modern Persecution; or Married Woman's Liabilities, as Demonstrated by the Action of the Illinois Legislature (Packard), 10, 168, 187

monomania, 73–74

Monroe, James, 175

Moore, Stephen R., 104, *105*, 125, 126, 191

moral insanity, 73–74, 76, 96–99

moral treatment, 4, 75–76

Morton, J. Lyman, 122

"The Mother's Legal Rights" (Packard), 157

Mott, Lucretia, 116

Mott, Rebecca, 157

Mrs. Olsen's Narrative of Her One Year's Imprisonment at Jacksonville Insane Asylum (Olsen), 151, 153

"Mrs. Packard on Dependency" (Hartog), 13

Mrs. Packard's Reproof of Dr. McFarland (Packard), 112

The Mystic Key (Packard), 183–84, 188

National Association for the Protection of the Insane and the Prevention of Insanity, 14, 188, 189

National Association of Social Workers, 188

National Conference of Charities, 188

Nebraska legislative reform efforts, 190

Neely, Mark, Jr., 13, 179

Newark Sunday Call, 191

The New Englander, 39

New England reform heritage, 69

New Hampshire legislative reform efforts, 174, 175

New Haven Daily Morning Journal and Courier, 128, 130, 131

Newkirk, A. B., 60

New York legislative reform efforts, 167–68

New York Times, 196

New York Tribune, 167

Nichols, Charles H., 99, 175–76

Nineteenth century overview, 3–7

North American Review, 188

North Carolina legislative reform efforts, 190

Northeast region legislative reform efforts, 169, 172–73

Nostrand, A. H., 126

Notable American Women, 1607–1950, 12

Noyes, John H., 42

Oak Lawn Retreat, 151, 195, 223n34

Oglesby, Richard J., 134–35

Olsen, Sophia, 86–87, 151

Oregon Daily Bulletin, 187

Oregon legislative reform efforts, 186

Orr, John, 105

Out of Bedlam: The Truth about Deinstitutionalization (Johnson), 14

Packard, Arthur Dwight (son), 52,
101–2, 161, 163–64, 184, 199
Packard, Clara Fish (daughter-in-law),
172, 192–93
Packard, Elizabeth, *37, 124*; Anti-Insane
Asylum Society, 153–54; bible class
episode, 53–56; birth and childhood, 16; brain fever, 16–17; business
acumen, 198; Chicago fire impact,
162–63; Chicago home purchase,
155; child custody rights, 160–61;
children, 26–27; controversies and
contradictions, 7–9, 197–98; conversion experience, 26–27; as critic of
institutions, 197–98; death, 197; as
defined by sex, 5–6; description, 191;
diagnoses of mental illness, 73–74;
divorce, 95, 110–11; Dix contact
and relationship, 86–87; education,
16; external oversight of asylums
position, 159–60; feminism, 47–48;
Illinois newspaper support, 135; Illinois relocation from New England,
43–45; impact on jurisprudence of
insanity, 1–2; impact on psychiatric
profession, 14–15, 100; importance of
work and life, 197–98; independence,
88–89; institutionalization in 1836,
16–19; institutionalization in 1860,
60–67, *62*, 78–90; intellectual and
spiritual influences, 16, 25, 26–27,
29–31, 33–34, 39–43, 46–50; Iowa
relocation, 36–39; libel suit, 190–91;
love affair, 50–53; marriage, 24–25,
26–27, 39–40, 44–46, 57–59; McFarland relationship, 141–43; network
of like-minded individuals, 178–79;
Ohio relocation, 32, 34, 35–36;
overviews, 2–3, 197–99; pamphlets,
112; political intuition, 198; prose
style and writing content, 113–16,
152–153; religious explorations, 54–55,
56; research overview, 8–15; scholars
denigrating, 12, 14; scholars favor-

ing, 11–12, 13, 14; social history, 3–4;
Spiritualism, 181; spirituality, 183;
Springfield, Illinois home purchase,
139; symbolic resistance, 62–63;
teaching career, 16; testimony at Illinois Hospital for the Insane legislative hearing, 141–43; as writer, 113–17,
127–28, 180–82, 183–84. *See also*
institutionalization of 1860–1863;
legislative reform efforts
Packard, Elizabeth (daughter), 28,
162–63, 185, 187, 196, 199
Packard, George Hastings (son), 28,
101–2, 161, 163, 184, 199
Packard, Ina (granddaughter), 196
Packard, Isaac (son), 28, 101, 155–56,
160, 161, 184
Packard, Samuel Ware (son), *155*;
achievements and accomplishments,
101, 155–56, 184–85, 199–200; birth,
28; Colorado relocation, 163; marriage, 172
Packard, Theophilus, *37*; Calvinism,
20–21; Chicago relocation in 1869,
161–62; childhood and education,
19–20; children, 26–27; conversion
experience, 25–26; death, 191–92;
declining years, 185; defense against
Packard allegations, 122, 125–26, 128,
130; depression, 22; diary, 21–22; divorce, 97, 110–11; financial difficulties
of 1860s, 100–101, 160–61; genealogy,
203n10; health, 20, 22; Illinois relocation, 43–45; institutionalization of
wife in 1860, 60–67; intellectual and
spiritual influences, 25–27; Iowa relocation, 36–39; marriage, 23, 24–25,
26–27, 44–46, 57–59; Massachusetts
relocation in 1864, 109; Ohio relocation, 32; ordination, 21; overview,
1–2; personality, 38, 39–40; on sanity
trial verdict, 28, 109
Packard, Theophilus III (son), 100, 112,
161, 184, 192–93, 196

Packard and Cooper, 156
Packard's Law, 165–67
Parigot, J., 121
Patterson, R. J., 143, 179
Penfield, Mary, 162
Personal Liberty Law, 136–37, 193–95
petition of unlawful restraint, 102–3
Phillips, Wendell, 123, 124, 171–72, 176, 178
Pinel, Philippe, 4, 75–76
postal rights for the institutionalized insane, 172, 174–75
Presbyterianism, 44, 54, 71, 146–47. *See also* Calvinism; Congregationalism
The Principles of Nature; Her Divine Revelations and Voice to Mankind (Davis), 42
The Prisoners' Hidden Life, or Insane Asylums Unveiled (Packard), 151, 152, 153, 154
The Private War of Mrs. Packard (Sapinsley), 12–13
"Project of a General Law for Determining the Legal Relations of the Insane" (Ray), 119–21
"Project of the Law" (AMSAII position paper), 176, 177
property rights, 110, 111, 125, 132, 156
Protestantism. *See* Calvinism; Puritanism
Psychiatric Persuasion: Knowledge, Gender and Power in Modern America (Lunbeck), 14
psychiatry, 69–70, 70, 74–77
Puritanism, 25–26. *See also* Calvinism

Quakerism, 116
Questions of Power: The Politics of Women's Madness Narratives (Hubert), 12
Quinby, Mrs. C. A., 170

Rand, W. H., 160
Ranney, Mark, 165, 166–67, 177

Ray, Isaac, 97–98, 100, 118–19, 143, 168
Reade, Charles, 118
Reynolds, Albert, 177
Rhode Island legislative reform efforts, 170–71
Rice, Fordice, 46
Rice, Laura, 46
Ricks, John B., 139
"The Rights of Children" (Packard), 157
romance novels, 29–30. *See also* "female gothic" literary style
Rothman, David, 74–75
Rumsey, Sarah, 59

Sage, Leland L., 38–39
sanity trial, 104–7, 109
Sapinsley, Barbara, 12–13
Schrock, William, 191
Scull, Andrew, 63
Second Great Awakening, 24, 25, 33. *See also* Calvinism; First Awakening
Seneca Falls Women's Rights Convention, 115, 116
Severance, Miriam, 109
Sewall, Samuel E., 123, 124, 125, 126, 128, 160–61
Shaffer, Arthur, 11
Shirley, T. G., 79
Simington, I. L., 107
Smith, Gerrit, 49–50, 128
Smith, Josephus, 56
social history, 3–7
South Carolina legislative reform efforts, 190
Southern region legislative reform efforts, 190
Spiritualism, 1, 46–50, 122, 179, 181–82
spousal authority, 109–10. *See also* married women's rights
Springfield State Journal, 157
Stanton, Elizabeth Cady, 64
Starr, Charles, *102*, 102
state legislative reform efforts. *See* legislative reform efforts

Sturtevant, Julian, 145, 222n3
Swedenborgianism, 42, 109
Szasz, Thomas, 11

temperance movement, 192–93
Thoreau, Henry David, 86
Three Years' Imprisonment for Religious Belief (Packard), 153
Tilton, Theodore, 182–83
Tocqueville, Alexis de, 31
Tomes, Nancy, 64
A Treatise on Domestic Economy (Beecher), 30–31
true womanhood, 51–53
Tuke, William, 4
Turner, Jonathan Baldwin, 145, 222n3
Tyler, John E., 97, 99, 124

Unitarianism, 91
Universalism, 91
Unlawful restraint petition, 102–3
Ure, John, 191

Vanderventer, J., 165
Vermont Asylum for the Insane, 4

Waite, C. B., 157
Wakeman, T. B., 139
Walker, Clement, 124, 176
Waller, Altina, 183
Ward, Jasper D., 135, 139
Ware, Elizabeth Parsons. *See* Packard, Elizabeth
Ware, Mary Tirrill (mother), 16
Ware, Olive, 132, 219–20n3
Ware, Samuel (father), 16, 57, 132, 219–20n3

Washington, D.C. federal legislative reform efforts, 173–74, 192, 227n52
Washington Territory legislative reform efforts, 186
Way, Joseph H., 105–6
Whitefield, George, 26
Whitlock, H. G., 139
Who Qualifies for Rights? (Failer), 14
Wines, Fred H., 178
Winter, Kari J., 151
The Woman Hating Party in the Idaho Legislature Exposed! (Packard), 186–87, 188
womanhood, 51–53. *See also* women's rights
Women of the Asylum: Voices from Behind the Walls, 1840–1945 (Geller and Harris), 12
women's rights, 6, 46–50, 156, 157, 209n41. *See also* domestic feminism; feminist consciousness; married women's rights
Women's Rights Convention of 1848, 115, 116
Wood, Mary Elene, 13, 79–80
Woodhull, Victoria, 182–83
Woodward, Samuel B., 17–18
Worcester Hospital for the Insane, 17–18
Wright, Frances ("Fanny"), 49, 206n34
The Writing on the Wall: Women's Autobiography and the Asylum (Wood), 13

York Retreat, 4
Younglove, J., 102

*The University of Illinois Press
is a founding member of the
Association of American University Presses.*

Composed in 10.25/13.25 Minion Pro
by Celia Shapland
at the University of Illinois Press
Manufactured by Sheridan Books, Inc.

University of Illinois Press
1325 South Oak Street
Champaign, IL 61820-6903
www.press.uillinois.edu

Linda V. Carlisle is an associate professor
in Library and Information Services at
Southern Illinois University Edwardsville.